Mary Adelaide Walker

Eastern Life and Scenery

Vol. I: With Excursions in Asia Minor, Mytilene, Crete, and Roumania

Mary Adelaide Walker

Eastern Life and Scenery
Vol. I: With Excursions in Asia Minor, Mytilene, Crete, and Roumania

ISBN/EAN: 9783743384149

Manufactured in Europe, USA, Canada, Australia, Japa

Cover: Foto ©ninafisch / pixelio.de

Manufactured and distributed by brebook publishing software (www.brebook.com)

Mary Adelaide Walker

Eastern Life and Scenery

EASTERN LIFE AND SCENERY

WITH

EXCURSIONS IN ASIA MINOR, MYTILENE,
CRETE, AND ROUMANIA

BY MRS. WALKER

IN TWO VOLUMES
VOL. I.

LONDON: CHAPMAN AND HALL
LIMITED
1886

Many of the following chapters are from unpublished MSS., others have been collected from "Good Words," "Temple Bar," "London Society," "The Morning Post," *&c. Several have been translated into German, and some of the papers, written for a French periodical, appear now for the first time in English.*

CONTENTS TO VOL. I.

I.—LIFE IN THE SERAÏ.

My First Portrait. — Difficult Installation. — "Shimdy! Shimdy!"—The Handsome Circassian.—An Unfortunate Costume.—"Where is the Soul?"—The Lay Figure.—The Wedding Dresses of Two Sultanas.—The Portrait of an Imperial Princess.—A Seraï on the Bosphorus.—Waiting.—The Sultana.—In the Harem.—Diamonds and Difficulties.—Halaïks and Hanums.—Excellent Order of the Household.—Oustas, Calfas, and Children.—Lining the Quilts.—Draping the Antary.—Prosperous Slaves.—Backshish and Presents.—Entangled Music.—"Caveh Alti."—The multiplied Work of the Imperial Kitchen.—The Teachers of the Harem.—A Caged Bird.—"Destour!"—The Dinner Trays.—The Military Band.—Circassian and Georgian Beauties.—Souzy-Dil and her Violoncello.—Deilfèrat and her Double-Bass.—The Class of Tumblers.—An Evening Entertainment.—The Pantomime.—The Ball and the Red Bandanas.—Portrait of a Seraïli.—Beautiful Jewellery 1

II.—IN STAMBOUL.

The Bridge.—Place of Executions.—The Old Seraglio.—Alaï Kiosk.—The Guilds of Constantinople.—Their Patron Saints.—An Old Stone.—Bab-Houmayoun.—Fountain of Ahmed III.—His Inscription.—St. Sophia.—Construction and Destruction.—The Samaritan's Well.—The Hindoo's Tree.—The Atmeïdan 42

III.—DIVAN YOLOU AND THE BAZAARS.

A fine Street View.—The Burnt Column.—The House of Busbek.—The Noor Osmanieh.—Kebabs.—Bazaar Touters.—Hadji Osman.—Fading Splendours.—Seal Engravers.—Spoonmakers.—Mosque of Sultan Bayazid II.—Ramazan Bazaar.—The Petted Pigeons.—Merchants from the far East.—Bric-à-brac 58

IV.—PERA.

The Grande Rue.—Street Commerce.—A Quiet Corner.—Bulgarian Milkman.—Maltese Goats.—Snails and Cuttlefish.—"Milk-drinking Lambs."—"Koush Conmaz!"—Caramanian Mutton.—The "Djighirdji" and Marco.—A Dog's District.—The Bear and his Leader.—The Schekerdji.—Mohalibé.—Oil, Lemon, Soot, and Charcoal.—A humble Devotee.—"Sakas."—The Buffalo Cart.—A Greek Funeral.—A Quiet Time.—The Fire Gun.—Great Fire of Pera 72

V.—EVERYDAY LIFE IN A HAREM.

The Family of the Pasha.—A Tiny Woman.—A Sucking General.—Tchaousch Hanum.—The Eldest Daughter.—Turkish Beds.—Nomadic Furniture.—Concerning Household Matters.—Risk of Fire.—The Duties and Condition of "Halaïks."—Female Pedlars.—Life on a Farm in Asia Minor 99

VI.—EVERYDAY LIFE IN A HAREM.

Djenàniah Calfa.—Djémilé.—"A Sad Coquette."—Entangled Interchange of Sentiments.—An Adventure.—Reflections.—Portrait of the Hanum.—A Venerable Fiancé.—Collection of Antiquities.—A Brick Tablet.—Cylinders.—Seals. Gems and Coins.—Legend of Nimrod.—Moses.—Dream of a Sultan.—Isolation 113

VII.—A STRAY THREAD.—FROM YALI-KIOSK TO YEDI-KOULE.

A Feeble Line of Rail.—A Simple Booking-Office.—Patient Passengers.—The Panorama unwinds.—Byzantine Remains.—Gardens of the Old Seraglio.—A Calm Decay.—Remains of the Great Palace of Constantine, of Justinian, of Heraclius.—Beautiful Fragments.—Ruins of a Palace of Theodosius the Younger.—Koum-Kapou.—Vlanga-Bostan.—The "Pomegranate Gate."—Monastery of St. John Studius.—Yedi-Koulé (the Seven Towers).—Camels.—The Fortress and State Prisons.—The Industrial School.—The Golden Gate 129

VIII.—THE LAND-WALLS OF CONSTANTINOPLE.
NO. I.—THE TOWER OF ISAAC ANGELUS AND THE PRISONS OF ANEMÀ.

The "Sebil-Khané" and the Steam Mill.—The Blachernœ.—Five Miles of Towers and Battlements.—The Tower of Isaac Angelus.—State Prisons of Anemà.—A walled-up Gate 140

IX.—THE LAND-WALLS OF CONSTANTINOPLE.
II.—TEKFUR-SERAÏ.

Eghri-capou.—The Stamboul Taksim.—Origin of "Sou-Terazi" (the Water Towers).—Interesting Remains.—Tekfur-Seraï.—The Hall of the Emperors.—History of a Diamond, the "Tchoban Tashy." 147

X.—THE LAND-WALLS OF CONSTANTINOPLE.
III.—FROM TEKFUR-SERAÏ TO THE SEA OF MARMORA.

Kerkoporta.—Useless Destruction.—View from the Top of the Wall.—Kachrié Djami.—The Land-Walls of Constantine.—The Adrianople Gate.—The Lycas.—The "Riven Tower."—An Ancient Burial-place of the Gothic Guard.—A Monster Cannon : its requirements, its vengeance, and its fate.—Mevlaneh Capoussy.—Silivria Capoussy.—The Burial-place of Ali of Janina.—The Golden Gate.—A Railway Arch !—The last Tower of the Land-Walls 156

XI.—BALOUKLI AND THE FESTIVAL OF THE FISHES.

Up the Golden Horn.—The Okmeïdan.—Aïwan-Seraï.—The Greek Burial-ground.—An Animated Scene.—Dancing

Hamals.— Laborious Enjoyment.— Greek Dancing.— Solemn Gaieties.—Tchinganas.—A Funeral.—The Church of Baloukli.—The Miraculous Fishes.—The Fragments of a Festival. 168

XII.—VILLAGE LIFE IN TURKEY.

Round the Meïdan.—The Meïdan.—The Grey Wooden House.—The **Imām's House** and the Battle of the Broomsticks.—Ibrahim.—The Rose-Coloured House.—The Ruined House.—The Yellow Konak.—Two Cottages . . . 184

XIII.—THE TURKISH GIRLS' SCHOOL.

The Normal School of Yéré Batān.—Opening Ceremonies.—A small "Medjliss."—The Drawing Class Room.—A First Lesson.—Art Students, their Ways and Manners.—Discord.—A "Tender Infant."—Practice better than Precept. — "Yavash." — Cracked Konaks.—Djénab.—Déli Fatima.—Working for the "Imtihan."—Emine.—Fetiyé and Muniré.—A Circassian Mother.—Djémilé and Her Work.—Camma, the Abyssinian.—The Examinations.—A Visit to the Home of Djenab.—Black Coffee and Gossip. — The Marriage-maker. — Anarchy. — The Poor Old Mudir 221

XIV.—THE IFTAR.

Turkish Society.—Ramazan.—The Iftar.—Djémilé and Zeheïra.—How to sit round a Dining-table.—Bouyouroun."—A Varied Repast.—"Aschourah."—The Young Hanums.—Sabiha and the Little Boys.—Neighbourly Visits.—Hospitality 249

XV.—THE GREAT BURIAL-GROUND OF SCUTARI.

The Rustic "Café."—Dreamy Influences.—The "Mézarlik." Three Little Donkeys and their Driver.—Ali Baba's Wife.—The Oil Jars.—Copper Mangals and Metal Lamps.—Allah-edeen.—Alnaschar's Eggs.—A Dream rudely broken.—A Turbé, Tombs, and Shrines.—Reverence.—Beautiful Epitaphs.—The Tomb of a Horse.—Its Extraordinary Efficacy.—The Use of a Long "Tessbih."—Gloomy Depths.—Lingering Rays 271

XVI.—THE HOWLING DERVISHES.

The Téké.—A Venerable Scheïk and his Little Son.—Discriminate Salutations.—Devotees.—Growing Excitement.—A Pause.—Infant "Faithful."—Frantic Devotion.—A Holy Santon 282

XVII.—A STEP EASTWARDS.
NO. I.

On the Road to Nicomedia.—In search of the Tomb of Hannibal.—Church of St. Euphemia.—Elastic Railway Arrangements.—The Bay of Kalamitza.—Ayasma of St. John Chrysostom.—Fanaraki.—A Summer Palace of Justinian.—"Kaïsh Dagh."—Maltépé.—Tomato Paste.—Cartal.—Pendik.—The Gulf of Ismid.—Station of Guebsch 290

NO. II.—GUEBSEH.

The Ruins of Eski-Hissar.—The Baths of Yalova.—Crusaders.—The Baths of Pythia.—The Turkish Peasant.—Guebseh.—Beautiful Mosque.—The "Mezarlik."—A Hanum of the Good Old Time.—A Native Repast.—The Camel Stables 299

XVIII.—IN THE SERAÏ.
NO. II.

Once more in the Seraï.—A Pretty Scene.—In the Visitors' Room.—Neat Needlework.—Souvenirs of former Gaieties. The Invasion of Crinoline.—Art under Difficulties.—The Pocket Sketch-book.—The old Negress and the Sud'na.—Peaceful Pictures.—The Call to Prayer.—The Sejjadé. The Namaz.—The Prescribed Hours.—The Tessbih.—A Dying Halaïk.—Marriage of the Ibrikdar Ousta.—Prosperous Servitude and Undesirable Freedom.—Ghevhéri 307

XIX.—THE MIDDLE BRIDGE.

An Unfashionable Lounge.—Shores of the Golden Horn.—Churches and Church Mosques.—Black Sea Boats.—Caïques and Mahones.—A Pasha's "Five-pair."—Sandals.—A Man-of-War's Boat.—The Bazaar Caïque . 322

XX.—FACTS, FANCIES, AND FOLK-LORE.

Festival of the Firstborn.—Turkish Caudle.—Tchinganas.—A Splendid Bed and Cradle.—Naming the Infant.—Precautions against the "Evil Eye."—The use of Incense.—Dog-bread.—A Faulty Pattern.—Polite Spitting.—The Value of Old Shoes and of Blue Beads.—Breadcrumbs and Scraps of Paper.—Infused Writing.—The Seven Holy Nights.—The Night of Terror.—The Night of Power.—Aschourah and Névrouzié.—Invention of Confectionery.—Garlic and Onions.—A Kurd's Appreciation.—Shem and his Bees.—Balkiss, Queen of Sheba, and her Difficulties.—Solomon, a Basket-Maker.—Concerning Mangals.—The Origin of the Deluge.—The Old Woman of Kufa.—Carrier Pigeons, and the Fate of Yezid and Djebada.—Dyvits invented by Enoch 330

INTRODUCTION.

In order to form some idea of the changes that have taken place in Constantinople since the Crimean war, let us look back thirty years. Can we at the present time fully realise the different conditions of men and things as they existed here at that long-past date? Can we still trace, in the steep but yet practicable highway suggestively known as "Step Street," the tortuous cascade of stones that, passing through a ruined archway, served at that time as main thoroughfare between Galata and Pera? Can memory reconstruct the venerable wall, the towers, and the broad moat where now we see populous streets and solid modern dwellings? Can we even remember the old approach to the steamer bridge, so narrow that the opposite houses seemed to knock their crooked roofs together?

Thirty years ago the streets throughout the city

were unlighted, without written names, the houses without numbers; there was no organised fire-brigade; no local post, no telegraph, railway lines, nor tramways; no street cabs but the crazy *talikas;* wild dogs the only scavengers. At that time the narrow sombre alleys in the heart of Pera were the scene of almost nightly assassinations. Galata and Tophauch were utterly unsafe after sunset. The artist may indulge in a quiet lament over the picturesque " bits " and stray remnants of Eastern type and character that have perished in this flood of practical improvements, but old residents daily and hourly appreciate the material comfort that they have brought to the everyday life of the city.

Thirty years have wrought changes also in the life of the harem, through a growing appreciation of the benefits of education and employment; but in many cases the efforts made by Turkish women to assimilate their habits and manners with the freer mode of life usual to " Frank " women, being—too often—ill-directed, serve rather to discredit our Christian rules and customs in the estimation of the old-fashioned and most respectable Mussulman families.

A slight sketch of the constitution of Turkish

homes, of the harem, and of slavery forms one chapter of the present volume. Every rule and custom of harem life mentioned in it will be found exemplified in the varied scenes that have been drawn from notes of personal experience during a residence of nearly thirty years in the East. I have selected those more particularly connected with my work as an artist, which brought me amongst scenes that would have been quite inaccessible to the tourist or the visitor.

Some of the interesting remains of antiquity described in my rambles and excursions have since been partially destroyed; a few have been utterly swept away. Of these last the residence of the old German Ambassadors, the ruined Kerkoporta, the fine archway of Tekfur-Seraï, and the noble tower at Vlanga-Bostān, are the most to be regretted; but yet enough remains of imperishable beauty, of archæological interest, of historical truth and legendary lore, to render Constantinople one of the most attractive cities in the world.

SKETCHES OF EASTERN LIFE AND SCENERY.

I.

LIFE IN THE SERAÏ.

My First Portrait.—Difficult Installation.—"Shimdy! Shimdy!" —The Handsome Circassian.—An Unfortunate Costume.— "Where is the Soul?"—The Lay Figure.—The Wedding Dresses of Two Sultanas.—The Portrait of an Imperial Princess.—A Seraï on the Bosphorus.—Waiting.—The Sultana.—In the Harem.—Diamonds and Difficulties.—Halaïks and Hanums.—Excellent Order of the Household.—Oustas, Calfas, and Children.—Lining the Quilts.—Draping the Antary.—Prosperous Slaves.—Backshish and Presents.—Entangled Music.—"Caveh Alti."—The multiplied Work of the Imperial Kitchen.—The Teachers of the Harem.—A Caged Bird.—"Destour!"—The Dinner Trays.—The Military Band.—Circassian and Georgian Beauties.—Souzy-Dil and her Violoncello.—Deilfèrat and her Double-Bass.—The Class of Tumblers.—An Evening Entertainment.—The Pantomime.—The Ball and the Red Bandanas.—Portrait of a Seraïli.—Beautiful Jewellery.

It was in the spring succeeding my arrival at Constantinople, and shortly after the close of the Crimean war, that I was asked to undertake a portrait of the wife of one of the chief functionaries of the palace. I paid a preliminary visit, and found the pasha exceedingly courteous and most anxious for the success of the work, as it was to be followed by a likeness of one of the sultanas.

My "subject," a handsome Circassian, appeared delighted at the prospect of a new method of killing time; but she was evidently under the impression that two or three days of labour on my part, and of patience on her own, would be all-sufficient to complete the work—a three-quarters life-size in oils.

We began. The arrangement and sketch of a portrait are always matter for anxious thought, even with civilised models accustomed to the requirements of an artist; to set up an easel for the first time in a Turkish harem was terribly perplexing, and to this day I have an acute remembrance of the trials of temper and of patience, the discouragements and weariness that were endured, before that portrait was accomplished.

As it would be quite contrary to the rules of orthodox Mussulman society that a lady should visit a painter's studio, or expose her portrait in any way to be seen by men, it becomes necessary to execute the whole work within the harem, even to the last finishing touch of varnishing and framing—a labour of difficulty and fatigue rarely undertaken by a lady artist in the case of very large canvases.

I found myself obliged to pass the greater part

of several weeks in the harem of R—— Pasha, and, as time seems to be of no account with this easy-going people, as soon as the novelty of the sittings had worn off, I frequently waited an hour or two, sometimes even the whole day, in momentary expectation of the young hanum's appearance. "Shimdy! shimdy!" said the slaves good-humouredly, in answer to inquiries. In the early days I used to fancy that "Shimdy! shimdy!" (literally translated, now, directly) meant — well, let us say, now, directly; but I soon learnt to understand it as meaning any time within the twenty-four hours; and therefore, starting on a voyage of discovery, in search of my recalcitrant "subject," usually found her reposing beside the tandour, busy at a game of cards.

The tandour is a wooden framework placed over a brazier of charcoal, and covered with a padded quilt; it is frequently surrounded by a circular couch, and the quilts are drawn up over the persons reclining on it.

I can recall every line and curve of that first portrait; I see the oval face, the soft, dark, almond-shaped eyes, the delicate aquiline nose and well-formed mouth of the handsome, imperious-looking Eastern lady. Her dark hair was cut nearly short, according to a fashion then in favour, and a small gold cap, bordered with a wreath in gold filigree, work, was placed on one side, a massive tassel drooping on the shoulder; her dress, a deep rose-coloured satin embroidered in gold.

Out of such materials a graceful picture ought surely to have been produced, but nothing could persuade my model to fall into an easy attitude. The gold-embroidered costume, which, comprising a trailing skirt and very ample "schalwars," hung in exquisite folds as she sat with one foot raised upon the sofa, had been fashioned in the upper part into an imitation of a "Frank" bodice. This was (at that time) a daring innovation on the usual style of Turkish dress; the hanum was consequently very proud of her stiff, unbending waist, and insisted on being represented as sitting perfectly upright, and with her elbows squared to the utmost, in order that each side of that objectionable waist might be clearly defined. The drooping hand, exquisitely formed by nature, which would have slightly modified the outline, was twisted into a constrained front view for the purpose of exhibiting the full splendours of a monstrous diamond ring disfiguring the little finger.

The grand question of shade had next to be solved, and, in spite of many an energetic remonstrance, the softening tones were gradually reduced to imbecile weakness; in short, I yielded, spoilt my work, and contented my model. But there was yet a further dilemma to be encountered. "Ah! that is all very well," said a friendly Nubian slave, patting me on the shoulder, while she gazed at the finished picture. "Yes, there is our Hanum Effendi and the beautiful dress and the diamonds; but madama djim, cousoum!" (my lady, my lamb) "*where* is the soul?" Here was a responsibility quite unlooked for, not at all included in the agreement. Was I, then, to engage to find souls for all the Mussulman portraits which I hoped to achieve in the future? The prospect was uncomfortable; I took refuge in silence, and my inquiring friend turned to examine the lay figure. "Vaï! vaï!" said she, shrinking back; "is it alive? No!" Then, creeping nearer and touching one of the hard fingers, she uttered a loud shriek and fled. "Amān! amān! the madama has brought into the house a skeleton covered with cotton!"

Some slave girls, lounging about, followed her retreat with hearty laughter; *they* knew better, for the life-size figure had been their plaything on its arrival. They speedily penetrated the mystery of the iron framework, and had already contrived hopelessly to dislocate several of the joints.

The transport of this lay figure, on its road from Pera to the caïque, had occasioned some consternation in the streets. As it was borne along, carefully enveloped, on the shoulders of an Armeniun porter, people told each other that it was a dead halaïk, or slave, about to be cast into the Bosphorus, and shrank from contact with the uncanny burden.

The konak of R—— Pasha was a handsome building, containing spacious and airy halls. The furniture of the selamlik was extremely simple; but the harem was fitted up with much luxury, and one room of it deserves especial mention, now that the taste for Western fashions is filling the homes of Stamboul with articles of Austrian and French manufacture. This room had been freshly decorated for a newly married daughter of the pasha by a former wife. A few chairs and a large girandole from Vienna bore witness to the beginnings of innovation; but the rest of the furniture—the divans, curtains, and portières, composed of rich crimson silk velvet, with a bordering a foot deep, in raised gold embroidery — retained much of the gorgeousness inseparable from our ideas of Eastern homes.

It was at this time that an exhibition was made in Stamboul of the wedding trousseaux of two of the imperial princesses; they were arranged in some spacious rooms in the Mint. Such a display will never be repeated here; times and fashions have altered, and it is worth while to recall, in a few words, this last glimpse of Oriental magnificence.

To enumerate the "antarys," the "schalwars,"

the "keurks," the "feràdjés;" the dainty slippers, boots, and gloves; the headdresses and the hand-mirrors, all embroidered with gold and heavy with jewels, would involve a wearisome repetition. Every article, either of wearing apparel or of household use, was formed of the most costly materials that could be adapted to it; even the very dustpans were of solid silver; the coffee zarfs, tchibouk rings, ashpans, bathing-clogs, thickly encrusted with precious stones.

A sketch of one or two of the costumes will be sufficient to indicate the style of the whole trousseau, and to prove the lavish extravagance which has helped to bring this country to its present deplorable condition.

One of the dresses principally remarked for its costliness and elegance of design was made of poucean satin. The trains were then worn exceedingly long, and the whole of the antary, which, at the back, measured between three and four yards, was thickly covered with a running pattern exquisitely wrought to represent branches of fuchsia: the leaves in gold, the stamens of the flowers in fine pearls, and the petals in diamonds; the keurk, or fur cloak, lined with the most costly sable, was enriched in the same manner; the rest of the toilette *en suite*. Another robe of pale blue satin was thickly sprinkled with pearls, and trimmed round with a broad edging like heavy lace, also entirely composed of fine pearls. Each toilette of the trousseau —and they were countless—besides the antary and schalwars, had a cloak of the same, lined with rare furs of a colour to harmonise with the hue of the materials; with headdress, boots, slippers, glove, and even pocket-handkerchiefs to match.

These recklessly costly garments were probably never worn, partly on account of their excessive weight, and also for the sake of the newer fashion of silks from Paris. The trousseaux were subsequently carried home with great state and ceremony, to be laid aside unused; notwithstanding which one of the bridegrooms, Il Hami Pasha of Egypt (so said the talk of the harems) desirous of outdoing the magnificence of his imperial father-in-law, presented his wife, after their marriage, with a robe infinitely richer and more bejewelled than anything that had been previously given. It is difficult to realise how he may have accomplished this feat.

It is affirmed that on the occasion of a former marriage in the imperial family the procession of trousseaux and presents continued during the space of one entire week.

My next large work in a harem was a portrait of a daughter of the Sultan, married to the son of a celebrated statesman. A day was fixed for the introduction to the princess, then at her summer palace on the Bosphorus, and I went there accompanied by an interpretress.

The palace is familiar to all travellers on the beautiful waterway: a white building backed by a richly wooded hillside. The interior is vast, airy, and beautifully kept. On the ground-floor an immense hall, completely covered with fine matting, is surrounded on three sides by large rooms, the handsomest apartments, overlooking the water, being appropriated to the principal women, the hustas of the Sultana's household. On the fourth side of the hall a broad and lofty staircase leads to the state rooms on the upper floor, inhabited by the princess.

The part of the building devoted to the use of the Pasha is a wooden yali of much less importance, communicating with the palace by a long gallery. An intermediary room at the extremity of this passage is intended as a waiting room, in which the husband, after sending in due notice of his visit, awaits the answer of his imperial spouse. This ceremony is observed in all families. There may be visitors in the harem, or others whom the master of the house does not see unveiled, and notice is therefore necessary in order that they may retire. But I return to the interview with the Sultana, remarking that if I dwell somewhat lengthily upon matters and incidents connected with this particular household, it is because the harems of the imperial family are exceedingly difficult of access, and consequently little known, excepting to those to whom, for reasons of business, the doors are readily opened.

Very few foreign ladies succeed in obtaining admittance as simple visitors into one of these seraïs, but I had once the fortunate opportunity of introducing into the charmed circle a lady whose social rank, if not her world-wide reputation as an artist, might have secured her an interview with the Sultana, but no official effort would have gained her admittance into the class-rooms, in which the girls were being trained in music and dancing, and where the most effective, because unconscious, " subjects " were to be found; therefore Madame " Henriette Browne," wisely avoiding all attempts at a ceremonial visit, came quietly with me to the palace. We sat for some time watching the groups so fascinating to an artist, and soon afterwards the art exhibitions of Paris and London were graced by the works of her delicate brush, chiefly inspired by the thoughtful studies made in this seraï on the Bosphorus.

The harem " kapoudji," or porter, received me on my first arrival, and, having duly investigated my right to an introduction, handed me over, together with my interpretress, to the care of a very tall, black agha, who led us by a seemingly interminable labyrinth of rooms and passages, landing us at length in a deliciously cool room and on a divan overlooking the water. Coffee was presently served.

The palace was very quiet, for it was warm summer weather. Most people were taking their midday siesta; and, in truth, the lapping ripple of the strong current, the measured thud of passing oars, the faint sound of music from a distant room, combined with the drowsy stillness of the atmosphere, all had a very soporific tendency as we sat and waited, as one learns to wait in Turkey.

After a time there arose a faint stir of life; it was a passing footfall beyond the door curtain, scarcely audible, indeed, on the fine matting; then a low murmur of conversation somewhere near at hand; now a slight unseen skirmish, as some young girl, not daring to venture in, peeped at the strangers with one furtive eye from behind the perdeh, and was suddenly plucked back with a reprimand; again a woman or a girl would wander in, and, sitting on the divan, or subsiding on to a padded quilt on the floor, would gaze at us, ask a question or two, and finish by asserting that "Shimdy! shimdy!" the princess would be ready to receive me.

At length the summons came. A tall, handsome Circassian walked in with an air of authority, announcing, "Our lady wishes for you." She leads the way up the broad staircase and across a splendid saloon crowded with gilding and glass, satin stuffs and French furniture.

The Sultana was seated in a large arm-chair beside one of the trellised screened windows; her attitude was carefully arranged; she bowed her head slightly, mindful not to disturb the train of her green silk antary, which had been draped about her so as to look as much as possible like the skirt of a Frank dress. At the time to which I refer no Mussulman woman had as yet ventured on the daring experiment of the genuine "fistan," or skirt, which is now almost universally adopted.

The Sultana—we will call her Zeïneb—is decidedly attractive; an exquisitely fair skin, unaided by powder or cosmetics; hair of the blond cendré shade so much admired in France; grey eyes with dark rims, and a charming mouth, are lighted up into positive beauty by the smile, which might be more frequent. At the time of her portrait she was barely nineteen, and had been married for some years. Her eldest child, a boy, lived but a few days, being probably one of the last of the little sons of imperial princesses doomed by inexorable and cruel custom, for reasons of State, to unavowed but certain destruction. Since that time the iniquitous practice, which had almost the force of law, has been abolished, being one among the innumerable changes for the better developed by the progress and civilisation of the last twenty years.

Zeïneb Sultana is very intelligent and clever, a perfect mistress of her own language, and an eager reader of the daily papers. She speaks with aristocratic gutturals, using a mixture of Arabic and Persian, which is very perplexing to lower mortals who may be struggling with the utterances of homely, useful Turkish. She has also, in common with the other children of Abdul-Medjid, remarkable musical talent; she is acquainted with all great political movements, in other countries as well as in her own, and has something to say with regard to most of our modern inventions.

In the lifetime of her easy, tender-hearted father this princess exercised considerable influence in affairs of State; but all the Sultan's unbounded affection for this daughter could not induce him to give her the husband of her choice. Political considerations made her the wife of a man whom she did not love, and who dared scarcely to raise his eyes in her presence.

While discussing the arrangements for the picture the Sultana sat immovable, speaking occasionally in an oracular manner, and with a voice less soft and musical than that of Turkish women in general. At length the day was fixed for my removal to the palace, and I withdrew. The princess bestowed a nod and a pleasant smile without moving one pleat of her draperies, or in any way changing her dignified attitude, but before we had reached the foot of the staircase shouts of laughter from the upper floor showed that she was indemnifying herself for the long restraint.

I became an inmate of the harem of Zeïneb Sultana, and during five or six months spent a great part of my time there with my drogmanesse—a middle-aged, good-natured Frenchwoman, who took snuff and spoke but indifferent Turkish.

One of the principal "oustas" having been—greatly to her dissatisfaction—dispossessed of her room on the ground-floor of the palace, it was converted into a studio. Our beds were carefully spread each night, according to genuine native fashion, on the floor of a large room adjoining.

Everything about this seraï is exquisitely clean and orderly, and this, indeed, is the case in all good Turkish houses. In matted apartments, where the furniture consisted of a long couch, a rug or two, some padded quilts, and a door curtain, there is no possibility of shelter for slovenly or neglected service; the least spot or stain would be at once visible; and nothing can be imagined fresher or pleasanter for an idle hour or two on a hot summer day than to rest in a genuine old-fashioned Turkish yali overhanging the Bosphorus, where the couches are spread with spotless lengths of white cotton and the breeze through many windows raises the light white curtains. There is a charm even in the cool, clean odour of the newly washed matting, and—alas! for the weakness of human nature in this enervating climate—in the " dolce far niente " that pervades the very atmosphere.

But the portrait of the Sultana was not accomplished, by any means, in this indolent, easy-going manner. The work under any circumstances would have required great industry, but this particular canvas—of a size to need a considerable extent of background—was completely painted, before it was finally pronounced as finished, quite three times over, as the varying taste of the imperial lady wandered amongst the different articles of dress, jewellery, or furniture which she took a sudden fancy to see represented.

The costume chosen for the important occasion was deplorable; no line of Oriental grace, or even of splendour, in the dress. She had robes stiff with gems, draperies of fairy tissue, yet she stood for her portrait in a dress of the poorest French silk, because it was "moda" "à la frança." It was a dead unlovely white, the upper part made like a European lady's ball-dress, while from the waist downwards it was fashioned into the orthodox antary and schalwars. The jewels were splendid, but their effect was utterly destroyed by the hard white, on which it was simply impossible to make the diamonds sparkle; for there were diamonds also, enough to purchase a principality. A diamond necklace of immense value encircled the throat of the Sultana, the precious stones cut as pear-shaped drops, each one as large as a filbert; large diamonds were in her ears; an enormous stone on the little finger; the Sultan's portrait set in splendid brilliants, and a large diamond star, an order, on the bosom of the dress. But the girdle surpassed all the other ornaments in value; it was a broad band composed entirely of diamonds, with a double clasp of the same, as large as a saucer. This clasp formerly fastened the cloak of ceremony of the Sultan her father, and the belt was, probably, the one given by him to his daughter at the time of her marriage, according to custom.

Such was the appearance of my imperial model: the ease, the grace, the dazzling magnificence of the East lost and dimmed by a painful striving after Western fashions. Nothing could destroy the glowing tender whiteness of the soft skin, or the silken gloss of the fair hair; but the dress caused a feeling of despair, and the pose was a further subject of discouragement. It was required to be as "full-face" as possible, that impartial justice might be done to the whole of the features; shade was highly objectionable. Then, again, the Sultana was short, and plump as a partridge; I was asked to represent a tall, slight woman. The lady, stepping down from her platform, examined the charcoal sketch in silence, then, taking a crayon, made a mark a foot and more lower down. "There," said she in a decided tone; "I am to be as tall as that. I am only sixteen, and sure to grow." She had dropped a few years in her calculation. The arm had to be lengthened in consequence of this suddenly improved stature, and Zeïneb Sultana was so obliging as to assist the corrections by stretching the soft white limb and jewelled hand as straight and stiff as a figure of wood.

I objected at first to such unintelligent dictation; tried to reason. Zeïneb Sultana stamped her foot, said I did not care to please her, and that the portrait must be done according to her wishes, or—not at all. I could not risk the "not at all," and, with many an inward groan and rebellious struggle, submitted, with less difficulty than might otherwise have been the case, because the picture when finished would rarely, if ever, be seen by persons competent to judge the merits of a painting. As the features of women are veiled, so also, according to orthodox custom, must a female portrait be hidden from the gaze even of the men who perform the rough work of the house. The ultimate fate of the picture is either to lie hidden away in some dark closet, or, if too large, and destined to remain in one of the sitting-rooms, curtains are fastened on to the frame. This portrait of Zeïneb Sultana was eventually honoured with a large curtain of rich white silk.

Life was not unpleasant in this imperial seraï. The Sultana, if capricious and unreasonable on the subject of the portrait, treated me in all other matters with marked consideration; the women and girls were most of them very friendly. The poor Georgian, indeed, whose room I had unwittingly appropriated, looked at times rather gloomy; and the khasnahdar ousta, who liked things in their accustomed order, gently shook the corner of her jacket one day with a resigned air, as if to say, "Amān! amān! will the work *never* be finished?" But on the whole the painting-room was a sort of lounge which the girls by no means disliked. They would wander in by twos and threes, particularly in the evening. Some were soft and gentle, some bright and full of fun, none rude or uncourteous. The tiny children toddled in in search of "scheker" (sugar), of which a small store was known to exist in a certain cupboard; and on one occasion little Zerimicelle managed to appropriate a gold pencil-case with great adroitness, but I lost nothing further.

There were two little girls much petted by the harem in general, Ta'asnevin and Ghevhèri: they had been bought as infants by the Sultana. Ta'asnevin, a lovely fair-complexioned, blue-eyed child, promised to become beautiful; she was to be educated as a present to the Sultan at some future time. Ghevhèri had proved sickly; she was almost crippled, and, as little hope could be entertained of her growing up in any way attractive, she was adopted by her mistress and received the title of "hanum," being, in consequence of that adoption, no longer a slave.

The harem consisted of about one hundred women and girls, including several negresses whose quarters were separated from the rooms given to the white slaves. The organisation of the service in this establishment deserves especial notice, as it is, in many respects (though on a greatly reduced scale), the same as that of the Great Seraglio. Seven principal women preside over the feminine community, the chief and most important personage being the khasnahdar ousta, or treasurer. This lady inhabits a richly furnished and beautiful apartment at one extremity of the great hall. She superintends the expenditure and keeps the accounts, besides entertaining all visitors whom the Princess may not feel disposed to receive. The Khasnahdar Ustad (pronounced ousta), at the time of my residence in the palace, was a woman no longer young. She had been with the Sultana almost from her birth, and was much beloved by her, as by the whole household, for her gentleness and sweet temper. The second in the hierarchy is the Tchamashir Ousta; she is answerable for the linen and for the laundry arrangements. Then follow the Chashinguir Ousta, who directs the service of the table, and would formerly have performed the duties of "taster;" the Ibrikdar Ousta, whose office it is to overlook all matters concerning the drinking-water, the lighting, warming, mangals, &c.; the Càvedji Ousta, who has all connected with pipes and coffee in her charge; the Killardji Ousta, or keeper of the stores; and, finally, the Espapdji Ousta, whose cares are devoted to the Sultana's robes.

Each ousta superintends a certain number of calfas, who in their turn take the responsibility and training of the children. The calfas divide between them the lighter duties of the service of the house, six or seven girls at a time being on duty during a week: they give out the dinners, serve the coffee and sweetmeats, attend to the tchibouks still used by elderly ladies, sweep the matting, lay out the beds, etc. All the serious cleaning is performed by the negresses.

We may remark, in reference to the number Seven, that it is here regarded as a mystical and typical number, set apart, as it were, both in religious observances and in the usages of everyday life. Thus, there are seven holy nights and seven days of public festivity at the two Baïrams; the

Sultan is allowed seven kadinns, enjoying the position and privileges of wives; there are seven principal officers of the Court, as there are seven female Court functionaries; every corporation or guild also is governed by seven chief officers.

At the approach of Baïram, or of any festival for which numerous visitors may be expected, the great central hall of the palace, usually so quiet, presents a lively scene. Twenty or thirty girls are busy with the "yorghans" or quilted coverlets, which they prepare with clean sheets for the occasion. The upper sheet of a Turkish bed is always sewn on to the yorghan, the edges turned over and neatly tacked; this can only be done conveniently upon the floor, and the soft tone of the matting becomes suddenly warmed up by patches of bright colour, as the yorghans are spread out for the operation: gay chintzes and flaunting patterns of impossible flowers, striped silk and cotton stuffs from Broussa and Damascus, beautiful tissues from Bagdad of deep rich hues or tender half-tints with flashes of gold or moonlight sheen of silver thread woven into the silk; here and there are laid the coverings for the pillows, thickly embroidered at the ends with flowers of coloured wools or silk and gold.

Some women come on to the scene with bundles of clean sheets poised upon their heads; the workers crouched on the floor bend over their employment;

many look on and give that easy help — advice; children flit about the hall, animated by the unusual bustle of preparation. The tchamashir ousta, with anxious face, and large keys dangling from her girdle, issues her orders to her subordinates. The girls are all good-humoured; there is a great amount of chattering, and all, even the idle ones, have tucked up their antarys tighter than usual to have their movements unimpeded, and in honour of the occasion.

The tucking up of the antary or long-trained dress, that only free women can allow to sweep majestically behind them, is accomplished in various modes, according to the fashions of the different harems. The style adopted by the attendants of Zeïneb Sultana was the same as that in favour in the Great Seraglio, and not used elsewhere. The three tails of the skirt, twisted into a ball in front, was an arrangement by no means always graceful or becoming, but sometimes, when carelessly drawn up, the draperies took the classical outline and folds of old Greek statuary.

All the women in this harem, as belonging to a sultana, wear at the back of the head, on occasions of any ceremony, a round of red cloth the size of a crown piece, with a small blue tassel hanging from it: this is intended to represent the fez, the distinctive badge of the Ottoman subject.

All the members of Zeïneb Sultana's household

receive a monthly present of money, according to their rank and age; the leading girl in each class, such as the chief dancer and the chief musician, possesses a set of beautiful diamond stars as a mark of distinction. In a harem of this rank such women as are careful, and who resist the allurements of the Greek and Jewish pedlars, may easily amass a considerable sum of money, as, besides the monthly allowance (which is very liberal), and the presents given at Baïram and on all great festivities, it is customary for visitors to leave backshish for distribution on a scale of generosity, or rather lavishness, almost ruinous to the giver. For instance, the mother of the Sultana, whose visits—of two or three days—occurred twice and sometimes thrice in the year, invariably left 300 Turkish pounds (over £297) to be shared amongst the attendants.

According to the strict letter of the law, slaves cannot possess property, and if their monthly allowance, which is an established custom in all great houses, were withheld, or the ornaments and savings of the slaves retained in the event of their quitting the family, they would have no legal cause of complaint; but this is one of the many instances that occur in Turkish life, in which custom, good feeling, the opinion of the neighbourhood, and the sense that *noblesse oblige* is stronger than established law, and it is rarely that slaves who have been well conducted are denied the entire possession of what they have been once allowed to consider as their own.

In a harem such as those of the imperial princesses, composed of one hundred women and girls in constant companionship, without relief to the monotony of their lives from intellectual occupations, or, indeed, from much occupation of any kind, it might be inferred that the vacuum and weariness of the day must inevitably be enlivened by frequent quarrels amongst themselves. If so, the battles rage silently, for in all that vast establishment, to the whole of which I had free access, I heard once only the sounds of woe and wailing—a little girl was being beaten by one of the calfas. The deepest quiet usually pervaded the place, broken sometimes by the sounds of rather boisterous laughter; but the habitual expression of most of the halaïks is melancholy and listless. Some of them, indeed, such as the moon-faced musician, Dilber Ada, cherish ambitious dreams, and see already within their grasp the high rank and title of Validé Sultana, but the greater number are content to count as the summit of human prosperity the post of favourite attendant of their mistress; and to attain this distinction, to supplant the reigning favourite, many intrigues are carried on; for this end the heartburnings and the strife smoulder, though unperceived by the stranger.

The order of the day is much the same in the palace of Zeïneb Sultana as in the households of lower rank; it is soon described. Turkish women rise early, and in the first freshness of the morning the measured sounds of sweeping the matting of the spacious hall warns us shortly to expect the irruption into the sleeping-chamber of two or three stout girls, who roll up the beds and clear us up without mercy. Perhaps we linger, declining such early attentions, but our peace is hopelessly gone, for in one corner of the room there stands a crazy old piano, which has great attractions for the idlers and presently one Circassian nymph, then a second, frequently even a third, will wander in and proceed to jangle out some native melody. Did I say melody? All three of them are at work at once, each picking out and pursuing, with desperate tenacity, her own particular air, utterly independent of the thrilling results of her neighbours' favourite fancies.

Then little cups of black coffee make their appearance, sometimes preceded by a tray of small saucers of olives, cheese, sweetmeats, and fried eggs. This is called the "caveh alti"; but many take only the black coffee until the midday meal, which is almost as elaborate as a dinner. The hour of dinner depends upon the time of sunset; it is always served after the prayer time, which ends the day. The announcement of dinner is made in a characteristic manner: one of the sofradjis (waiters at table) simply makes her appearance at the entrance of the room with a long folded napkin embroidered with gold at the ends hanging over her right arm; she says nothing, but it is perfectly understood that dinner is served.

The repasts of the household during the lifetime of the father of Zeïneb Sultana were furnished by the imperial kitchens at Dolma Bagtché, and as the dishes had to perform a journey of ten or twelve miles, their condition on arriving was not tempting to the appetite; neither were the dishes themselves delicate or choice, which is not to be wondered at when we reflect that about an equal number of men —the household of the Pasha, and inhabiting the selamlik—were provided for in the same manner, and that similar provision was made for all the married members of the Sultan's family, also from the imperial kitchens. The usual mode of sending out these dinners is in covered metal dishes, on a circular wooden tray covered by a thick leather cap, the whole finally tied up in woollen cloth. These trays may be constantly seen about midday and towards sunset in the neighbourhood of the Sultan's dwelling, and of the residences of wealthy people, borne on the heads of stout aïwass. This system of providing the table of married or dependent members of a household is very generally adopted by heads of families. In Zeïneb Sultana's establishment several cooks are kept on the premises for the work of furnishing more delicate viands for her table and for those of the khasardar ousta, the visitors, and of the principal women. When the Sultana dines in company with her husband, they are served at table by two elderly and remarkably ugly women, selected for the purpose.

The Pasha sees none of the younger slaves of the harem. On his passage through the apartments they are carefully warned to retreat, and there is a general flight, like the scattering of a covey, until he is fairly out of sight, the favourite hiding-place being some perdeh or door-curtain, commanding a good surreptitious view of the staircase. The same flight took place whenever the Sultana's young brothers arrived on a visit; but in the presence of the Padischah the necessity for veiling the face or for the concealment so rigorously observed on all other occasions is not in force, the law of Islam giving to the Sultan the right of gazing on the unveiled features of his female subjects. There is a story current that upon a certain festival of Baïram, many years ago, the elderly wife of some great man whose privilege it was, together with other ladies of her rank, to salute and compliment the Sovereign, being indisposed, despatched as her representative a young and pretty woman. The complimentary message returned by the Sultan to the invalid lady was gracious and considerate in the extreme. He begged that for the future she would consult her health, and feel herself absolved from the great fatigue of coming in person to the Baïram reception.

During the course of the morning, in the palace of Zeïneb Sultana, instruction is given to most of the children. Three native teachers are employed—a muezzim, an imām, and a female khòja, according to the age of the scholars, who learn Arabic and Turkish, reading and writing, sometimes a little arithmetic. The female teacher gives religious instruction to some of the elder girls. A few of them listen willingly; two or three of those in the neighbourhood of our room would even rise twice in the night to perform the supererogatory prayers, which are announced about midnight and a short time before daybreak.

Several European teachers are also employed for the different classes of music and dancing, which are held in a separate part of the building. A lady teacher has always two or three pupils for the piano; and there are occasional lessons given on the kānoon and the ood, stringed musical instruments much used in Egypt and Syria.

As the afternoon wears on, duties and lessons being over for the day, the great hall becomes animated by gliding figures; the doors into the garden are thrown open, and in twos and threes the bright groups saunter along without yashmak or feràdjé; for the boundary walls, of immense height, are further provided with screens of trellis-work, shutting out the view of the garden from the neighbouring hillside.

Each Thursday a detachment of girls joyfully put on the shrouding veil, and wrap the gay-coloured cloaks about them; they are taken in carriages, under the care of a calfa, and protected by an agha or an aïwass, to make an excursion to some spot of favourite resort. They return at sunset.

The Sultana herself seldom leaves her palace in state, but she flutters her poor clipped wings in the garden and the grounds, which run up a great part of the hill. The garden contains a miniature lake; it has its little island also, connected with the mainland by a yard or two of bridge, the whole strongly suggestive of the famous willow-pattern landscape. In the days which I am now recalling, the princess would row a tiny boat round and round until, tired of the monotony, she calls for her horse, riding with a side saddle; but again it is round and round, though on a somewhat larger orbit. Then the horse would be put into harness, and in an elegant little vehicle, still went the Sultana, driving round and round. What wonder that she sometimes burst the trammels and, with one or two attendants, went off to see some giant, or dwarf, or other attraction for the people, in which the mass of Turkish women delight, but in which her high rank forbade her to take interest.

The sunset gleams are fading; the miniature lake, the trim garden, the wooded hillside are bathed in shadow, while the golden light still sparkles and glitters from the opposite shore. The majestic beat of the many-oared caïques is heard from beyond the boundary wall. The lingering groups turn inwards from the garden and spread about the great hall, for the news circulates that dinner has arrived. Suddenly there is a cry, "Destour! destour!" (clear the road!) the girls fly and disappear; a black agha enters, followed by an aïwass who bears on his head a large dinner-tray. It is deposited on the ground in one corner of the hall; the aïwass vanishes without raising his eyes; the girls return: the sofradjis or table-women cluster round the tray and prepare to serve the table of the khasnadar ousta, which has been placed on a low stool, surrounded with padded quilts; other dinner-trays are laid in various parts of the halls and passages, and all dine in succession.

To complete the idea of life in Zeïneb Sultana's harem, let us take two or three scenes recalled from sketches made at the time. It was many years ago, but with the exception of great changes in the matter of costume, there is little, if any, alteration there in the actual routine of the daily life.

There is a rough sketch of a large, bare room lighted by many windows; fifteen or twenty women and girls, arranged in a semicircle, are playing on various instruments; in the centre, a common-looking man, in spectacles, seated before a music desk, beats time. This is the Sultana's military band—Circassians and Georgians principally—and they are taking their music-lesson under the guardianship of a tall black, who lounges near one of the doors. The music-masters form part of the orchestra of the Pera Theatre.

This is a good opportunity for judging the much-vaunted beauty of Circassian women, for these slaves have been carefully chosen, and combine an amount of personal charms rather above the average; and yet it is impossible, upon the whole, to deny that the idea of their loveliness is much exaggerated, according to our Western standard of feminine attractions.

The flute-player on the left-hand is the Ibrikdar Ousta—a tall woman, past the bloom of early youth. She shows the true Circassian type: a fair skin and delicate colouring, light chestnut hair, bluish-grey eyes, dark lashes, and a very slightly arched nose. These features should produce beauty, but they are too often marred by prominent cheek-bones, a wide mouth, and an ill-setting of the head upon the throat. In some instances, where these defects do not exist, the beauty remains, and may go far to justify the wide-spread reputation of Circassian women; but much of it also is due to the shrouding yashmak, that conceals the blemishes whilst it leaves unveiled the beautiful eyes, the carefully trimmed eyebrows, and a part of the pure soft brow. The hands, which may also be exhibited, are exquisitely small, soft, and delicate; the disfiguring custom of dyeing the finger-nails and palms with henna has long since passed out of fashion.

To be fair, with light hair and blue or grey eyes, is to be beautiful according to the idea of beauty in the East; if, in addition, the siren's eyes be very prominent and her face round and puffy—moon-faced, in fact—then her attractions are complete, even though the features may be entirely without expression. Dilber Calfa, sighing fastidiously into a tiny reed, near the centre of the musical group, has just such a combination of charms. Her countenance is quite unintelligent, showing no trace of thought or line of grace; but she holds her head very high, perfectly convinced that some bright day the Padischah will appreciate her claims to distinction, and that she will forthwith depart to the dubious delights of the Grand Seraglio.

Near to the proud " moon-faced " beauty is seated

the Georgian, Souzy-Dil. Her instrument is the violoncello. She is dark, her raven hair ripples back from a forehead of ivory; but her finely-cut, delicate features, the sensitive mouth, and, above all, the bright intelligence that lights up her charming face, are but slightly esteemed beside the colourless contour of Dilber's vacant countenance. Souzy-Dil has a very decided musical taste, and a great desire to learn from the " nocta" (notes), but she is condemned to pick up by ear, and to scrape on her violoncello the senseless tunes that form the chief study of the Sultana's band.

Not far from Souzy-Dil stands Deilfèrat, a blue-eyed, dark-haired, high-coloured girl. She is tall, yet she has need, indeed, to stand to her instrument, for she is working with all her strength at a monstrous double-bass; while Yildiz (the star) crouches on the ground at her feet, holding a small Turkish viol. She is not using it, but is adding to the general din a few impromptu words of so-called song. Yildiz is an Abkhasse, one of a fierce mountain tribe; she has none of the softness of the ordinary Tcherkesse. The Abkhasses are cast in a strong mould, reminding one somewhat of the Chaldean type. Her eyes are immensely large, with a deep fringe of silken lashes sweeping her olive cheek; when raised they have a look of some wild mountain animal.

This military band has been organised without

any thought of feminine weakness: one girl struggles with the coils of a French horn, another sounds the trumpet, two or three are exhausting their lungs on flutes; the bang of a drum and clash of cymbals are heard amidst the uproar. Some of the simple airs are prettily enough executed, but when the orchestra deals with more difficult music the effort at combined effect is utterly abandoned; each has quite enough to do to master her own rebellious instrument without troubling herself, in addition, about those of her companions. The result need not be described.

When this military band performed before the Sultana, an effort was made to put the musicians into characteristic costume—a tunic and pantaloons of white woollen stuff faced with blue, with little shakos to match. They made quite a martial appearance. While practising with the masters, the women threw a strip of muslin over the head and shoulders, extremely picturesque and becoming, though hardly answering the supposed purpose of veiling the face.

In a room on one side of the large hall in which the band is practising, another class is busily at work preparing a pantomime. In the opposite chamber dancing, both Turkish and French, is being taught; and, on the ground floor, may be seen a different set of pupils earnestly studying tumbling and the tight-rope! The imperial mistress had seen tumblers exhibiting at one of the great festivities, and had been so much charmed by the performance that she instantly determined to add that accomplishment to the list of studies desirable for her household. Some very young children were selected for the purpose, and it was sickening to witness the contortions of the tender little limbs under the guidance of a villainous-looking teacher, a Jew. Little Zerimicelle, in a miniature suit of blue and silver, with fleshings and spangles quite *en régle*, usually formed the apex of a hideous human pyramid, supported by an immensely stout and strong Georgian lass, clad, or rather unclad, in the orthodox style of the street mountebank.

Here is another scene. A vast hall, the ceiling supported on columns of many-coloured marble, the walls gorgeous with slabs of malachite, agate, and alabaster, rose-coloured porphyry, and lines of lapiz-lazuli; the floor, a beautiful parqueterie of inlaid woods; mirrors, gilding, dazzling lights from high branched stands of richly wrought silver.

A few women are listlessly gazing at something which is taking place in the front of the picture. It is an evening entertainment in honour of some hanums who have arrived on a visit. There will be dancing, music, and the pantomime, to be followed by an imitation of a ball " à la frança."

In the centre archway, the Sultana, tired of sitting

in the stiff armchair (which she adopts on occasions of ceremony, as more fashionable than the lounging couch of the country), has risen, and stands looking at two little girls dressed as clowns. They execute a sort of comic dance. The music is in accordance with the youth and feeble powers of the performers; it is not exhilarating. The dark Georgian ousta looks gloomily on, leaning against a column. The good old khasnadar has moved out of sight of the Sultana and subsided on to the floor, for etiquette would not allow her to sit in the presence of her mistress. By special order of the Sultana, chairs had been placed for myself and my companion, but the harem generally remained standing all through the long hours of the evening late into the night, or, when opportunity offers, they slip out into the corridor and crouch to rest on rugs or padded quilts.

These entertainments are not unfrequent at the palace; it is a very mild amusement, got up with infinite labour. But what can they do, these poor women, to while away the weary hours which they have not yet learned to employ more profitably? And they have the unwise habit of sitting up inordinately late. But to return to our soirée. The comic dance has been succeeded by several pieces of music, some Turkish, others from the operas most in vogue; then Turkish dances, and at length, after a pause, the pantomime begins.

Looking on the little piece of rough paper on which I took down at the time the names of the performers and characters of the piece, the whole scene lives again with the vividness of reality. There is Lahali Devran, the bright, affectionate girl, and our especial favourite; she is the young and dashing hero, who is nothing more poetical than a house-painter; there is Nazousta, the heroine; Melekpèr, the porter in the piece; and gentle, auburn-haired Nourmayàn, who represents the "heavy father." Souzy Dil is transformed into a harlequin; the "star" has become a columbine; while the chief dancer—they call her Razi Djeïlan (the antelope)—leads the ballet, supported by Belkiss, Niaziper, and Lahàlirenk.

The piece was some foolish trifle, forgotten as soon as ended, and which the poor girls with their utmost efforts could not succeed in acting intelligibly. The characters were well dressed, and the parts had been correctly learned; but how could they hope to render, with any approach to true colouring, scenes of European life, of which they neither knew nor could understand the simplest elements?

The theatrical performance was followed by the ball "à la frança," the great event of the evening. Much anxious thought and preparation had been expended on this display. The girls had frequently come into the studio to seek advice; half the number of the performers, to be dressed as young "tchelebis," were in special need of hints as to their behaviour under the unusual circumstances. My companion eagerly seized the opportunity of instilling some notions of politeness and deference to ladies; as, "for example," said she, "if a lady, while dancing, should chance to drop her pocket-handkerchief, her partner picks it up and restores it with a bow." This seemed to strike every one as a bright idea. On this, the eventful evening, the supposed company assembles. The young "cavaliers" look exceedingly well; their partners, in full ball dress of gauze and tarlatane and flowers, make a most creditable effect. They dance the mazurka, the galop, and the polka; the performance is excellent; finally, they take their places for the grand quadrille. At this moment it becomes startlingly evident that each fair dancer, in addition to her airy, floating draperies, is provided with a huge dark cotton bandana hanging at the right side, ready for action; it is the finishing touch of grace and refinement. They are quite new, bought expressly for the great occasion, and are conscientiously and carefully dropped at intervals all over the room, to be restored with intense gravity and the utmost show of polite deference.

Quadrille follows quadrille; the weary orchestra plays flaggingly; the Sultana has fallen to sleep on a couch; but as we slip quietly away the serious observance of the ceremony of the red bandana is still going on. They would have gone on the whole night through, those poor girls, rather than omit or slight so essential an incident in the manners and customs of polite society in "Franghistan!"

Amongst the Turkish portraits which followed that of Zeïneb Sultana, one—the likeness of an ikbal, or favourite of the Sultan, Abdul Medjid—is especially remembered.

A request came to me through one of the chamberlains to undertake immediately a small likeness of a lady connected with the Great Seraglio. The affair seemed rather mysterious, as no name was mentioned, and the work was to be executed, not in the house of the sitter, but in the house of a khasnadar of the palace, to which I was directed. The place had a questionable look. It is impossible to say from what this impression arose, but there seemed to be an absence of that quiet atmosphere of repose and decorum that prevails in all respectable Turkish houses, and I began the work with a feeling of distrust quite unusual under similar circumstances elsewhere.

The subject of the portrait proved to be a celebrated beauty, whose influence over the Sultan was said to be unbounded. The sittings were more than commonly troublesome, as the capricious " séraïli" took no heed of time or engagements, and frequently forgot altogether to come to the konak according to appointment. The little picture was a miniature in oils, to be enclosed in a case, by the particular desire of the sitter.

The charms of this fair Circassian consisted of a tall, well-formed figure, a delicate complexion, blue eyes, dark lashes, and bright chestnut hair; but the face was spoiled by the high cheek-bones and wide mouth which are common defects among her people. The appearance of the head was, however, striking, from the illumination of jewellery with which it was crowned—a magnificent *résille* of diamonds, covering one side of the hair, with a deep fringe of the same, mingled with rubies and emeralds, falling all around.

S—— hanum looked consumptive, and was no longer in early youth; although rather fanciful and uncertain, she was by no means ill-natured. The sum agreed upon for the picture was never paid; it remained, I am convinced, half-way to its destination, in the dishonest hands of the khasnadar, whose reputation was far from good. I may mention here the fact that in all my transactions with the Turks this was the only instance in which I failed to receive—with more or less of delay, but always, in the end, honestly and faithfully—the sum of money agreed upon between us.

By a coincidence, showing the untrustworthiness of newspaper reports, S—— hanum, at the very time during which I was quietly studying her features, was the subject of a sensational paragraph, describing her flight from the seraglio with an Italian, and the subsequent travels of the ill-matched pair in Western Europe.

II.

IN STAMBOUL.

The Bridge.—Place of Executions.—The Old Seraglio.—Alaï Kiosk.—The Guilds of Constantinople.—Their Patron Saints.—An Old Stone.—Bab-Houmayoun.—Fountain of Ahmed III.—His Inscription.—St. Sophia.—Construction and Destruction.—The Samaritan's Well.—The Hindoo's Tree.—The Atmeïdan.

To pass from Pera—the "Frank" suburb of Constantinople—to Stamboul, the heart of the Mussulman city, you must cross the bridge of Karakeny (the black village), so named, we may suppose, from the intense griminess of tone that distinguishes the busy neighbourhood of the Galata Custom House and of the quays fringing the Golden Horn. You reach the bridge through a surging crowd of vehicles and beasts of burden, of men and horses, of laden hammals, of people hurrying to their steamers, of sauntering pedlars crying out their wares, of agitated speculators clustering near the Stock Exchange, of idle loiterers looking for a windfall, all mixed up together in the roadway without any rule or "order of their going." You struggle onwards, pay the toll in passing, and are at length fairly on the bridge. You then look up for the first time since leaving the hill of Pera, and, if you have feeling for beauty of form and colour, you lose, in admiration of the scene, all remembrance of the past discomfort.

Let us take a day in October for an early quiet ramble in the ancient city of Constantine. It is just now veiled by a soft autumnal haze that lingers about the gardens and palace of the Old Seraglio, then, as the sunbeams gather strength and brilliancy, floats gently away, a golden mist, along the windings of the inner harbour. Everything seems to glow and brighten at this season, refreshed by the late rains after the languor of the long summer heat. Even the meanest object in the picture, the cobbler's crazy little stall, with the trailing garlands of wild vine, the pump under the blasted plane-tree, the blades of grass sprouting in some neglected corner about a broken capital or by the old sarcophagus (now a horse-trough), all glitter and sparkle in this clear Eastern atmosphere, as you turn from the crowded neighbourhood of the steamer bridge towards the battlemented walls of the Seraglio gardens.

There is a road now opened through the court of the Yeni-Djami. This is one amongst the numerous improvements which have been made in the matter of street traffic within the last fifteen years. Before that time, the busy stream of life ever flowing between the bridge and the populous quarter of the bazaars was crowded, pushing and struggling, up a rough, irregular flight of steps and through a narrow gateway, where it seldom failed to come into angry collision with some hammal bending under a load greatly too wide for the aperture.

It was on the open ground at the Stamboul extremity of the bridge that executions for capital offences formerly took place; happily, they were, and still are of very rare occurrence in the Mussulman city. Before the removal from this space of the dilapidated wooden buildings which encumbered the ground on the right hand, there existed, near the station at present occupied by the tramway cars, a ditch of sinister aspect filled with black mud and slime; it was crossed by a rotten plank, from which unhappy culprits were beheaded, their heads falling into the ditch; while others were hanged on the brink. The hollow has been long since filled up, and a stand of expectant street cabs covers now this spot of ghastly memories.

Leaving the crowded neighbourhood of the mosque, we follow, to the left, the quiet line of the tramway and turn downwards towards a lower entrance gate of the Seraglio. It is near the site on which formerly stood an antique pavilion, known as the Yali Kiosk, where ambassadors used to be received before obtaining audience of the Sultan. It was a quaint old place, with its heavy tent-like curtains of faded green, and deep projecting roof. It left a gap in the landscape when they swept it away to make room for the hideous though useful railway works now standing in its place and usurping its name.

We do not enter the gardens, although they are at times open to the public; the stern "yassak" (forbidden) of the sentinel is unanswerable, and bending our course upwards, follow the picturesque road that skirts the battlemented wall. The various buildings and the vast gardens of this old palace, erected by Mahomet II. (Ghazi), occupy the entire area of ancient Byzantium; they are inclosed within a high wall, which is strengthened at regular intervals by massive towers. There are eight entrance gates, of which the principal is the Bab-Houmayoun. The Old Seraglio, which is also known as the palace of Top Capou, was abandoned as a residence by Mahomet II., after the destruction of the Janissaries, and become the retreat of widows of the Sultans and of aged dependants of the imperial harem. It is now only occasionally used on the great festivals of Baïram, and the day of the adoration of the Hirka Scherif, or holy coat of the Prophet, which, together with the Sandjak Scherif (the sacred banner) and other relics, is preserved in the palace.

Upon the north-western angle of the wall of the Seraglio, and opposite to the entrance of the Porte (the Government offices, called Pasha Capoussy), stands the beautiful Alaï Kiosk, or Pavilion of the Processions. Let us pause here for a moment and conjure up the vision of a wonderful pageant—the march of all the guilds of Constantinople—that, during three days, poured in a continuous stream below the gilded lattices of the fairy-like kiosk, for the gratification of Sultan Murad III. and of the favourite ladies of his harem.

It was in 1634 : the Sultan, about to start for the siege of Bagdad, had caused the Sandjak Scherif to be taken from the chamber of relics, and the guilds were called together that they might accompany it to the water's edge. These processions, which may be compared with those of the ancient guilds of Flanders and Alsace, were abolished in 1769.

The establishment of guilds or companies, called "Esnaf," dates from the most flourishing time of the Bagdad Caliphate. Every profession, art, trade, or calling, is enrolled in one of these corporations, each company or craft being under the direction of a chief, elected by the body and recognised by the state.

Every guild acknowledges a patron saint. The traditions upon which their tutelary protection is claimed are founded, for the most part, upon events supposed to have taken place in the lives of the personages of Old Testament history. Thus, Adam, taught by the beavers and swallows, is considered as the first tailor, builder, and sawyer, as Hawa (Eve) is the patroness of bathwomen, having learned among the ducks and water-fowl of Eden; Cain, " the accursed," instructed by ravens, was the first gravedigger; while Abel is the protector of shepherds, and Noah of shipwrights, and so on through the list of nearly fifty great guilds with more than five hundred minor subdivisions.

On the occasion of the great processions, each trade carried curious and richly ornamented emblems and specimens of their craft, themselves being dressed in holiday attire; and the 200,000 men who are said to have passed in order before Murad III., seated in the Alaï Kiosk, must have produced a most remarkable and striking effect.

It is not difficult to imagine the wildly picturesque crowd in this, one of the most oriental-looking parts of the old city, but the picture is soon rudely shattered by the large metal placard of the Stamboul telegraph office; perhaps, also, by the passage at the same moment of a heavy tramway car; but as you wander onwards, still skirting the Seraglio wall, the dim past is once more recalled by a rough stone worked into the base of a massive square tower. A local authority, the Rev. Canon Curtis, surmises, from the fragmentary inscription on the stone, that it is part of a list of retired spearmen and runners, and was originally put up in the Agora, or market-place, of the ancient Byzantium. He believes this to be the oldest local inscription to be found in Constantinople.

From this point the road ascends abruptly between a lofty wall of the great mosque, that displays some beautiful examples of ornamental brickwork, and the grey battlemented towers of the Seraglio, draped and festooned with creepers, great tufts of vegetation, wild fig-trees, foxglove, and terebinth springing from the clefts of the rugged stone. At length the summit of the hill is reached, and you emerge from the shadow of the walls on the open space before the principal gateway of the palace precincts—the Bab-Houmayoun—and in front of the beautiful fountain built by Sultan Ahmed III.

The old gate has lately been considerably repaired—and spoilt—but the fountain retains all its charm of form and colour: the exquisite harmony of the rich arabesques that adorn the upper part, and the inimitable tracery of the gilt metal-work beneath. The imperial founder himself composed the inscription, which has been thus translated:—

"This fountain reveals to thee its age in these lines by the Sultan Ahmed. Open the source of this pure and tranquil water in the name of the Almighty, drink of the everflowing fountain, and give a prayer for the soul of Sultan Ahmed."

The first and outer court of the Seraglio, to which

the Bab-Houmayoun gives access, possesses many objects of deep interest. Unhappily, since the burning of the Government Pay Office, that stood on the right-hand side of the enclosure, the public are not generally admitted.

The vast buildings of the Imperial Mint are seen on the left as you pass the gate. The ancient church of St. Irene, now used as an armoury, occupies the northern angle of the enclosure; a small space on the outside of the church, surrounded by railings, contains several porphyry sarcophagi, tombs of imperial princes and princesses of the time of the Greek Empire. It is supposed that one of these is the tomb of Julian the Apostate. You see there, also, the gigantic head lately discovered in Stamboul, besides other fragments and relics.

Opposite to the entrance-gate of the Mint stands a gnarled, and hollowed, and time-worn plane-tree, spreading the shadow of its knotted boughs across the building. This tree, known as the Janissaries' tree, has a weird and sinister history. More than once the bodies of recalcitrant Governors of the Mint have swung from those rugged branches; and the ground beneath the spreading foliage of the great plane was the recognised rendezvous of the turbulent troops, who would pile up their soup-kettles here while waiting for the mess of Friday pillaw, served out from the neighbouring imperial kitchens. When things went wrong with them, the signal of rebellion was simple: they turned their cauldrons upside down and refused their food. Few sultans could brave this ominous "turning of the kettles," till Mahmoud II. abolished the corps of Janissaries, sweeping off the greater number of them in one fearful massacre.

At the further extremity of the area, the Orta Capou, or Middle Gate, leads to the second court of the Seraglio. In former times the Djellal Bashy (chief headsman) had his official residence in one of the flanking towers, and the deep nitches on either side of the gate received the piled-up heads of his victims.

Outside the Bab-Houmayoun, the walls and towers of the Seraglio can be clearly traced, descending the southern slope of the hill in an unbroken line, until they reach the shore of the Sea of Marmora. We will not follow them, but rather take the line of the street called the Divan-Yol, which commences here, and, turning round the vast precincts of St. Sophia, forms one limit of the great square of the Atmeïdan, or Hippodrome.

I may not venture on a description of the celebrated church-mosque—it has been frequently given by high and learned authorities—but merely notice that the original church of St. Sophia (the Eternal Wisdom), built by Constantine and subsequently enlarged, was twice burnt and frequently shaken by earthquake, and that finally the indomitable church-builder, Justinian, undertook the entire reconstruction of the edifice.

Dr. Neale (in his " History of the Holy Eastern Church "), speaking of St. Sophia, says that the Emperor Justinian "determined to erect a church which should excel all those then in existence. The execution of the work was committed to Authemius of Thralles, the first architect as well as mechanician of his time, and to Isidore of Miletus; but the emperor reserved to himself the power of suggesting, altering, or improving. Artists were collected from the whole world. Heavy taxes were imposed to supply the immense drain of money; the various salaries of the public teachers and professors were diverted to this channel. The riches of the East could hardly bear the expense of the undertaking. Ten thousand workmen were employed, and paid every evening in silver; Justinian, in a light tunic, was constantly at the works; the operations were pushed on with inconceivable speed, and costly presents flowed in from all sides to the rising pile.

"The church of the Eternal Wisdom was commenced at eight o'clock on the morning of the 23rd of February, A.D. 532, and was consecrated on the 26th of December, A.D. 537. The time occupied by its erection was thus five years, ten months, and three days. Justinian's pardonable exclamation is well known—'Glory be to God, who hath accounted me worthy of such a work. I have conquered thee, O Solomon!' The church then dedicated was, however, very different from the present building, and it needed a stern instructor to convince Justinian that the work must be strengthened. A series of earthquakes in the thirty-second year of that emperor overthrew the eastern hemisphere, and overwhelmed the altar in its ruin. The indefatigable prince recommenced the work, raising that part of the roof higher, and celebrated the second consecration in the thirty-sixth year of his reign, A.D. 561, from Christmas Eve to Epiphany." It was on the occasion of this partial rebuilding that four buttresses were added to the east front of the church. I find it mentioned elsewhere—on what authority is not stated—that "when Justinian rebuilt the church of St. Sophia the mortar was charged with musk, and to this very day the atmosphere is filled with the odour."

A few years back the ground before the west front of the mosque presented a very different scene to the animated picture of Justinian's ten thousand workmen employed in rearing the massive pile.

It was in 1869; a great fire had swept over this quarter, and, by the destruction of a considerable block of wooden dwellings that encumbered the south side of the mosque, had brought into view a group of exquisitely wrought columns supporting a remnant of an architrave. Near this another shaft, hitherto preserved from the action of the weather, remained, notwithstanding its centuries of existence, white and pure as if but newly chiselled. Other columns were prostrate and broken, and workmen were preparing to reduce them to the state of "metal" for the new macadamized road. Some splendid capitals lay about awaiting the chisel that should turn them into mere blocks of useful marble, while mounds of material already collected showed large fragments of verd-antique, of porphyry, jasper, and costly marble, still retaining traces of the delicate workmanship that formed them to ornament the precincts of the stately monument. Ancient bricks and tiles, also, were lying about in profusion, printed in the old Greek characters; they happily had attracted the notice of the learned, and the workmen were endeavouring to sell the fragments at fabulous prices, casting down and shattering the relics at the slightest hesitation on the part of the purchaser. Two or three Croats, seated in the shadow of one of the gigantic buttresses, were steadily reducing the fragments of old brick to powder. They had stationed themselves near to the mouth of an ancient well that exists at the base and in the thickness of the buttress. This is thought by some to be the "Samaritan's Well," which is known to have been about this spot. It took its name from the ring which was once attached to it, and had belonged, so said the tradition, to the holy well of Sichar, in Samaria, whence it was transferred by Justinian to his new church. As the Mussulmans never destroy a Christian ayasma, or holy spring, it is probable that this now dry well may be the one referred to.

The immediate vicinity of St. Sophia has been much cleared and improved of late years, both the west and south sides of the building, formerly choked up by labyrinths of shabby houses, being now cleared; and the structure rises nobly above its trees and "turbés." The broad opening to the south is planted with young sycamores on either side of an excellent road.

A pretty little garden, also, has been laid out at the entrance of the Atmeïdan. As it does not interfere with the few remnants of antiquity still to be seen in this part of the city, it may be acknowledged as an inoffensive embellishment.

We stroll into the Atmeïdan and stop at the Hindoo's tree; only a blasted, gnarled old trunk with feeble tufts of foliage straggling about the blackened branches, in which a Hindoo some years since had contrived for himself quite a comfortable little dwelling. He had fitted in an iron door and a tiny window, carpeted and papered the rough interior, and disposed about a multitude of small luxuries, amongst which he squatted all day long, supported by the charity of the neighbouring houses. This crafty, dark-skinned "dryad" had arranged with much ingenuity some planks suspended outside the trunk and among the twisted roots, supporting bright-flowering plants. In hollows of the branches hung cages full of birds. Now the tree is untenanted, the door wrenched off, the plants and the cages gone; but if this be the same tree that figures in accounts of a revolt of the Janissaries under Mohammed IV. in 1655, it has borne heavier and sadder burdens than birds and flowers, when the revolted troops marched to the Alaï Kiosk, preceded by their inverted kettles, and forced on the Sultan the immediate execution of several of the chief functionaries of the State. Two of the strangled bodies, the chiefs of the white and black aghas, thrown from a window, were seized upon by the mob, dragged to the Atmeïdan, and hung up on the tree outside the wall of the mosque enclosure. On the following morning the corpse of another victim, a beautiful and talented woman of high rank, was thrust into a sack and suspended between the aghas.

In the outer court of the mosque of Sultan Ahmed we remain awhile to rest. We are in the city, near public offices and crowded dwellings. The Divan-Yol is the Oxford Street of Stamboul, and yet what calm, what deep repose there is within the gates of the mosque enclosure, removed scarcely a stone's-throw from this populous highway. The throbbing life of the great city ebbs and flows around the bazaars and in the busy streets of Akaï Seraï; there is a feeble pulse of traffic here and there along some other thoroughfares, but away from these you find yourself suddenly in a region of almost unbroken quiet.

We sit on an old block of granite in the deep shade of a gigantic plane-tree. All the soothing influences of the surroundings are full of rest—the broad masses of transparent shadow cast by the beautiful mosque, the snow-white minarets raising the delicate tracery of their triple galleries against the tender blue just flecked with cloudlets, the gentle murmur of the leaves of the stupendous planes, the feeble twittering of birds, the vision of a bright-tinted woman gliding noiselessly across from sunlight to shadow, a group of mollahs slowly mounting the broad outer steps, some infant Moslems lazily flicking about the falling drops of the half-ruined fountain; all is quiet and restful, with a feeling of calm, of dreamy "kiéf," that the busy, toiling, onward feet of our western city life knows little of. But we must not linger; let us pass out to the Atmeïdan once more. We gaze at the Obelisk, with figures clear and sharp as when Moses may have looked upon their mysterious imagery in Egypt; then upon that other obelisk, the Colossus or pillar of Constantine Porphorigenitus, ever seeming to totter to its destruction; upon the twisted snake column of Delphi, that bears upon its antique bronze the list of Grecian tribes engaged in the battle of Platæa; and upon the massive building standing opposite. It is painted now, and whitewashed, but in its coating of grey stone was once, they say, a palace of the Roman quaestors.

III.

DIVAN YOLOU AND THE BAZAARS.

A fine Street View.—The Burnt Column.—The House of Busbek.—The Noor Osmanieh.—Kebabs.—Bazaar Touters.—Hadji Osman.—Fading Splendours.—Seal Engravers.—Spoonmakers.—Mosque of Sultan Bayazid II.—Ramazan Bazaar.—The Petted Pigeons.—Merchants from the far East.—Bric-à-brac.

THE principal objects of interest in this part of Stamboul are clustered about the head of the street called Divan-Yol, that skirts one end of the great square of the Hippodrome. At the farther extremity an ancient building, in which the collection of the costumes of the Janissaries is now displayed, covers one of the numerous cisterns for which Constantinople was so justly celebrated. A better-known cistern, the Bin-bir-direk, or "thousand and one columns," is reached through a shabby wooden doorway upon some vacant ground in the near neighbourhood.

A hundred yards or so forward, on the slope of the hill, stands the mosque and mortuary chapel of the celebrated poet and statesman, Fuad Pasha. This quarter is known as Fazli Pasha, and beneath it wind tortuous burrowings, underground galleries in every direction, sustained by massive subterranean walls and vaults of enormous thickness and solidity.

The line of the Divan-Yol, as seen from near the mosque of St. Sophia, presents one of the most striking street views of Constantinople. In the foreground —above a row of antique wooden houses and little shops—towers the old Sou-térazy, or water-tower, until lately draped in ivy, with fig and mastic trees springing from the disjointed stones, and a strange, ruinous dwelling of grey planks clinging to the summit. These effective touches have all been cleared away; but it would take even ruder treatment than that to spoil the picture. An irregular entrance to the once-celebrated cistern of Constantine, the Yéré-Batàn-Seraï, that gives its name to the quarter, is in the courtyard of an old konak not far from the base of this Sou-térazy.

The Divan-Yol follows with slight deviations, but under different names, the backbone of the line of hill through the entire length of the city from east to west, between the Seraglio and the Gate of Adrianople. It begins to rise at the Atmeïdan, till it passes before the marble front and gilded gratings of the Mausoleum of Sultan Mahmoud; then, level for a short distance, it ascends once more, where that interesting relic of past splendours, the Burnt Column, points the vista with the warmth and richness of its time-tinted shaft of porphyry, girdled with bronze. Transferred hither from Rome by Constantine, it was erected in this, his Forum, for the embellishment of his new capital. The silver statue of Apollo, designed by Phidias, which once adorned the summit, was afterwards injured by lightning, and finally blown down in the reign of Alexis Comnenus. The column itself has stood the test of fire over and over again, been repaired and bound with metal hoops, has been for centuries threatening to fall, but stands there yet, a relic of the strength and majesty of ancient Rome, and of the vanished glories of her Eastern rival.

On the opposite side of the street another ruin stands, picturesque in the desolation of its aspect, its massive arches overgrown with rampant weeds and branches. It was the palace of the German ambassadors, and was once inhabited, about the middle of the sixteenth century, by the learned Busbequius or Busbek, the ambassador sent to Soliman the Magnificent by Ferdinand and Maximilian. Busbequius is held to be the first introducer of the tulip into Western Europe; he brought some bulbs to Prague, from whence they afterwards spread over Germany. He wrote an account of his travels in Turkey, in which he mentions finding the tulip on his road hither from Adrianople.

What changes in the aspect of the Divan-Yol since the days when Busbek gazed upon the crowd passing along the highway beneath those now ruined windows! How different from the humanity which thronged it then is the crowd that gathers in it to-day! The old types are extinct, but, arrayed in the genuine dress of the period, their effigies may be viewed in the Museum of the Janissaries. The ruined palace is now inhabited by tinkers and dyers, and standing as it does in a great thoroughfare, from which all remains of antique beauty are being rapidly improved away, one trembles for the impending fate of the gaunt old monument.* In this part of the street are many fine specimens of iron-work grating, in enclosures of mosques, turbes, and médressehs; the designs are intricate, and often very beautiful.

We have passed beyond the " burnt quarter," destroyed by the great fire, which, in 1865, swept all before it, from the water-edge of the Golden Horn, right through the city, to the water-edge of the Sea of Marmora, on the other side. The new buildings which have arisen in the place of the former wooden and very picturesque houses are ugly, tasteless, and ill-adapted to the climate—a senseless imitation of the most ignoble type of Western architecture. It is a relief to quit the glare of stucco

---

* This picturesque ruin was entirely destroyed in 1883.

and unshaded glass for the softened gloom of narrow streets and tent-like eaves, with tones of grey and brown, and moss-grown walls and flickering dashes of amber light, and wandering wreaths of vine.

Out of the Divan-Yol for a time, turning towards the mosque of Osman, the Noor Osmanieh, in a neglected corner of whose outer court stood, until recently, a large porphyry sarcophagus, converted into a water-tank; it was called the tomb of the Empress Irene. The Noor Osmanieh is one of the mosques usually allotted to women during the month of Ramazan. Stop here at a well-known kebab shop, a dingy little hole close to the iron gateway of the bazaars, where, if you can consent for awhile to ignore the conventional trammels of polite society, and to take up a position on one of the very ricketty wooden stools standing about, you may eat kebabs in perfection, hot, savory, and succulent from off the skewer. This dining-saloon, which, besides the stools aforesaid, contains a bench or two, one decanter, two tumblers, and a saltcellar, is open to the street, and affords a pleasant lounge to the tawny dogs of the quarter, who take a profound though melancholy interest in the business of the establishment, wistfully watching the kebabs as they pass from the block to the skewer, and thence to the gridiron, until lost to view in the jaws of the customer. Dogs of large practical experience snap up many a stray morsel, heedless of the expulsion which ensues, for they soon steal in again, and resume their post of observation.

The genuine kebab consists of small pieces of mutton, cut with due regard to proportion of fat, and impaled, eight or ten pieces together, on a skewer. They are roasted rapidly on demand, and are served on flaps of native unleavened bread, with pepper, salt, and a sprinkling of chopped herbs. Sometimes the pieces are arranged in gradually increasing dimensions, topped by a lump of the fat tail of the Caramanian sheep, which pours down during the process of cooking a gentle cascade of grease over the skewerful, on a system of basting-made-easy.

Entering the bazaars we are beset by the Jewish touters. "Tchelebi! Dis vay, dis vay, for Broussa gauze? Ah! for bracelets? Ah! oil of roses? Table carpets? Persian rugs, boxes, towels, Broussa towels? Dis vay, tchelebi! What you want?"

You have entered the bazaar for a quiet saunter, to enjoy the picturesque, Oriental aspect of the place, and for a time you steadily ignore the attacks of these pests. One urges you to turn to the right; you turn sharply to the left, plunge into a maze of narrow alleys, and there, at the first cross-road, waits your tormentor, quite cool and utterly unquenched. "You take too much trouble, tchelebi," says the touter; "dis vay, dis vay!" It is sorely trying to the temper. Having long experience we may contrive to dodge our Jews a little, or (when impracticable) to endure, with a faintly successful air of unconsciousness, until—well advanced in the avenue of the Broussa stuffs—we run to earth in the shop of a genuine Broussa merchant.

Hadji Osman has grown very prosperous of late years, and slightly patronising; he was more malleable in his former little shop, or in the magaza where he stows his bales, somewhere in the weird recesses of an ancient khan. Many a stiff struggle over the delicate tissues has been gone through in that gloomy den, with its heavily grated window, and the padlock on the door half a foot in diameter. The conclusion of the conference was usually satisfactory, but never attained without an exhaustive amount of expostulation, accentuated by the final argument of a dignified withdrawal (effected with great difficulty down a steep and ruinous staircase), this move producing a recall and capitulation; peace and the bargain were concluded over little cups of black coffee at the expense of the Hadji.

The bazaars have greatly lost in attractiveness within the last few years, through the rapidly increasing spread of European fashions. The famous slipper tcharshi, once so dazzling with its rows and festoons of dainty, gold-embroidered papoushes, brightening the whole arcade, is now altogether uninteresting; a few of the gaily ornamented slippers are still displayed in glass cases for the benefit of strangers; but the general brilliancy is extinguished in an overwhelming flood of black boots, so that the place is scarcely worth a visit.

In the dirty, narrow alley that leads from one end of the Bit-Bazaar, or old clothes' market, towards the open space before the mosque of Sultan Bayazid, are found the stalls of the talisman and seal engravers. The engravers of Stamboul were renowned in former times, and their art being exercised by men of some learning, this guild was amongst the most respectable in the city. The calling was hereditary, and the number of engravers very strictly limited. At present they make but a poor appearance. Their glass cases exhibit amulets, stones, and small jewellery, amongst which are bundles of little sticks like lucifer-matches, with a so-called turquoise stuck on the end. The genuineness of these gems is more than doubtful, as the imitation of the turquoise is so perfect that the merchants themselves are deceived by the crafty Persian dealers.

At the farther end of the alley the spoon-makers, working in boxwood, horn, and tortoiseshell, sit cross-legged upon the counter of their rustic-looking shops, which is seat and frontage and workshop all in one. Most of them are hard at work at their trade, only suspending their labours to serve customers.

The spoons displayed in glass cases are extremely elegant, both in form and style of ornament; there are the spoons with tortoiseshell bowl, the handle of ebony inlaid with silver, coral, and mother-of-pearl. Others have the bowl of cocoanut, ivory, fine horn, or even of agate, and most of the slender, delicately turned handles are tipped with a little branch of coral to avert the evil eye. The most beautiful ornamental spoons are made in Persia of pear-wood; they are very large, but exceedingly light and richly carved; they are sold by the dealers in curiosities.

Leaving the bazaars by the lane of the spoon-makers you come at once to the precincts of the mosque of Sultan Bayazid II. During the month of Ramazan it is in the courtyard of this mosque that the merchants from the far East—from Bokharah, Turkestan, India, and China—spread their tempting wares. They set up their stalls along three sides of the gallery surrounding the quadrangle and about the paved court in the centre of which stands the Fountain of Ablutions. This fair is especially picturesque, the merchants themselves being as worthy of attention as their merchandise. The fountain is a circular building, with a deep-eaved roof, shaded by a group of cypress and other trees, and by a wandering wild vine. Some men are engaged in ablution, preparatory to their devotions; others, passing in a many-tinted stream beneath the half-raised curtain of the richly fretted doorway, disappear into the solemn shadow of the interior. Around the court beautiful columns of verd-antique, green jasper, and porphyry support the roof of the raised gallery, one division of which serves as the refectory of the wild pigeons that roost in the cypresses, and are fed by the bequest of the founder, and by the benevolence or the curiosity of the passer-by. Give a trifle to the man sitting all day long in the corner beside the grain-bin, and before the handful of seed is thrown out the pigeons are in full descent, struggling and pecking as if their lives depended on that particular dole. As this goes on with little intermission from sunrise to sunset, the digestive powers of the Ottoman pigeon would seem to be fully as healthy as those of his British brother. The pigeons have their little drinking-pail and their bath at the farther end of their dining-hall, and their dominion is never invaded by the stalls of the merchants, however great may be the pressure elsewhere. These wild pigeons are the descendants of a pair of birds bought by Sultan Bayazid of a poor widow who implored his charity; he made a present of them to the mosque, endowing them and their descendants to the last generation—a strange exhibition of gentle feeling in the man who, amongst other crimes, hunted to his death his own brother, the accomplished and unfortunate Prince Djem!

The stalls of this year's fair are numerous and well filled. A spicy, aromatic odour pervades the quarter where the sweetmeats are sold; the swarthy, turbaned vendor is half hidden behind his piled-up delicacies, which prove more tempting to the eye than the palate. There are lumps of pressed dates, pistachios from Damascus, bananas, rahatlakoum, dried fruits, boxes of honeycomb, cakes of unknown composition, and an infinite variety of sugared pastes, and mighty almond bohosses. An opposite neighbour, in a white turban, very much depressed and worn with his Ramazan fast, presides over a stall of china cups and bowls, mingled with charms and amulets in little saucers, with spices, nutmegs, jars of preserved ginger, and aromatic gums. There is a Bokhara merchant, of crafty, eager countenance, owner of a stall well spread with beads and chaplets, with tails of musk-rat, bottles of perfume, strange stones, amber, and little bits of roughly-cut cornelian. On the ground below this stand sits a boy selling lengths of orris-root for toothbrushes and toothpicks. The use of toothbrushes made of bristles has been recently introduced among Turkish ladies, although they have set aside with difficulty the prejudice against hairs which may be those of the unclean beast.

In the most sheltered corner of the gallery Hadji Hussan Hindi, the Indian merchant, sets up his Ramazan stall, bright with the delicate, fanciful toys of China and Japan; the best matting also is to be found here. The next-door neighbour makes a show of Arabic, Persian, and Turkish literature; his little temporary shop is furnished with a couch or two and some stools, whereon are seated mollahs smoking narghilés and tchibouks, and sipping coffee as they dip into the illuminated volumes. No one ever seems to purchase at this stall; indeed, throughout the bazaar, the idea of selling their wares would appear to be altogether below the dignity of the proprietors. They will answer a question as to price reluctantly—not omitting, however, to state four times the true amount for those restless, inquisitive strangers—but it is a matter of supreme indifference whether the answer may lead to a deal. One of the most superbly disdainful amongst them is an elderly man wearing the green turban of a descendant of the Prophet. Year after year he comes to the same place; he is very grave and solemn, utterly inflexible in the matter of bargaining, and with a steadily ascending scale of prices and equally steady decline in the quality of his goods, which, with the usual display of gums, essences, uncanny-looking amulets, are further adorned with dangling specimens of outlandish basket-work, and with garlands of little packets of henna for dyeing the toes and fingers of unfashionable Stamboulees.

On the farther side of the colonnade there are stands of rare and costly porcelain, where chance now and then brings beautiful specimens of Dresden china and Venetian glass, and sometimes stray bits of furniture of the genuine Louis XV. period; it is the paradise of the bric-à-brac hunter. The smoker has his temptations in the form of pipes and amber mouthpieces, or the delicate red clay productions of Tophaneh; while, sprinkled about in odd corners, are humble displays of Adrianople soap in company with caviar, and a fearful black sausage, made of buffalo flesh and garlic—a dainty produced by the makers of pastourma, or dried beef, in Roumelia.

A few years ago a quiet visitor to the bazaar might buy, for a few piastres, many a trifle of real artistic merit, but the influx of too demonstrative tourists has utterly spoiled the market; those palmy days have vanished, though the place itself has lost nothing of its rare charm. The Eastern form and rich, harmonious colouring of the merchants' dresses are not as yet quenched in dull, prosaic broadcloth. Strange figures, many-tinted, flowing, supple, glide in and out amongst the columns. In the centre of this slowly-moving crowd the cool trickle of the fountain mingles with the softened chant of the faithful from within the mosque, and with the murmur of the petted pigeons; the tall cypress bends its stately head, the vine-garlands wave a gentle dance of shadows on the rough pavement, and on the coarse canvas of the merchants' stalls. There is an indolent fascination about the place; but, passing out by the narrow gateway, one steps forward a century or two into the midst of a crowd of well-appointed carriages, waiting for pashas who are performing their afternoon namaz in the mosque.

IV.

PERA.

The Grande Rue.—Street Commerce.—A quiet Corner.—Bulgarian Milkman.—Maltese Goats.—Snails and Cuttlefish.—"Milk-drinking Lambs."—"Koush Conmaz!"—Caramanian Mutton.—The "Djighirdji" and Marco.—A Dog's District.—The Bear and his Leader.—The Schekerdji.—Mohalibè.—Oil, Lemon, Soot, and Charcoal.—A humble Devotee.—"Sakas."—The Buffalo Cart.—A Greek Funeral.—A Quiet Time.—The Fire Gun.—Great Fire of Pera.

PERA is the "Frank," or, as some would say, the Christian suburb of Constantinople. The name is derived from a Greek word signifying "beyond," as it is beyond and opposite to the city of Constantine, now more especially known as Stamboul. Pera is built on the steep slopes of a little promontory which separates the Golden Horn from the Bosphorus, and, extending also for a considerable distance along the sharp ridge of the hill, it commands on all sides exquisite views of the surrounding country. The winter residences, called here the "palaces," of the Christian embassies, are situated on or near the main thoroughfare, the "Grande Rue," or High Street, and the suburb contains many handsome and luxurious houses belonging to Greek, Armenian, and foreign families, besides shops of all nationalities well stocked with merchandise imported from the West.

Pera, with the business quarter of Galata at the foot of the hill, is the most polyglot town in Europe: here each of the different foreign communities lives its own life, administers its own justice, works its own postal system, circulates its native coin, maintains its national churches, has houses, furniture, and servants, as if still living in the fatherland; and although beyond the limit of the diplomatic circle, there is little social intercourse amongst the groups by which the nationalities of Europe are represented, the shops stand in goodly rank and file along the narrow Grande Rue, which is almost the only line of street between Galata and the upper portion of the " Frank " town, and it is undeniable that there exist here greater facilities for procuring articles of foreign (*i.e.* un-English) manufacture than in any of the great capitals of civilisation. English, French, Italian, German, Swiss, and Greek display the goods for which their respective countries are most renowned, while three wonderful bazaars seem to offer to the public a little of everything that can benefit the human race. Then there are the churches and chapels of all denominations, which have their entrance on or near the principal street; and while the air resounds with the bells calling

Christian people to their places of worship, it is hard, indeed, to believe in the Moslem "fanaticism" which is such a favourite party cry of the day: had people a true knowledge of the subject about which they discourse so freely and so ignorantly, they might realise, with considerable astonishment, the fact that in no country of Europe, England and France excepted, is religious liberty for Christians of all denominations so freely and completely given as in Turkey, the Sultan or the Government giving the ground for most of the churches and charitable buildings, admitting, entirely free of custom-house dues, all goods imported for the use of the Christian missions, and protecting and, as far as possible, keeping order amongst so-called religious processions that too often afford, by their violent and indecorous behaviour, a humiliating contrast to the sober and quiet demeanour of their Turkish guards.

It is not, however, the Pera of the diplomatic or controversial world that interests us at present, but the polyglot city, its street merchants and street cries in many languages, and the trivial incidents of its daily life, which give so peculiar a character to the aspect of the place.

Almost the whole of the itinerant commerce of Constantinople is carried on by peasants from the provinces and the tributary states, who come up to the capital to seek their fortunes, remaining for various periods ranging from several months to as many years, according to the distance and difficulties of transit from their native villages, where they have left their wives and families. They revisit their homes from time to time, then return to their labours, until having amassed a sufficient sum on which to retire, they settle down in the Memleket (the native place) to cultivate the ground, and end their days amongst their own people.

These street merchants and labourers are estimated at between 60,000 and 70,000, of whom a small proportion only are genuine Turks, the greater number being Armenians; the last, a sober, honest, and industrious body of men, are the " hammals," or street porters, who are also employed as the guardians of banks, counting-houses, and shops, besides which they take service willingly as household drudges in their leisure hours. Other Armenians are the " sakas," or water-carriers, and in both capacities they are members of an organised society, under the direction of a chief of their own appointing. It is amongst these hammals that the descendants of the ancient kings of Armenia may principally be traced; and the name of many a humble individual staggering under his load, or counting the coppers gained by his hard day's toil, is high-sounding enough to suit the most exalted destiny: Tighranes and Argashenz (Artaxerxes), it may be, carry between them the portantine or sedan-chair which is their joint property; Tiridates, Balthazar, and Arisdaghez are bringing water to your cistern, while Mithridates stands by with a leathern hump upon his shoulders, ready for the first load that may offer.

The Albanians are also numerous; they are the sellers of mohalibé, khalwah (sesame-seed and honey), salep, and of a sort of fermented acid drink much favoured by the Turks. The bakals (grocers) and the makers of stovepipes and of iron-work in general come from Kaïserieh (Cæsarea in Asia Minor), while Maïtos, opposite the Dardanelles, and other places in Roumelia, send us carpenters, and Yanina and Salonica, masons.

The woodcutters are mostly Turks from the neighbourhood of Trebizond and the interior of Anatolia, and it is also the Turks who manufacture and sell the sweetmeats so attractive to the public of all ages. Greeks and Bulgarians arrive from the barren slopes of the Pindus mountains to pass a season in selling fruits and vegetables; and many engage as milkmen, and as journeyman gardeners, carrying about plants and flowers out of which they make a lucrative trade.

The Persians are the principal donkey-drivers of the capital; they and their patient little beasts form an important element in the moving panorama of the street scenes, as, in default of sufficient roads and proper vehicles, it is the fate of the little donkeys to stumble along, encased in monstrous planks, or bearing their heavy panniers loaded with brick and stone. The Kurds work as hammals of an inferior degree; they are much employed about the quays and custom-house in unloading vessels, and are supposed, in a general way, to be devoted to coal; while the Montenegrins and Croats flourish spade and pickaxe in companies and under the orders of a chieftain, to whom they pay feudal obedience.

There is, in Pera, an unpretending stone house on the sharp slope of the hill, looking towards the Sea of Marmora, and under the shadow of the rough height which is crowned by a Government school; it stands away from the neighbouring street, but an irregular pathway, a kind of short cut towards the upper end of Pera, passes before the door. People remark that it is a very "quiet" corner. It is, in fact, so quiet, so out of the way, that all the noises which strive in vain to obtain a hearing in the crowded and bustling Grande Rue, take refuge here, and unaided imagination would fail to realise the cries, the shouts, the barks, the growls, the laughter, and the lamentation which find expansion and relief in this, our very quiet corner. To gain some idea of the polyglot sounds, the fantastic and picturesque groups—the comedy of life, in short —that passes across the stage of this little open-air theatre between sunrise and sunset, let us take a day —at hazard—and note the different scenes which the revolving hours bring forward.

It is spring-time, about six o'clock in the morning; already, in the grey dawn, the first faint murmurs of awakening town-life have breathed in the mournful-sounding cry of the Bulgarian milkmen coming slowly in from the surrounding villages with great cans, jogging along on horses or mules; they are the pioneers of the almost countless street-sellers of the city. The voice of the soutdji dies in the distance, as a flock of Maltese goats run jingling by on its way to some pasturage on the outskirts of Pera. Then a bright, merry call wakes up the neighbourhood: "Frangiolà! frangiolà! franiolàdji—i!" It is the itinerant vendor of rolls, who has his customers among the small houses round about. The quarter rubs its eyes, gives itself a shake, and is wide awake and on the move; for, by this time, men and beasts of burden, street-sellers, and building materials, begin their customary progress around the hill of Galata Serai.

In Pera, everything can be procured at the street-door, from the most necessary elements of daily food to the most needless articles of fashion—these last, perhaps, rather out of date and behind the times, but none the less highly appreciated by the simple neighbours of our "quiet corner." There are sounds of active bargaining going on below. On the doorstep, a large basket, decked all round its border with bunches of poppies and elder-flower, takes up the entire space. It is a charming little bit of the fresh country, very tastefully arranged with beds of bright green foliage; but the contents of the basket, although equally suggestive of fields and gardens, lacks the charm and the grace of the floral bordering: it is—snails! fine, fat, juicy snails, briskly alive! They overflow their boundaries, and some are making a stately progress, with horns erect, over the stone entrance-step; they are picked up by the Greek servant, upon which they retire promptly into their native seclusion. But this modesty will not save them, for they must form part of a Greek Lenten dish, much esteemed by that ancient people, almost as much so, indeed, as the cuttle-fish, which they eat in great quantities during the same season; and the worthy man who intends a treat of the last-named delicacy for the family supper, does not shrink from carrying home the loathsome creature, suspended by a string, with all its livid-looking tentacles flapping, as he walks along, reflecting on the rich flavour of the "ink" sauce with which it is to be dressed. The bag of dark-coloured fluid which is found in the body of the cuttle-fish, and called by the natives "ink," is the sepia well known to the artistic and commercial world.

What is that old man calling for sale? "Lambs!" says he in Turkish; "little lambs! home-raised, tender, milk-drinking lambs!" The basket on his back displays only green stuff; green balls of some sort ornament the rim. They are artichokes—young artichokes, cut probably in the market-gardens which fill a great part of the moat beneath the ancient walls of Constantinople; and the merit of being home-grown, which is insisted upon by all the vendors of spring produce, may be explained by the fact that the greater proportion of the early fruit and vegetables is supplied from Broussa, Smyrna, the Greek islands, and even from Egypt, where they come in much earlier than in this cooler climate, but being gathered too soon and badly packed, they arrive faded and flavourless, very inferior, indeed, in quality to those that are truly "home-grown." What is there in the undeveloped artichoke to evoke poetic fancies? In Paris they are offered by the mysterious cry of, "La tendresse et la verdurette!" —here they are "sucking lambs!" We cannot pause to solve the question, for the man has wandered away with his little green "lambs," and it is again a gardener that follows him down the path. He holds beneath his arm a large bundle of green weeds, telling the public that "Birds do not alight upon it! birds do not alight upon it!" So be it; but how does this ornithological fact interest us?

The honest man is offering some wild asparagus, and the descriptive name of the plant is the Turkish suggestion of the feathery lightness of the green sprays.

After poesy comes the prosaic fact of a hideous burden borne by a miserable and much-enduring horse, whose load is hidden by a ghastly blood-stained cloth; it is the itinerant butcher's stall, with a stock of goat's flesh and Caramanian mutton of inferior quality. Sloping planks on either side form both the shop-front and the block, on which the uninviting viands are cut up. There are butchers' shops in Pera which furnish the tables of the better classes with excellent meat, the beef coming principally from Odessa; but the wandering meatman is the purveyor of humble households, who patronise also the trade of another individual somewhat in the same line of business, the "djighirdji," or dealer in liver and lights. He comes forward balancing a long pole duly garnished with dangling hearts and pallid lungs. The street-dogs sympathise keenly with the national taste, and a pack of the yellow, dusty creatures follow the fascinating garland, licking their lips in eager anticipation, but not, as yet, daring to advance to the assault. Perhaps the man will stop at that piece of open ground and share the treat amongst them, as animals are frequently fed in this way through the bequests of pious Mussulmans; but no, he is moving onward. The stir in the canine kingdom has aroused Marco, the patriarch of the tribe, a tawny brute, whose rough old body shows the scars of many a hard encounter; they call him the "king of the quarter," and few in dogdom venture to resist his will. He rises and shakes himself, then moves forward with a sublime indifference to learn the cause of the commotion. "Ah, ah! those dangling bits look good!" He mounts a little hillock for nearer inspection, and a drop of blood falls on his nose. It is too much! He forgets himself and the dignity of his position, springs upwards and tears away a large sheep's heart, upon which, in one wild moment of combined attack, the whole of the long pole is stripped. The man turns gently round; his merchandise has vanished, and, without a word, he calmly retraces his steps: it is his " kismet."

In the meantime our dogs enjoy their feast, gazed at with hungry envy by the members of a neighbouring tribe gathered near their boundary-line, for the invisible frontier which separates the various states of the wild-dog kingdom is as clearly defined and as strictly guarded as if laid down by commissioners and international law. Many a tough and hard-fought battle takes place at the entrance of a street within a stone's throw. It is the recognised limit of another band or family, and woe to the grown-up dog who, tempted by the allurements of the rubbish thrown out in readiness for the morning dust-cart, shall venture to creep quietly towards an enticing bone. The clamour which instantly echoes through the neighbourhood warns the intruder; he retreats within the limit of his own domain, then turns to defy the enemy, strongly supported by his tribe, and bleeding, limping forms retire after a few minutes of fierce and desperate encounter. A young puppy, if very small and ignorant, is permitted to stray across the boundaries unscathed; he is sniffed at, then with supreme contempt, ignored; but a grown dog is expected to know and to obey the unflinching laws and regulations of dogdom.

"Tam! tam! tam!" the sound of a native drum comes from the narrow alley beside the house; the dogs burst into a chorus of defiance in howls, and cries, and smothered growls. The noise is deafening; our little Maltese throws itself against the window with a shriek of impotent fury. No need for inquiry; we know that a wandering bear has paused on its weary round, to rest and exhibit in the "quiet corner." Yes, there he is, held at the end of a long chain by his owner, an Asiatic peasant. The two have travelled from the gorges and forests of Mount Ida in Bithynia, and it is hard to say which of the combatants presents the wildest appearance when they begin to struggle together for the gratification of an admiring circle of idlers, principally composed of Greek maid-servants, whose heads are dressed in tumbled muslin, trailing down the back over a cascade of uncombed hair, while their feet are shod in heelless slippers. Some bacalâkis also have joined the group, grocers' boys on their way to collect orders; they pause to share in the excitement, and to watch for the glorious opportunity for a sly pinch or a wrench of the tail of the furry monster as he lumbers heavily about; but the little crowd dissolves as if by magic when the poor peasant holds out his shabby tambourine for halfpence. What a study for a painter, this bronzed visage of the Asiatic mountaineer, with his dark eyes glowing through a forest of ebony locks escaping from a tattered turban! His teeth gleam like pearls in a copper setting as he catches a lump of bread, which he faithfully shares with the hairy comrade who sits beside him, panting, weary, and very limp.

An elderly Turk next appears upon the scene; he carries on his head a large tray with a raised back, and, under one arm, a three-legged wooden stand, which he presently sets up with the tray upon it. This is a "schekerdji," or "sweetstuff" man, and the bright, many-coloured display consists of sugared-almonds, lemon-drops, rahatlakoum, sweet mastic, preserved apricots, and every variety of native-made bon-bon, all tastefully arranged, and preserved from flies by means of a large pliable whisk that waves like a plume of feathers at the head of the board.

Another collection of sweet temptations much carried about is of the "stick-jaw" description. The black, brown, red, white, and yellow substances are disposed on a flat metal dish, divided into compartments radiating from the centre, where there is a revolving stick which the appreciative twirl round, and the dealer, with an iron skewer that serves for all, scoops out a halfpenny or a farthing lick from the sweet at which the point may stop. But these dealers are generally Persians. Our Osmanli is of a superior order, and he gravely waits the approach of customers; they quickly gather round, amongst them two little Turkish girls under the charge of an old man in a cotton dressing-gown and large white turban. The little maidens are on their way to the day-school of the quarter, for their gold-embroidered school-bags are slung over their shoulders, but they stop soberly at sight of the scheker, and enter upon a serious bargain on the subject of candy, exacting, with much show of experience, the largest lumps obtainable for ten parás. They are, however, slightly distracted during the negotiations by the rival charms of the mohalibé which an Albanian is dispensing at a neighbouring house-door. Mohalibé is a sort of cold jelly composed of ground rice and milk; it is served in saucers, powdered with sugar and sprinkled with rose-water: in the proper season a lump of clotted cream, called caïmak, is added. There is nothing prettier and more tempting than the mohalibé trays, when the white jelly is covered with a clean, wet cloth and surrounded with gaily-coloured and gilded saucers, while a richer display of ornamental porcelain rises in tiers at the back. Then there are the slim metal arrow-shaped spoons, and the Oriental-looking flask of rose-water with its slender neck. The costume of the mohalibédji completes the picture: he wears the broad Albanian fez with a ponderous dark blue tassel, and a large striped cloth is bound round him like an apron.

While the little girls are consuming their sweets, the turbaned guardian, like a true old Turk, fond of an easy life, and especially gentle and indulgent towards children, has patiently subsided on to his heels, and is sipping black coffee, provided by a wandering cafedji who has set up a little brazier of lighted charcoal on the open ground in hopes of custom from a band of workmen employed in levelling a part of it. Not far off, a barber is in full work, all the labourers seeming suddenly impressed with the necessity of having their heads shaved, much to the inconvenience of the numerous passers-by, as the barber is operating on the edge of the pathway. But no one thinks of police supervision or street order in this out-of-the-way quiet corner, and so everyone does just as he likes; and the hungry are consuming masses of greasy pillaw, green lettuces, and raw onions all round and about.

"Ya, moubârek!" ("Oh, ye merciful!") cries a voice in rather a supplicating tone, "nine lemons remain to me! Only nine lemons!" The owner of the voice has sold the greater part of his stock-in-trade, and invokes the pity of the public to clear out his basket. "My soul! my lamb!"—to an idler who is gazing vacantly upon him—"only nine lemons!" Does he dispose of his fruit? We cannot say, for the streets are by this time full of life and movement, and the place of the lemon merchant is now occupied by a Bulgarian carrying a large crate filled with live poultry. The poor birds mingle their lamentations with the piteous cries of a bunch of fowls which he holds in his right hand, tied together by the claws, and head downwards, and with the screams of terror from a fine goose in an equally painful situation on the left. "Callo la—thi!" calls out the Greek oilman, with a prolonged and unctuous intonation. "Callo ksìthi!" cries, in a sharp incisive tone, another individual, who drags behind him a little donkey laden with small barrels of vinegar. "O—djak—dji—i!" This last announcement, majestic and impressive, proceeds from a being of gigantic height, black from head to foot, who bears, as a sceptre, a vast bundle of dishevelled brooms. His aspect is formidable, but he is only the chimney-sweep of the quarter, a mild and perfectly harmless creature.

Presently there labour along the pathway two heavy sacks of charcoal; someone is beneath them, as is proved by the stifled call of " Kumûr var!" ("There is charcoal!") the two-legged beast of burden stating the fact, without strength or energy left to press it further on the public notice.

Twelve o'clock: one of the hours of Mussulman prayer. The call of the muezzin is heard from every minaret of the hillside and of the valley beyond, which is a Turkish quarter of the town, and some amongst the labourers respond to the call, leaving work to rub their hands and feet with earth in default of water, according to the injunctions of the Koran. There is a little hillock covered with fresh blades of grass and tangled wild flowers; it stands back from the pathway, and a poor workman chooses the spot in order to perform there his "namaz" without interruption; he has no prayer carpet, he simply turns towards Mecca and begins his devotions. Every change of attitude in the Mussulman prayer has a special meaning, being accompanied by pious phrases and ejaculations; it may, therefore, be interesting to note his movements, although the murmured words are, of course, quite inaudible. He stands at first upright, with his arms hanging down, his bare feet a little apart; next the hands are raised, open, on each side of the face, the thumbs touching the lobe of the ear; this is the introduction. The worshipper begins the prayers by placing his hands together, the right uppermost; then bows low from the waist, his hands slightly spread upon his knees; then raises himself for a moment and afterwards kneels down, and, with his hands on the ground before him, touches it with his nose and forehead; without rising, he then sinks backwards—this bowing is performed twice—after which he rises in one movement (the feet still remaining on the same spot), and stands again, the right hand clasping the left, and all the previous attitudes are repeated four or five times. At one period of the devotions, the worshipper, sitting back, turns his head first over the right shoulder, then the left, with murmured salutations supposed to be addressed to the good and evil angels of his destiny; finally, he stands, holding his hands before his face as if reading, then gently strokes face and beard, and the namaz is completed; the poor man slips on his worn old shoes and, sitting down, begins tranquilly to eat his dinner, a large lump of coarse dry bread.

While watching the flowery hillock with its

humble devotee, we have been for some time aware of a heavy tramping sound, audible above the noises of the street: an irregular procession of Armenian water-carriers is slowly making its way upwards, recalling a subject which in the summer season weighs heavily on the minds of the inhabitants of Pera, a problem as difficult of solution as the dreaded " Eastern Question "—it is the question of the water supply. These Armenians are the authorised sakas; they climb the stairs, each bearing slung across the shoulders a sort of leathern box, narrowing towards one end, from which a flap of leather, when raised, lets out between two and three gallons of yellow turbid water; in the dry season even this can hardly be obtained, although the price charged is very high. As each summer comes round the terrible insufficiency of the supply to the needs of the overgrown suburb is the leading topic of the moment: projects and plans without number are brought forward, talked over, and abandoned, leaving us at length, as before, to the tyranny of the sakas, the bitter enemies of the Kurds and Persians, who strive to meet the wants and to gain a scanty pittance by the aid of their water-jars and little barrels, filled drop by drop at the half-dry fountains. The independent housekeeper, defying the sakas, will assert the right to purchase of the Kurds or of any who may offer water for sale, and the bare-legged Armenians leave you with a haughty disdain; but the irregular supply failing, perhaps you entreat them to return. No, the fountain of the quarter is shut, they say; they can attend to regular customers only. There are indications of a change in the weather, and the cistern beneath the house will be partly filled; but at the first symptoms of such relief from the pitying rain, the irresistible string of leather "courbas" once more appears on the scene; deaf to all prohibition, they carry the kitchen by assault; they fill, they inundate everything, and leave no room for collecting a poor little pint of the precious element without expense.*

The Jews take here, as everywhere, a prominent part in all street commerce. Here is one of the Yahoudys (men of Judea) bending under a heavy bale while he waves the "archine," or rod for measuring his unbleached calico, which he calls vigorously as he goes, "Américànico;" his comrade passes lightly along with boxes filled with what the French call "mercerie," or, it may be, a glass tray of tawdry trinkets suspended in front of him. Next, there is a Maltese dealer in straw hats and sponges; he has an impudent, jaunty look, and wears his hat very much on one side, while the two men who follow shortly afterwards form the most striking contrast that can be imagined. Two turbaned natives of Morocco, grave and quiet, they have no need to

* See note at the end of the chapter.

proclaim the contents of their bundles: it is well known to consist of fezzes and brilliant stuffs for scarves and waistbands, and that the bags thrown over the shoulder of that slim Persian, who comes next across our little scene, are full of gaily painted boxes, which can be bought at a very low price, but are rarely to be found without scratch or damage, owing to the long and difficult land journey through which they have been jolted.

Scraping, groaning, shrieking sounds, the agonised cries of unoiled wheels endeavouring to drag forward a lumbering buffalo cart. It is the removal of a neighbouring Armenian family that is flitting early to the Islands or to Belgrade. The araba upholds a veritable mountain of mattresses and cushions, together with enormous sacks made of camels' hair, into which all the smaller articles are collected. The heap is crowned by a few straw chairs and an invalid table or two. The start is accomplished, but, after a few yards, the ground rises a little and the buffaloes, in spite of the utmost exertion of their dogged strength, stop short amidst a tempest of blows and cries. Spectators gather round, most of them with the benevolent offer of advice; one or two put shoulders to the wheel, and again the araba is under weigh, surging ominously from side to side.

Sharp cries now pierce the murmurs of the streets, a woman's shrieks; they ring through the neighbourhood. These cease, and the low sound of a religious chant swells up gradually from the narrow lane; it becomes sharp and nasal as the procession, turning into the roadway, proceeds in the direction of the Greek church. It is a funeral; and, according to the custom of this communion, the poor body, alive perhaps the day before, is carried dressed as for a festival, and the face uncovered. It is a sad and often a revolting spectacle, these corpses, scarcely cold, decked out in gaudy colours, shod and gloved, and bedizened with artificial flowers. The little children look like waxen angels, but the disfigured countenances of those who have succumbed to long and painful illness should be at least veiled; this is only done in cases of smallpox and other alarming epidemics. Not long since, the well-known funeral cries were heard. A woman, a near neighbour, was being borne from her cottage for interment; she was clothed in the dress which she had been seen to wear on the previous day in perfect health, but instead of the pale hue of death, a glow was on her features—the forehead even was flushed. The miserable creature had been strangled the evening before by her only son. They buried her, and some sort of inquiry was made by the police, but it was conducted with such astounding apathy and negligence, that the murderer was able to return to the desecrated home to seek his property and then depart. "It can't be helped," observes a Greek servant, shrugging his shoulders; "it is all finished now."

The shadows are by this time beginning to lengthen, and the unconscious actors of our imaginary stage have greatly altered in style and character. The street merchants have almost disappeared; the beautiful flock of silky Maltese goats, brought back from their morning's round, are feeding on the rough hillocks under the care of the goatherd, who is stretched fast asleep upon his back amongst the grasses. Perote ladies drag their dresses through the dust as they proceed, armed with the seductions of their Parisian toilettes, and followed by a servant, to accomplish their daily task of visits; and as the first grey tints of evening gather over the picture, a straggling but scarcely interrupted stream of men winds slowly up the hill—the merchants and their clerks from the counting-houses and stores of Galata returning to their homes in the higher and more healthy neighbourhoods. Many of these ride, and the barefooted, panting "suredji," or horse-boy, can scarcely keep pace with his steed, though he hold on with all his might by the horse's tail.

The report of a cannon announces the close of the day—twelve o'clock, Turkish time—and at the same moment, throughout the city, thousands of watches are consulted and regulated; after which everyone dines, and Pera becomes silent, with the exception of the main street, along which a restless throng of pedestrians, carriages, and sedan-chairs press towards the theatres, or to the balls and receptions of the various embassies. In the quiet quarters of the town, excepting an occasional furious outbreak among the dogs, few sounds disturb the stillness of the evening hours. There is one cry, however, which, beginning late, echoes at intervals, and with various degrees of strength and distinctness, far on into the night. In winter it is " salep," which, in a plaintive tone, is offered to the public. During the summer it is " caïmakli dondourma—a !" (" penny cream ices ! "), and, looking out, you see a lantern like a wandering meteor flickering through the gloom and settling here and there upon a doorstep.

And there is yet again one other signal which too often breaks upon the solemn hush of night—the dreaded boom of the fire-gun, quickly followed by strokes of an iron-shod staff upon the pavement. You listen with suspended breath to the cry of the beckdji, " Yangheun va—ar ! " (" There is a fire ! "), then the name of the locality and of the " mahalle " or quarter. It may be " Stambouldah Sultan Mehemetdeh "—meaning the district of the mosque of Sultan Mehemet, in Stamboul ; or it may be " Escudardah," " Hissardah," or " Bebekdeh," or any of the villages fringing the Bosphorus or the Golden Horn. You feel that the fiery enemy is far off ; but if the hoarse voice of the night-watchman announces "Beyogloundah," meaning Pera (called in Turkish "Beyoglou," or the son of the Bey), then it behoves you to rise, to ascertain that the fire may not be sweeping onwards to engulf your own cluster of houses. Within a year or two the organisation of a fire-brigade, under the Hungarian Count Szechényi, has done much to check the spread of this terrible scourge, which, in 1870, destroyed in a few hours nearly the half of Pera. On that fearful night, a change in the direction of the wind might have converted into a mass of glowing embers the whole of this busy, populous Christian suburb of Constantinople, but the lower half of the town, overhanging the quarters of Galata and Tophaneh, was spared. The gale, continuing steadily from the same point, and increasing in force as acres of burning houses strengthened the fiery blast, bore full upon the British Embassy as if impelled from a gigantic blowpipe. No human exertion could have saved the building, and the stream of death and ruin rushed down the crowded hillside till stopped by the waters of the Golden Horn. In this ghastly furnace, in which whole companies of the brave but ill-organised "touloumbadjis," or native firemen, perished, no fire-brigade could have worked with success; but on the edges of the burning stream the touloumbadjis exerted themselves effectually. Not, however, without previously driving terrible bargains with the distracted owners of house and property. Nearly £1,000 was paid down in gold to save a large wooden building standing near a corner of the High Street, of little value in itself, but which, by its position, forms the apex of a vast triangle of crowded dwellings covering the slope towards Galata, which must have been entirely destroyed if that one building had caught the flames. It was in consequence of this great fire of 1870, and of the alarm afterwards felt at every recurrence of the fire signal, that the new brigade service was at length established, many of the former touloumbadjis being enrolled in it. When reduced to discipline and order, their courage and energy are found most valuable in quelling the flames, instead of being very frequently exerted, as hitherto, in breaking one another's heads. It often happened under the old *régime* that two rival companies of half-naked firemen, rushing wildly through the streets, yelling and shouting and carrying all before them, would meet at some cross road and, setting down their little painted pumps, engage in a free fight, utterly oblivious of the conflagration to which they were both bound.

With the exception of this great disaster, there occurs, happily, on the occasion of fires, very little loss of human life. Most of the native houses, built of wood, are low, having one or, at the most, two stories. The furniture, consisting almost entirely of mattresses, carpets, and bedding, is made up into bundles on the first alarm and turned out of the windows, due care being taken for the reception of the property; but, in more than one instance, during the terror and confusion of the Pera fire, distracted householders, endeavouring to follow the native system, forgot this rather necessary precaution, and goods were showered down in haste to vanish amongst an admiring and appreciative crowd beneath.

Throughout the history of Constantinople, destructive fires have occurred so frequently that most parts of the city are said to have been renewed every ten years. The new houses are run up upon the ashes of the former buildings, and it is for this reason that, comparatively speaking, so few remains of great antiquity are brought to light. They lie buried fifteen or twenty feet below the present level of the ground, and it is only when excavating for the foundations of some structure of great importance, or in the cutting of a railway, that the workmen come upon the masonry and sculpture of Greek and Roman times.

NOTE.—Since the above was written the much-needed waterworks have been executed, and Pera now receives an abundant supply of water, brought from a considerable distance.

V.

EVERYDAY LIFE IN A HAREM.

The Family of the Pasha.—A Tiny Woman.—A Sucking General.—Tchaousch Hanum.—The Eldest Daughter.—Turkish Beds.—Nomadic Furniture.—Concerning Household Matters.—Risk of Fire.—The Duties and Condition of "Halaïks."—Female Pedlars.—Life on a Farm in Asia Minor.

I HAD been asked to undertake the portraits of two children of an officer of high rank in the Turkish army. The old warrior was at the camp at Schumla, and his wife was anxious that he should possess some visible reminders of the family ties left behind in Stamboul.

The konak of Z—— Pasha stands far back from the road, in an extensive but neglected garden. The lodge gates, newly built in the French style, might be supposed to lead to a handsome modern mansion, but rebuilding and embellishment have stopped at the gates, for the konak is a shabby, rambling, wooden edifice, quite out of keeping with the trim, rather pretentious entrance.

Everyone was impatient for the arrival of the tasvirdji (portrait-painter), as the work would be a novel amusement. I was welcomed with smiles by some women and girls clattering on wooden clogs about a sloppy stone hall, and at once escorted to a room on the first floor.

The hanum rose to receive me, making the temene, a politeness not always accorded to Europeans. This lady has an intelligent, expressive countenance, and is singularly well-mannered, quietly self-possessed, graceful, and ladylike. Another lady, past the bloom of youth, very dark, with magnificent black eyes, lustrous wavy hair, and a quick, bright expression, sat enveloped in a furred pelisse at the farther end of the broad divan.

The arrangements of the portraits were discussed, and it was finally agreed to begin work on the following Friday as, contrary to popular notions amongst ourselves, Friday is considered as the most propitious day for the commencement of any undertaking. Accordingly, at the appointed time, I was once more in the konak, and while waiting for the appearance of the children, who were being elaborately and anxiously dressed up for the solemnity, I took the opportunity of learning from a respectable-looking French girl, attached to the household as nursery governess, some particulars about the family.

Eminé Hanum, the lady of the house, is the buyuk hanum, the principal and, in that establishment at least, the only wife of the Pasha, to whom she has been married thirteen years. She is a daughter of a former governor of the holy places of Mecca and Medina. The dark lady, Ayesha Hanum, is a widowed aunt. There is an older daughter of the Pasha, also a widow, with two children; they occupy a separate apartment in the harem. One or two other female relatives with their attendants, and those of the principal ladies, complete the harem or female portion of the family.

While still waiting for my little models, two individuals came quietly into the room to inspect the stranger lady. They are white aghas, a variety amongst harem guardians very rarely met with; one of them very tall, sickly-looking, and polite; the other, a strange little specimen of humanity, like a withered child—a gentle, pallid face of thirty, with a growth of ten years old, a childish voice, and small deformed hands. The poor little creature is a djudjé, or dwarf, and buffoon. He seems to be on good terms with everyone, especially with the children, who have been at length brought into the room.

The eldest is a little girl of four or five years old, Eminé Faïka Lutfié Hanum, a plump, rosy-faced, bright-eyed little woman, very quick and clever, and very much spoiled. Her tiny violet antary and schalwars, the toque on her head, and the little tuft of white feathers, form quite a grown-up woman's costume. There is scarcely a difference here in the style of dress between two years old and twenty, excepting that very young children do not wear the yashmak, or the outer cloak (the feràdje); otherwise the component parts of their toilette, the materials and the form, are precisely the same as those worn by their mammas. With little boys this custom of dressing them in imitation of their elders has an intensely ludicrous effect. My other model, Mushaver Bey, scarcely two years of age, and not yet weaned, had been buttoned up into the full uniform of a superior officer, with sword-belt, fez, and epaulettes; and when, in the course of the sitting, he suddenly turned and took his natural refreshment from the bosom of his sud'na (milk-mother) the situation was irresistibly absurd.

The work went on pretty well, considering the difficulty of inducing Faïka to glance towards me; she usually preferred turning her back. But Mushaver Bey, too young to have a preference, stared placidly from his nurse's arms, with his sword-belt all awry and his epaulettes in very unregimental condition.

I frequently passed the night in this harem, and had thus the opportunity of seeing many friends and acquaintances of the family, who would drop in towards evening for a neighbourly chat. Some of them came by invitation; others, according to the old-fashioned, hospitable custom of the past, arrived unexpectedly, sure of a welcome, and quite prepared to dine and pass the night, and if their quarters suited them, to remain a day or two longer. They would group themselves round the mangal (the brazier), some on low cushions, others on the ground, warming their hands over the smouldering charcoal, smoking cigarettes, and talking. One voice predominated in harsh, startling, manly tones. I drew near to examine the speaker. She was a fearful woman, her coarse, masculine features made more hideous by the loss of an eye, and by the blood-coloured handkerchief bound down low over her dark brows. She talked volubly, crouching by the mangal and using fierce gestures of explanation for my benefit, relating how she had cut and slashed the Moscovs during the Crimean war. This woman is a Bosniac, with some craze and a good deal of cunning. They call her Tchaousch Hanum, for she served in men's clothes in the regiment of Omer Pasha during ten years, and had gained the rank of corporal, when she was wounded and her sex discovered. She was, of course, at once dismissed; but they give her a little pension, and she passes her life wandering from house to house, relating her military exploits and collecting presents. Without doubt she finds it a lucrative occupation.

The room in which Eminé Hanum passed the

evenings with her guests was a small, meanly furnished apartment, known as the "caveh odjak," in which a chintz-covered divan, a quilted cushion or two, and a mangal, sum up the amount of luxury with which they seemed content. A large and handsome suite of rooms furnished in crimson velvet, on the other side of the great sala, is reserved for occasions of ceremony.

One evening the eldest daughter of the Pasha wandered into the room with her little girl, Zara. She is exceedingly gentle and winning, but very much kept in the background by her stepmother, who is jealous of her husband's affection for this grown-up daughter, and would fain engross all of it for her own spoilt pets. The poor young woman is under twenty, and already twice widowed. She is to be a third time married after the Pasha's return. Her first husband was a handsome young aide-de-camp, who was sent into active service a month after the marriage, and was killed in the first engagement.

As the evening draws to an end the circle round the mangal has gradually thinned; the ladies have one by one glided away, and are probably spread about the floors of some distant rooms, in the tent fashion of their nomadic ancestors, which is slowly yielding to the pressure of Western civilisation in the form of iron bedsteads.

A well-made Turkish bed, although laid on the hard floor, and somewhat unyielding, is by no means uncomfortable. The coverings are arranged with great care and neatness: first a large wrapper is spread over the matting; on this are laid down two or three mattresses of finely carded cotton; a delicate sheet of striped Broussa cotton stuff, of linen, or calico, is spread in summer; in the winter a sheet of soft white woollen material is used. The coverings, or yorghans, literally quilts, as they are made of quilted cotton, are lined, with the upper sheet tacked on all round it. The yorghans, which are frequently covered with silk or satin, or even with silk and gold brocade, are folded on the bed in a peculiarly ingenious manner. There is no bolster. Two or three cotton pillows, flat, and encased in silk or in embroidered muslin, with a square of fine white linen laid across the pile, complete the arrangements.

In a small and well-ordered household the lady or her daughter comes to superintend the handmaidens; she will herself sprinkle the couch with rose-water before taking leave of her guest for the night. The mosquito nets used are frequently made of Broussa silk gauze, which is unrivalled for lightness and impenetrability.

All the furniture and goods of a Turkish family of the old school still retain a very nomadic character, and can be removed on the shortest notice. The rolling up of the bedding every morning in huge bundles; the wearing apparel kept folded in wrappers in the native wicker trunk covered with leather, the form of this trunk—without angles of any sort—adapted for packing on a horse or mule; the large sacks of camels' hair used in removals, all seem vestiges of the life and customs of the pastoral tribes that wandered from Turkestan six centuries ago, and founded the Ottoman Empire on the opposite shore of Asia. This simplicity of domestic furniture has its advantages. At the first alarm of fire everything can be turned out of window without injury; but it is very much opposed to our Western ideas of comfort, as the slave girls, unless carefully barricaded out, make an inroad into the sleeping-room in early morning. They sweep up bed and bedding before your eyes are fairly open; two or three maidens pounce upon the mattresses, the yorghans, and the embroidered pillows the instant they are unoccupied, and rolling the whole into the wrapper, bear it away to the vast cupboard constructed for that purpose in most of the rooms. The visitor is left stranded, and obliged to proceed, with the incongruous feeling of dressing in a drawing-room. These remarks apply to orthodox, old-fashioned households. Young feminine Turkey has its French or German bedsteads, its "armoire à glace;" its washstand, all marble and fine porcelain, "à la frança."

As a guest of Eminé Hanum, the greatest solicitude was shown for my comfort, and the only bedstead in the house was prepared for my use. It stood in a large dreary room, and the French girl, thinking I might feel nervous, dragged in her mattress and established herself in a corner. It was an opportunity for learning many details of household management, and of the daily life of the halaïk, or slave. The domestic organisation in this house is far from perfect. There are many servants. I inquired, " Is there no kiaya, or housekeeper?"

"No; the work goes on as it can. The hanum looks after it occasionally."

"Ayesha Hanum seems a managing person. Does not she superintend?"

"No; she is only a visitor, and brings her own attendant. The Kutchuk Hanum (the daughter) has four women of her own; all the rest of the slaves belong to the principal lady."

" Is she kind to them? She looks sweet and gentle."

"Yes," answered Josephine a little doubtfully. "I suppose they are as well off here as they would be in most houses. I remember one konak where there was a negress, the cook; a good creature, but rather clumsy (by the way, this negress had a beautiful black cat that she called Marsick). Well, she was one day bringing a lighted mangal into the room where the lady of the house was sitting smoking a tchibouk, and not in the best of tempers; the black woman stumbled, poor thing, and the lighted charcoal flew all over the matting. The hanum rushed from her divan, and, instead of allowing the negress to collect the burning pieces with all possible speed, she fell upon her, and began beating her with the whole strength of her delicate little hands. If I and some other women had not come in instantly the whole room would have been in a blaze."

"It is a source of continual astonishment to me," said I, "that there should be any houses left standing in Stamboul. What between the carelessness about the braziers, the quantity of old matting, and the ends of cigarettes thrown recklessly about, you ought to be in a continual conflagration."

"It is kismet," replied Josephine calmly. "I suppose we shall be burnt out some day. In well-ordered konaks a woman walks about the harem all night as female beckdji, or watcher."

"Tell me something about the slave girls," said I, waiving the subject, with an earnest hope that the burning out might not occur in my time. The stove-pipe was just then very hot. The house is old, and would catch like tinder. I felt a little nervous. "Tell me about the halaïks. What monthly pay do they receive?"

"Everyone here, black and white, myself included, receives two hundred piastres (£1 16s.) a month. That is pocket-money, as you know, for all are, of course, lodged and boarded, and chiefly clothed."

"Then they must put by nearly all this money. I think they are rather well off—richer than many servants in our own country, who, besides entirely clothing themselves, have often to assist their families; and these poor halaïks have no relations to help."

"No, that is true, madame; but they spend a good deal on trinkets, and those unprincipled female pedlars—mostly Jewesses—who hang about the harems, selling useless finery at four times its value, they take care to keep the girls' purses empty, and they naturally contrive to get them into their debt, and so obtain an injurious hold over them."

"There must be a great deal to do to keep such a rambling building as this in order," said I, wishing to elicit some further remarks.

"Oh, yes, plenty to do," replied Josephine, stitching away vigorously (she was sitting beside the stove working), "but, dear me, they are so idle, those girls, that they never do any really hard work. They get in 'rayah' women to do the scrubbing and scouring. The mangals are all sent into the selamlik to be lighted, and the brass candlesticks are also cleaned there. Each one takes her candlestick down to the door in the morning, and fetches it in the evening all ready. It is the same with the lamps and even with the night-lights; all that sort of dirty work is done for us on the men's side of the house. When there is anything disagreeable to be done by the girls it is the slaves last bought who have to do it."

"Are the slaves often changed?"

"Yes; they rarely work out their time of service in this house. I dare say you know, madame, that a slave by *custom*—for there is no *legal* limit—owes from fourteen to twenty years or so of service to her owner, after which time they remain with the family, doing as much or as little work as they may choose. Usually they are given in marriage, but in this house the Pasha gives them a marriage portion and a husband and home of their own at the end of three or four years. There will be several marriages here next spring if he returns in time."

And then we pass on to other subjects, and it is very interesting to hear Josephine relate her adventurous life in a wild district of Asia Minor, near Angora, where her father had the management of a large farm. It should have been a valuable property, but, owing to the want of roads and means of transit, it proved nearly worthless.

The French family lived there for ten years, the

only Christians in a population of Mussulman peasantry, and Josephine speaks warmly of the friendly neighbourly feeling, the kindness and constant hospitality, with which they were surrounded.

During all these years only sixteen European travellers passed by the tchiftlik, and these were principally French "loupeurs" in search of the "loupe," or knot of the walnut-tree, used by furniture and piano manufacturers in Paris. Erard, amongst others, has one or two of these loupeurs constantly employed at a high yearly salary, their expeditions being attended with much danger, as they are often the first to penetrate into the savage regions of the interior. These men, chosen for their courage and hardihood, have no eye for, or knowledge of, the relics of antiquity with which that country is thickly strewn. In the neighbourhood of the French farm the land was full of ruined fragments of marble and stone covered with inscriptions. It is probable that when road-making shall be begun in that part of the empire these interesting remains of a bygone civilisation will be broken up for metal. Should the blocks be needed for any less fragmentary use, they will be ruthlessly cut about, the inscriptions first carefully chipped and scraped away as being the dirty outside of the stone or marble.

It was from the neighbourhood of this farm that

a walnut knot was once taken; when opened it was found to contain in the centre a piece of money, a small cup, an engraved stone, and one or two other objects.

It was a wild life that the girls and boys of the French family led in that secluded "tchiftlik." And Josephine went on with her adventures while hunting the boars and bears, so common in that district, with other memories of farm life in Asia Minor, till the muezzin of the neighbouring mosque began his musical and melancholy call to the faithful of the sleeping city, and the clear voice gradually became a murmur as I passed into a tangled dream woven of bears and slave girls, of fearful amazons, and of officers in full regimentals still dependent on their wet-nurses for daily nourishment.

VI.

EVERYDAY LIFE IN A HAREM.

Djenàniah Calpha.—Djémilé.—"A Sad Coquette."—Entangled Interchange of Sentiments.—An Adventure.—Reflections.—Portrait of the Hanum.—A Venerable Fiancé.—Collection of Antiquities.—A Brick Tablet.—Cylinders.—Seals.—Gems and Coins.—Legend of Nimrod.—Moses.—Dream of a Sultan.—Isolation.

On arriving one morning at the konak I found the Buyuk Hanum, with a veil thrown over her head, engaged in reading the Koran. She must, she tells me, read it quite through during the Ramazan, and takes two chapters at a time, quite conscientiously, owning, however, that she does not understand it, being in Arabic.

This lady has had her mind considerably educated by foreign travel, and she takes great delight in relating her adventures when she accompanied her husband, the general, having with her only two female attendants. The poor women had a hard time of it; sometimes, in rough costumes and oil-skin cloaks, mounted on horses or balancing in panniers, they followed the march of the army, and on one occasion nearly perished in a snowstorm somewhere in Turkestan. They visited the fire temples of Bakou, the mounds of Nineveh, the wonders of Upper Egypt, almost every remarkable spot in the Turkish Empire, and both the hanum and her faithful companion, the chief waiting-woman, Djenàniah Calpha, have much to say about these places.

Djenàniah, a sensible, quiet woman of six or eight-and-twenty, is to be married in a few weeks. She does not speak of it herself. The future husband is a non-commissioned officer. They have known each other from their early youth, and shared in all the perilous campaigning adventures just mentioned, and there is doubtless a tranquil, undemonstrative sort of friendship between them, although, according to the rule of female seclusion, they are not supposed to have exchanged a word. I ventured a congratulation to Djenàniah on the near prospect of her marriage, but she looked down and made no reply. I found that in the Eastern code of proprieties such compliments are not acceptable to a bride-elect.

Once more in the usual sitting-room, I took a low stool near the mangal, in order to talk a little with Zeïneb Hanum, who was warming her hands over the embers. She is a native of Daghestan, and is loud in praise of her native mountains, joining chorus with a cheery old body from Heraclea, who was crouching near us singing the beauties of Trebizond—the high hillsides clothed with azaleas and rhododendrons, the fresh rills and grassy slopes, the rich pastures, and the deep shade of the spreading trees, under which the people from the town live in tents through all the fierce heat of summer. It is sad to think that so much sylvan beauty should be, for want of proper care and drainage, a very hotbed of pestilence and fever.

We have been very dull during the evening, for the poor little "sucking general" is seriously ill, and the hanum, who appears to be devotedly fond of her children, can think of nothing else. So we were sitting very silently, the native ladies smoking cigarettes, when a visitor glided into the room and sank on to a padded quilt on the floor—a pretty dark-eyed girl wrapped in a scarlet furred pelisse, with a twist of scarlet gauze upon her head.

"What a handsome, quiet-looking girl that is," I said to Josephine; "who is she?"

"She is our opposite neighbour, and often strolls in here. She is pretty, yes; but anything but quiet. She is the most terrible little coquette I know, and often gets us into trouble when we are out together."

"But how can she manage a flirtation? The parties of women of rank are always so much apart from the general public."

"Oh, there are a hundred ways when people are so disposed. For instance, a young lady goes to the promenade in her carriage; she is, as you know, never alone; her companion ought to be an elderly woman, but it is often some wild laughing girl like herself whom the young hanum manages to take as her escort; and this is how they contrive their amusement. The carriages are going slowly round and round, stopping every now and then; they do so in the square of Sultan Bayezid and at Kïathani. Well! some admirer comes near with a friend; he does not speak openly to the young lady, for he might chance to be marched off by the police if they were in a severe humour just then, but he addresses himself to his companion. 'Ah! if I could speak to that peerless beauty, the lovely wearer of the rose-coloured feràdjé, in the carriage lined with blue satin, I would say to her——' and so on. The friend perhaps murmurs something unintelligible, but the young lady remarks in a clear voice to her confidant, 'That is a perfectly graceful and adorable youth beside the carriage; his manner was charming while speaking to his friend. If I could converse with him I should say ——' "

" I can imagine," said I, " that the slow progress of the carriages at the promenades gives many facilities for this entangled interchange of compliments, and on that account the police, in a fit of indignation, forbid the procession every now and then; but, as such orders once launched are rarely enforced, the carriages soon reappear and circulate just as before. But in the country what did that bright-looking girl do to embarrass you?"

"Well, you see, there is a way of talking by signs from a distance. I remember once (we were staying then, for change and sea-bathing, near the Gulf of Ismid) our party had assembled in a meadow near the shore. We were sitting quietly together on the grass; that mischievous little Djémilé, being on a visit, made one of the group. The weather was very warm, and the yashmaks were a little loosened as we were quite away from the public road. Some young officers came sauntering along a pathway at some distance, and seeing a party of women laughing and talking, they began making signs, of which no one took any notice until Djémilé, thinking it great fun, made some sort of sign in answer; but when she saw that the young men, instead of continuing the dumbshow amusement, were coming forward to speak to her, she got frightened and jumped up, closing her veil and pulling her feràdjé about her. We saw what was the matter, and, passing the word to leave immediately, made the best of our way to the caïque waiting at the scala. The officers came behind, listening and trying to find out to what harem we belonged. We threw them off the scent, of course, and were heartily glad when once fairly in the boat. The young men tried to follow, but, happily for us, there was positively no other caïque to be got, so they were obliged to give up the chase, and we reached home terribly frightened. The Pasha would have been awfully angry if he had heard of our party returning with such an escort. Very much the same thing happened, also, in the Valley of Roses, above Buyukdereh. Djémilé Hanum does not now often go out with our harem."

"But I don't suppose she meant her signs and nods to lead to any serious adventure."

"Oh, dear no, not at all," replied my friend; "it was all a silly joke. Many women do themselves great injustice by this bold habit of making and answering signs; it means nothing but love of mischief from idleness and having nothing better to think about."

Poor women! What a vapid existence! No wonder harsh judgments are passed upon them. Every traveller who sees a yashmaked face smiling and nodding at him is either intensely flattered by his supposed conquest, or sets it down as an alarming risk of entanglement in some dangerous adventure. It simply means nothing more than a vain love of admiration, perhaps a mischievous wish to make the stranger look foolish. The traveller probably looks foolish enough, but he makes an extra wise entry in his note-book to the effect that all these poor women are hopelessly bad, and that there is no such thing as a respectable Mussulman home. He knows nothing—how can he know anything? —of the quiet, patriarchal families, whose women conscientiously avoid the places of universal resort, who are resigned to a monotonous existence, and who find their greatest pleasure in a simple family party, when with children and servants they wander off to some shady spot, and spreading carpets and matting, spend the long summer day, sauntering homewards towards sunset laden with great bunches of field flowers, a stout negress carrying the bundles, and the serving man, perhaps, bearing in his arms very tenderly the heaviest baby.

It is very difficult to form an unbiassed judgment concerning manners and modes of life so much differing from our own, but if unprejudiced persons amongst us could form even a faint conception of the false ideas prevailing here respecting ourselves, of the deplorable misconstruction put on simple acts at variance with their own rules of conduct, we might realise in some slight degree how much we also may be liable to misjudge female life in the East. What, for instance, must be the opinion of a Mussulman who finds himself for the first time in the midst of a European dancing party? What his estimate of, his mental comments on, the revolving figures, the uncovered shoulders, the bright, independent manner of our English girls in the present day?

We know how many a modest, virtuous girl, how many a matron whose pure life is the blessing of her home circle, may be found in those glittering ballrooms; but when young Osman confides to a friend his startling impressions of our domestic manners and customs, it were well not to overhear the conversation if we would retain some of our cherished self-esteem.

The portraits are finished. Some of the women crying, "Eïy! eïy!" gathered the fingers and thumb of the right hand together, waving it slightly upwards in sign of approval; a good-natured negress, with the best intentions, spat as she uttered her compliments to avert evil influences. Some patted me on the shoulder, and Djenàniah Calpha, who thought the work had been rather long about, gently shook the corner of her jacket, as glad to be rid of the business; but she had to take patience, for a week or two later I was again asked to go to the konak: the old General had signified his wish to have his wife's portrait executed immediately.

I found the household in a state of great excitement. The hanum had been up half the night manufacturing a "Frank" dress for the occasion. It was copied from a stray number of the "Modes Illustrées." The lady had cut out and fitted it herself, and her women were hard at work stitching the parts together. It is a handsome crimson velvet bodice trimmed with white lace, shapely and stiff with whalebone. Ah! how much more fascinating would be the easy flowing cotton "guidjélik," in which she usually indulges, than this ungraceful buckram attire! But it is "à la frança." I sigh and submit. The sittings begin; the hanum has had her soft chestnut hair dragged stiffly off her face, "à l'Impératrice," and is very nervous under the ordeal, trying so very hard to look her best that she loses all the charm of her really fine countenance. She has exquisitely soft, dark, almond-shaped eyes, slightly aquiline features, a delicate and refined-looking face. But her anxieties spoil her expression. In addition to the momentous subject of the likeness, her mind is troubled with the difficulty of finding a new cook, as her former one, for some reason, has insisted on being resold, a demand that could not be refused, and she cannot meet with one to her mind. I make a supreme effort to divert her, no one else venturing to speak, and I plunge into the subject of the various marriages shortly to take place in the household.

A former nurse of the little Bey is to be married to the kapoudji (doorkeeper) of the harem, an old grey-haired man, who has been for forty years in the Pasha's service. He knows his future wife very well, as he knows many of the young women and girls who have grown up under his eye. This young woman, however, has been but a few years in the house; her first husband, a Circassian, was killed in battle. How she became an article of merchandise was not stated, but she seems to have been sold cheap as wet-nurse for the youngest child. She is not at all pretty, and as Osman Agha, the venerable "fiancé," is very well off, it is considered an exceedingly good marriage for her, and the old gentleman goes through his courting with great propriety, bringing to the door of the harem little daily presents of fruit or other delicacies. Betrothal and marriage presents are regulated according to a very strict rule of etiquette.

Another bride-elect in this harem is a very nice-looking, fair-haired girl, a sort of widow of a brother of the Pasha. This man, before his death, had arranged his affairs with care, giving the odalisque her paper of liberty, and leaving her good store of furniture, jewels, and money. She is to be married shortly to a young Bey; the betrothal, which is, in fact, the only ceremonial part of the proceedings, had taken place some time previously.

Having directed my sitter's attention from herself and from her uncomfortable velvet bodice, the work goes on pretty well. The lady is pleased and very amiable, inviting me to gather violets in the garden to take home. I find there old Osman groping about for an offering to his betrothed, somewhat more poetical than his customary presents. The beds are full of blossom; in a few days they will make the violet preserve, a thick paste of highly perfumed sugar.

Before finally quitting the konak of Z—— Pasha, we passed a long evening in examining the treasures brought from Nineveh, Babylon, and many other places to which the hanum had accompanied her husband. They are usually kept in a fireproof magaza, a stone room detached from the dwelling-house. Some girls were sent down to bring up the most portable objects, and, crowding round the mangal— for the weather was chilly—Eminé Hanum, Ayesha, Djenàniah, and myself turned over the contents of several coarse canvas bags.

There were statuettes of alabaster and terra-cotta; one of them—a head—had the face white, the eyes hollow, the hair dark and very elaborately dressed; a small headless figure exquisitely draped, alabaster and earthen vases, objects in green enamel or glaze, and a brick, the size of an octavo volume, covered with arrow-headed writing, very small and close and as clearly-cut and fresh as if new. Next, we took out long chaplets of small cylinders and seals strung together, most beautifully engraved, the cylinders especially; they were thickly covered with seated kings, soldiers, prisoners, trees, animals, &c., the substance of the cylinder being agate, cornelian, crystal, and something like fine black marble. One heavy black cone, rudely cut in a different style, showed a design of branches with the crescent moon and star above it.

Other bags were full of coins, Roman, Greek, Byzantine, from Eubœa, Sardis, Pergamos, and Persia. Some were marked "Kufic;" others of the time of the Seleucidæ, Arsace, &c. Most of these coins had been examined and classed, in French. There was a splendid gold coin of Constantine, with the wall and gate of a city on the reverse side.

The most interesting portion of the collection consisted of gems, cameos, and intaglios of great beauty and considerable value; and one could not help regretting that it should have no better resting-place than a set of rough canvas sacks.*

To amuse and interest my kind model, who is really very patient under the unusual infliction of "sittings," I have taken to the harem a very curious little book: a coloured and illuminated geneaology of the Sultans from Adam downwards. Eminé Hanum is quite delighted with the representations of Nimrod, Moses, and Pharaoh. She begins relating their histories, which are so curiously embroidered with Oriental fancies that I note them down, as nearly as possible in her own words.

* The konak of Z—— Pasha was burned to the ground about two years later, and the valuable collections having been incautiously left in the mansion, were entirely lost.

NIMROD would build a tower in defiance of the Almighty—he wished to be as God—for which presumption he was to be punished. Accordingly, an immense fish came out of the sea, partly overthrew the tower, and vomited a stream of blood over the land. Out of this stream arose a lofty tree, and from its branches issued a swarm of little flies that buzzed about Nimrod and troubled him until he could endure the torment no longer. He takes refuge in his palace, shuts himself into an inner chamber, locks the door securely. Has he baffled his persecutors? No; there is one small fly that has flown in when he entered. It passes through his nostril into his head, and begins to buzz about his brains. Nimrod, in utter despair, orders a slave to knock perpetually upon his head with a stout club to deaden the intolerable noise. This goes on for some time without much success, until the slave (getting tired, probably) begins to reason within himself, that if Nimrod were really the deity that he pretends to be, the little fly could not have got the mastery, so with one powerful and vigorous stroke he effects a complete and permanent cure, by cracking open the skull of the mighty hunter, as represented in my book, where the bald head is very red and swollen. The Tower of "Babil" is seen in the background.

Moses.

After the history of Moses and Aaron—the rod that budded, and all the plagues of Egypt—Eminé Hanum continued—

"The Angel Gabriel appeared before Pharaoh in the dress of a common man, to state that he has a slave who has become so arrogant that he endeavours to assume power over his master; what is to be done? 'Kill him instantly!' replies the monarch. Gabriel entreats that the advice may be given in writing, receives the written paper, and departs. When the Israelites have passed through the Red Sea, Pharaoh follows in pursuit; his horse draws back, the angel appears again and enters the passage, the horse of Pharaoh following. In the midst Gabriel stops, turns round, and holds up the paper. 'I am lost!' cries Pharaoh at that sight, and the returning waters close over him."

After these histories Eminé Hanum relates a dream of the late Sultan Abdul Medjid.

"This padischah had built for himself a handsome turbé at the head of the mausoleum of his celebrated ancestor, Sultan Selim, the conqueror of Egypt. Before it was quite completed he dreamed that Selim appeared and thus addressed him, 'How can you presume to place yourself at my head? Are you a greater padischah than myself? What mighty deeds have you accomplished? What countries have you subdued? How have you made your name glorious? You are unworthy of that place of honour.' The poor weak, tender-hearted Sultan awoke quite overpowered by the stern rebuke; he abandoned the handsome resting-place in course of construction, and humbly built himself a smaller turbé at the feet of his haughty grandsire, but the effect of the dream did not pass away. He languished from that time, and died shortly afterwards."

Poor Abdul Medjid! unhappy padischah! In those earlier days a sultan deemed himself so highly exalted above the moving world suffering or rejoicing around him, that no glow of human sympathy could reach the altitude of the Unkiar (the manslayer), and Abdul Medjid, who was no manslayer, but a feeble, soft-hearted man, to whom it was agony to sign a death-warrant, must have bitterly felt the weight of the golden fetters of his exalted rank. I have often seen his pale, melancholy face, as he drove slowly and drearily along between his marble palace of Dolma-Bagtché and the toy kiosk of Flamour. People said he was intemperate and weak. He had at least the merciful courage to suffer his nephew to exist. Until then all princes, excepting those of the direct line, died in their infancy. It was a wicked custom, having almost the force of law, but when a little son was born to the Sultan's younger brother the child was kept in safety with his full knowledge and permission, although it was not until the accession of the father, Sultan Abdul Aziz, that the son was publicly acknowledged.

VII.

A STRAY THREAD.—FROM YALI-KIOSK TO YEDI-KOULÉ.

A Feeble Line of Rail.—A Simple Booking-Office.—Patient Passengers.—The Panorama unwinds.—Byzantine Remains.—Gardens of the Old Seraglio.—A Calm Decay.—Remains of the Great Palace of Constantine, of Justinian, of Heraclius.—Beautiful Fragments.—Ruins of a Palace of Theodosius the Younger.—Koum-Kapou.—Vlanga-Bostan. — The "Pomegranate Gate."—Monastery of St. John Studius.—Yedi-Koulé (the Seven Towers).—Camels.—The Fortress and State Prisons.—The Industrial School.—The Golden Gate.

LOOK at a continental railway map. Three little black threads steal out of the south-eastern fringes of Europe, and, turning upwards, strive to reach the tangled network of Western railways. Two of them break at the Danube; the third, wandering across Roumelia, splits into feeble strands that lose themselves among the gorges of the Balkans. Beyond the Turkish frontier black threads begin once more; they thicken and increase, ever seeming to struggle westward; they tangle, they separate, they join, they start apart, they cross, they loop, they weave a wondrous web, till, leaping the narrow belt of sea that will not long divide them, and reaching in a huge cluster our great metropolis, they are tied round and bound together by metropolitan, and underground, and district lines, and daylight station routes.

But our stray, wandering thread, known as the Adrianople Railway line, though it lives in the hope of a brilliant future, is feeble yet and undeveloped. There is quite a touching simplicity about its little itinerary, which can be comprehended at a glance; yet its first section, that running round the southern limit of Stamboul, and skirting the Sea of Marmora, presents, perhaps, more subjects of historical interest than any similar length of railway elsewhere.

We start from the Stamboul terminus, an unimportant building, formerly a government workshop. The ticket is easily procured at the solitary ticket-place, where the clerk has full time to take things easily, and even to be polite. In front, on a row of wooden benches, a few third-class passengers are crouched, waiting for the hour of starting; Oriental types, some in turban and caftan, others wearing heavy sheepskin caps and furred pelisses, though we are in midsummer. They are gravely discussing the strange perversity and ignorance of the Franks, who do not know how to calculate time according to the simple and primitive method of the sunset, and must needs put everyone out by starting their infidel carriages at hours always changing and impossible to understand. One patriarch, in a green turban, discourses with the air of a man who has travelled; he slowly draws from his ample shawl-girdle a large round case, from which he extracts, with tender respect, a silver watch not unlike a pumpkin in early youth, and proceeds to calculate the time that he has already passed in waiting— two hours and more! An active Frank would be wild with impatience, but the Oriental submits to circumstances, and waits; he is always to be found waiting. Is not " waiting " the dominant principle of life and business in Turkey, as it is the soft and subtle poison that corodes the one and too surely undermines the other?

The waiting-room with its " Farreplan " on the wall and the row of railway trucks seen through the windows, takes the traveller in imagination far from the picturesque capital of Islam, but, at the first turn of the wheels, the East is once more revealed in the irregular picture of ruined walls, of mosques and minarets, and of the azure waters of the glittering Bosphorus.

The panorama gently unwinds. Galata, with its noble Genoese tower; Pera, rising over the steep hill; the cypress-covered slope of the Petit Champ des Morts, disappear as the train, gliding round the point of the promontory, passes over the now buried ruins of an orphanage, mentioned in the writings of Anna Comnena. From this spot the line opens out, in its progress through the most interesting part of the city, an almost uninterrupted series of fragments of the capital of Constantine and of his successors. Here a battlemented ruin; there blocks of sculptured marble, broken columns, half-buried capitals, remains of vaults and arches where the close and solid workmanship, in alternate layers of stone and courses of brickwork, leave no doubt as to their Byzantine origin. Those which border the line before it reaches the lighthouse are said by some authorities to mark the old palace of Boukoléon; beyond the lighthouse the walls and towers show numerous fragments of Pagan temples worked into the foundations.

Now we are skirting the wild, neglected gardens of the Old Seraglio. There are pleasant vistas of grass-grown slopes, with cypresses and sycamores, minarets, cupolas, and pointed roofs, mingling together in picturesque confusion. It was the summer palace of former sultans. The winter palace at the foot of the hill, with its heavy overhanging roofs, its high walls and impenetrable gardens, covered, till within a few years, the tongue of land that separated the Sea of Marmora from the entry of the harbour. What tragedies have been enacted here of which the faint rumour only reached the outer world! What dreams of ambition or of love! what wild hopes! what agonies, intrigues, treacheries, despair have trembled and thrilled around those dark solemn cypresses, those venerable plane-trees! The sack and the silken cord were not always "things of the past" in this beautiful and terrible seraglio of the "Grand Turk." A long black funnel, reaching from a postern gate far out into the sea, served (so said the legends) as a means of disposing of unhappy victims in those past times; it has lately disappeared; by the aid of fire and hurricane all this has been changed. The site of the Winter Seraï is laid out as a garden, and the shriek of a railway engine pierces now the still gloom of the once mysterious palace grounds.

Before leaving the precincts of the Seraglio, the line skirts a rough enclosure, in which some wild animals and a few miserable-looking ostriches stalk helplessly about in the shadow of the heavy pile of St. Sophia that towers above the summit of the cliff; the Seraglio is bounded on this side by round, octagonal, and square towers that reach to the shore, and trace the limit of the site of ancient Byzantium.

In this part of the city, so lately surrendered to the encroachments of material progress, everything around remains in the condition of calm decay which characterises the old quarters of Stamboul. On one side we see sarcophagi and broken shafts of columns lying on a waste ground amidst ruined hovels and crumbling walls; then a brighter gleam, as an opening in a dark alley shows a graceful fountain with its richly-toned, though faded, Arabic inscription; on all sides remnants of colossal masonry; a range of half-buried arches; and soon, on the right hand of a cutting, the massive grandeur of the vaulted piles that mark the celebrated palace of Constantine the Great, of Justinian, and of Heraclius. This superb edifice, that extended from the site of the fountain before St. Sophia, covered with its sumptuous buildings the whole area now occupied by the mosque of Ahmed and the side of the hill down to the shore. The accounts of the pomp and splendour of the imperial receptions held on this spot seem like a fantastic dream; what now remains? Some monstrous blocks of fallen masonry; some arches cut by a rail; some traces of a workmanship unequalled in massive grandeur in this, our nineteenth century. Two sculptured lions, supporting the stone balcony of a ruin overhanging the sea, were lately taken down, and found a refuge outside the Church of St. Irene, but the beautiful columns of porphyry and green marble that ornamented one part of that ruin fell before the pitiless strokes of the railway navvy. The clear water bathing this desolate shore shows—among black rocks and granite boulders—fragments of columns of pure white or soft rosy marble, finely chiselled capitals, a block of delicately sculptured frieze. It is right to observe that the plan and execution of a line that has done so much to destroy many of the most curious vestiges of the ancient city, are due exclusively to European engineers, and that the Turks, in this instance at least, are guiltless of this irremediable barbarism.

We pass the corner of a mosque, the little St. Sophia, formerly the Church of Sergius and Bacchus; then, crossing a green level space that was once a harbour (the Port of the Palace), traced still by the ruined line of wall amongst the houses, we come to a wide breach on the left hand, and to a point of view almost unique for delicate harmony of colour and beauty of outline—the Sea of Marmora, bounded by the faint tracery of the blue mountains of the Anatolian coast, and the sparkling snows of Kaïshish-Dagh (the Monk's Mountain), the Olympus of Bithynia. Two islets, dimly visible in the transparent haze, and a large ship at anchor, seem to sleep on a calm sheet of molten gold and azure. In the foreground a brown and green mass of ruins decked with tossing weeds, some fallen columns, a finely chiselled capital, a massive tower—all that remains of a palace of Justinian and of the Palace of the Eagle, erected by Theodosius the Younger.

The train stops at Koum-Kapou (the Sand Gate) in the midst of a quarter laid waste by the fire of 1865, and the meagre stone houses that have arisen on the ashes of the wooden city contrast most disadvantageously with the genuine Turkish style of building. These modern dwellings, ill-built and narrow, with their scanty supply of windows and almost flat surface, are far from equalling in point of health the roomy, airy tenements of the olden time, with irregular angles and deep eaves, throwing broad masses of cool shadow, and catching the wandering breezes through countless windows and many an unmade outlet. There is a real feeling of repose, as you leave this unattractive neighbourhood, to find yourself once more rolling across old Stamboul, through market-gardens, groves of pomegranate and of fig, and patches of Indian corn. The land is everywhere sprinkled with traces of the Greek Empire. Now, it is the Vlanga-Bostan that the line has cut in two, and few people pause to remember that this name of Vlanga, or Vranga, is derived from the celebrated Gothic guard of the Greek emperors, the Varanghians, and that the "bostan" is the filled-up harbour for their galleys. Two fine square battlemented towers on the shore point out the entrance of this port.

In the midst of these gardens, in which pomegranate-trees abound, giving the name of Narli-Kapou (the Pomegranate Gate) to one of the city entrances in the immediate vicinity, low-roofed houses garlanded with vines, and water-wheels of the most complex and indescribable form offer a picture of endless charm and variety, from out of which rises the ancient church and the remains of the monastery of St. John Studius (now a mosque), surrounded by cypresses and planes. One of the numerous old cisterns still exists beneath this church · its roof is supported on columns.

The train still rolls quietly on, and you are thinking dreamily of that old Byzantium of times long past—of that crumbling and picturesque Stamboul that is even now rapidly vanishing, when you are brought up with a start, and poetic reveries evaporate in the centre of black trucks, heaps of coal, and prosaic engines at the station of Yedi-Koulé (the Seven Towers). You hear the frenzied agitation of the telegraph signal within the little office; some Turkish women shuffle hurriedly into a carriage reserved for their use; a waterseller offers his refreshment, "Like ice! like ice!" idlers gaze through the wooden barriers, and a flock of geese, superbly indifferent to consequences, patter slowly all about as the train begins to move. At the same moment a string of camels emerges majestically from a narrow lane; they turn in the same direction, treading solemnly, and with a calm contempt of all sublunary matters expressed in their half-closed eyes. They are laden with undignified sacks of charcoal destined for St. Stefano, a few miles beyond the point at which the line soon afterwards passes through the old walls of Constantinople near the Seven Towers and the Golden Gate.

The castle of Yedi-Koulé, built by Mohammed II. in 1458 on the foundations of an ancient fortress, was frequently used as a state prison, especially for foreign ambassadors in times of political difficulty. Many of the inscriptions, in divers languages, cut in the base of the great tower to the left of the entrance, record the sentiments and the sorrows of the unhappy captives; and the world is indebted for some valuable literary works to the enforced leisure protected by those massive walls.

Works of a different kind were established within the enclosure about ten years ago by the energetic Grand Master of the Artillery, the late Khalil Pasha —an industrial school for poor girls of all nationalities. The scheme in itself was excellent, but the founder's engineering tastes introduced into it works more fitted to the hand of the stout artisan than to the delicate, supple fingers of Eastern women. For a few years the sound of the hammer and anvil, the screech of the drill, and the scroop of files, mingled with the hum and rattle of looms and the rustle of cartridge-papers. On the death of Khalil Pasha the enterprise flagged, and it is now almost a nominal establishment.

The celebrated Golden Gate, through which the

emperors passed in triumphal procession, may be still recognised by the two massive square towers of white marble on either side of an archway supported by Corinthian columns of spotted green marble. These are mentioned by ancient authors, and there can be no doubt as to the authenticity of the remains, although, until within a few years, they had not been recognised, for the towers were covered with plaster, and the fortress being a military station and gunpowder magazine, strangers were not permitted to approach it. When the military were removed and the industrial school was opened in the interior court, a close examination discovered the solid blocks of marble under the whitewash on the towers, as well as sculptured Roman eagles supporting the cornice, and a labarum carved upon the keystone of the archway on the side towards the city.

VIII.

THE LAND-WALLS OF CONSTANTINOPLE.

NO. I.—THE TOWER OF ISAAC ANGELUS AND THE PRISONS OF ANEMÀ.

The "Sebil-Khané" and the Steam Mill.—The Blachernœ.—Five Miles of Towers and Battlements.—The Tower of Isaac Angelus.—State Prisons of Anemà.—A walled-up Gate.

A visitor to the land-walls has the choice of three ways by which to reach the usual starting-point at the northern extremity of the city. He may come by water; by the road that skirts the Golden Horn; or by a long round leading downwards through Eyoub; but he must reach the same spot—the little guard-house in front of the fine steam-mill at Haïvan Seraï.

A few steps farther back there is a Turkish fountain and small Sebil-Khané, a building where cups of water are kept ready filled for thirsty passers-by. It is here that the best view can be obtained of the two lines of battlemented walls that meet at this point. The spot is full of suggestion.

To the left hand, above the tangled branches and dank weeds of a neglected burial-ground, rise massive towers, the ruins of palaces and prisons, filled with the echoes of the splendour and the crimes of a once mighty empire. Beside you, the Turkish fountain with the faded beauty of its arabesque adornments; the feeble trickle of water, oozing through cracks and fissures unrepaired; the passive benevolence of the Sebil-Khané, and the sense of inevitable decay—the decay of pure inertia—are strangely symbolical of the present. On the other side of the road, the great steam-mill, with its throbbing roar of engines, and ceaseless hum of work, telling of active life and energy, seems to typify the principle on which alone hope for the future may be founded—in industry and useful enterprise wisely encouraged and conscientiously developed. And if the rigid lines of the vast building jar somewhat harshly on the dreamy beauty of the spot, it speaks of something higher and better than mere pictorial effect—of honest labour honestly rewarded, gaining bread for many a hungry household; and it stands as a beacon towards which all who suffer, in that poor and suffering neighbourhood, turn with a prayer for sympathy and help, which is never made in vain.

The best season for visiting the walls is in the spring or early summer, while the fruit-trees fill the moat with their snowy blossoms, and the graceful foliage waving about the ruins, feathers their hard ruggedness with sprays of tender green; but the group of towers at the angle of Haïvan-Seraï should be examined while the leafless branches permit a clearer view. The two lines of strongly fortified wall can be then distinctly traced: the inner and older line built by Heraclius iu the seventh century; the outer wall raised two centuries later by Leo V., called the Armenian.

The ancient palace and the fortress of the Blachernœ, as also the Church of the Holy Virgin, were comprised within the wall of Heraclius. Of these little now remains, except a fragment of a wall of the castle erected by Manuel Comnenus in the twelfth century, and the Holy Fountain, to which the Greek emperors, on the day of the Feast of the Purification, were accustomed to go in state, attended by the Varanghian Guard, to bathe in the sacred source.

From this, the extreme northern limit of the city, begins the magnificent line of ruined towers and battlements known as the land-walls of Constantinople, stretching five miles across, from the Golden Horn to the Sea of Marmora; five miles of ruins that are unrivalled in picturesque beauty and historical interest; a triple line of defence, in some parts clearly defined, in others veiled by clinging ivy or tangled in a maze of leafy boughs, springing from the clefts and rents of the stupendous masonry.

The towers are round, square, hexagonal, or elongated; some are riven to their base by earthquake; others, smooth and seemingly untouched by time. In the entire length, six gates in actual use give access to the city, while an equal number, long since walled-up, can be distinguished half hidden by the growth of trees or by the fallen blocks of neighbouring ruins.

On leaving Haïvan Seraï, you pass a little guardhouse, and turning sharply to the left, follow a narrow pathway—between old houses and the enclosure of a tract of vegetable gardens—to a spot where a low wall, broken away on the side towards the city, lays bare an open patch of ground. Suddenly you find yourself gazing upward at the imposing mass of ruins formed by the Prisons of Anemà and the tower built by Isaac Angelus, a contemporary of Richard Cœur-de-Lion.

The lofty wall and buttresses of the dungeon, with the towers standing high upon foundations of enormous strength, have a stern majesty of effect that is enhanced yet softened by the tender grace of luxuriant foliage crowning the ruined battlements, and draping the grey stone and blackened marble with veils of ivy and falling boughs of terebinth, for the high wall is built against the side of a precipitous hill, and the tower is roofed by the garden of a Turkish konak. The beauty of outline is completed by a fine cypress shooting out of the green wilderness upon this summit.

The tower of Isaac Angelus, serving formerly as a bastion of the Blachernœ, is a square mass of building, formed, it is said, of the materials of temples previously existing in this suburb. All its proportions are majestic: three arched and very lofty windows—partly veiled by ivy—yet show, in the black depths of their ruined outlines, the thickness and solidity of the walls; and mighty shafts of marble columns, once the supports of balconies, project irregularly from the face of the huge pile, which is raised upon its terraced foundations fifteen feet above the level of the ground.

The tower of Anemà has one narrow window on its principal front, but the opening through which you reach the celebrated state prisons of the Greek Empire is near the inner angle of the great wall. The name of the founder of the Anemà is unknown, but the first person imprisoned here for a length of time being named Michel Anemà, the name remained to distinguish this place, which was subsequently but too well known to many victims of imperial jealousy and court intrigue. Here, Andronicus, the son of John Paleologus, was first blinded and then imprisoned, with his wife and child, by order of his father, at the instigation of the Ottoman Sultan Murad. After ten years of captivity, Andronicus escaped, and, aided by the Latins, made war upon and conquered his father; then cast him, together with his brothers, into this same dungeon.

Within the great waste enclosure of the towers stands a wooden house, where people wishing to explore the prison may procure lights and perhaps a sort of ladder. It was on a bright morning in the early spring that we stood beneath the evil-looking opening made in the upper part of a long blocked-up window, full twelve feet from the ground, and, waiting while the old Armenian slowly knocked on another feeble rung to the rickety ladder, we had time to remember the agreeable fact that snakes of formidable size have fixed their residence in this eligible locality, and to admire the harmonious growth of nettles, long wet grass, and poisonous weeds, with which the earth is carpeted. It needs a spirit of investigation of unusual vigour to urge you to climb up into the uncanny hole, as, whatever may have been its original purpose, it is, at the present time, strongly suggestive of drainage; but it is the only known entrance. "We crept up," said one of our party, "through a very low and fearfully dirty passage, which leads into a high and rather spacious chamber. Here we lit our candles, and began to wind through passages, up and down, but mostly ascending, until our further progress was barred by a wooden grating overhead, through which the daylight came faintly, bringing with it a volley of angry Turkish from the indignant proprietor of the garden on the summit of the tower. We found that we were about to look through the flooring of his summer-house, and a gentle shower of potsherds and cabbage stalks, coming through the grating to accentuate the protest, we prudently beat a retreat, turning along passages that run in the thickness of the great wall. It is here that the dreariest and most fearful prison cells are situated; large iron rings still remain, fixed into the stone; the windows have been built in; gloomy depths, branching off from the main passage, pass into the bowels of the earth; and in one place, a well, or oubliette, yawns, almost in the pathway. We reached, at length, a point where the inner wall, fallen to ruin, stopped our farther advance, and, turning from the dreary gloom of these ghastly galleries and cells, we gladly scrambled back to air and sunlight."

As you cross the vegetable garden, on the return to the little pathway, a few yards farther along in the direction of the Horn will bring you to an ancient gateway of fine proportions, built of heavy blocks of marble, marked in many places with the cross. This entrance, which has been walled up in ancient times, is thought to be the Gate of Gyrolimni.

IX.

THE LAND-WALLS OF CONSTANTINOPLE.

II.—TEKFUR SERAÏ.

Eghri-capou.—The Stamboul Taksim.—Origin of "Sou-Terazi" (the Water Towers).—Interesting Remains.—Tekfur-Seraï.—The Hall of the Emperors.—History of a Diamond, the "Tchoban Tashy."

THE most comprehensive view of the northern portion of the walls is obtained by following the rise of the hill on the right of the road, after passing the little guard-house; then, by a pathway leading downwards, you come out in front of the first gate on this side of the city, Eghri-capou, or the Crooked Gate, formerly called the Gate of Charsia or Calligaria. The outer gate, that stood at a right angle with the line of wall (whence its name of Crooked), has been quite lately destroyed, but enough of the masonry is left standing to point out its position, and to preserve the remembrance of this entrance, which is frequently mentioned in the accounts of the siege and fall of Constantinople.

The road leading direct to Eghri-capou runs between a range of magnificent towers in excellent preservation, and the tall cypresses of the Mussulman cemetery, which begins about this point, and continues, with slight interruption, to border the highway along the entire distance to the Sea of Marmora.

Immediately after passing Eghri-capou, you find in an angle of the grey-stone wall on the left hand, a fountain and a watering-trough, on one side a small door, and, probably, the turbaned "sou yoldji," or guardian of the waterway, sitting key in hand, on a bench in the shade. He will take visitors in for a modest consideration, and you pass into a vaulted stone chamber almost filled with a tank of gurgling, rushing water. On one side a raised platform, furnished with old matting and sheepskins, is the couch of repose of the sou yoldji. This is the Stamboul Taksim, or distributing chamber, for the supply of water, similar in principle to the building at the head of the high street of Pera. The water is conveyed from the reservoirs of the Upper Bosphorus, a distance of nine miles, by a succession of aqueducts and sou-terazi (water-towers); in ancient times it was collected within the line of walls, in a vast cistern, now ruined; after the conquest, the Taksim was removed outside, and the present chamber was built by Sultan Suliman, in connection with the grand system of reservoirs and conduits constructed by Constantine the Great and his successors. The invention of sou-terazi, used to facilitate the flow of water over a long and unequal surface, is ascribed by some to the ancient Romans; other authorities affirm that the idea is due to the Arabs, who introduced similar works into Spain. In the Taksim of Eghri-capou, the supply of water rushes into the tank through a vaulted opening in the farther angle, and is distributed throughout Stamboul by one large and two smaller channels, the first, feeding the fountains in the quarter of St. Sophia and in the lower parts of the city, the others going in the direction of the Seven Towers.

Leaving the shade of the great trees overhanging the Taksim, the road rises gently towards the Greek burial-ground, and from its grassy slopes you may enjoy one of the most charming points of view in all this line of marvellous pictorial beauty. In the foreground, the soft green of the grass is broken here and there by marble slabs, dotted with browsing sheep, and flecked with tender shadows of softly waving branches; then, beyond the grey masses of the stern battlemented towers, the blue waters of the Golden Horn sparkle through the rich foliage of the gardens at their feet and melt into the lilac distance of the hills beyond.

A splendid tower forms the angle of the line of walls at this point; it is almost uninjured by time. Some battlements have fallen away or been thrust down by the vigorous growth of leafy boughs that crown the summit, but the rest of the mass shows little sign of age; the upper part is built in alternate courses of brick and smaller stones, while the lower half and the foundations are formed of immense blocks of stone and marble.

In the recess beyond this tower, a walled-up gate with some remains of marble columns on either side, was once an entrance to the Church of St. Callinikos, and the walls continuing, strengthened with towers, another similar walled-up gate appears, the gate of the "Incorporeal"—a celebrated church that in the time of the Greek Empire stood on this spot. No vestige of it now remains, with the exception of this gateway, and the ruins of three windows in the wall above it, in one of which a sculptured tablet, lately destroyed, showed four letters signifying, as is said, "King of kings and Lord of lords." The whole of these ruins fell many years since into the hands of the Jews, who set up glass-blowing works and other industries about the premises.

In the upper corner of the open space stands one of the finest monuments yet left to testify to the former splendour and importance of this now desolate spot: a noble mass of masonry, with delicate ornamental work, and belts and cornices of marble, bronzed by centuries of ardent sunbeams, that stands in warm relief against the soft deep blue of an unclouded sky.

This ruin, a large square building pierced with

many windows, and standing high above all surrounding objects, is a landmark familiar to many under the name of the Palace of Belisarius, but sometimes more correctly called the Palace of Constantine, as, according to high authority, it was founded by Constantine the Great. Rebuilt and restored by Justinian, it was lent to his famous general Belisarius; some say that it even served as his place of imprisonment. It was at that period called the Tribunal of the Hebdomon—a quarter extending from this point downwards as far as the shore, and without the city, until enclosed in the time of Theodosius II., who extended the circuit of the land-walls. The Hebdomon was so named (according to White) because the seventh stone marking the number of stadia from the golden central indicator in the Hippodrome, stood upon this hill. Dr. Déthier believes it to be due to the fact that the seventh cohort of the Gothic guard was stationed in this neighbourhood. The Turkish name of this place is Tekfur-Seraï (the Palace of the Lords)—Tekfur being a corruption of a Byzantine term for the Governor; before the conquest the Turks called the Greek Emperors "Stamboul Tekfury"—the Lords of Stamboul.

In the beginning of the thirteenth century, the treasures of art contained in this palace shared the fate of all that had most contributed to embellish and enrich this magnificent capital of Constantine the Great: they were utterly destroyed by the Latin invaders, who left of it nothing but the bare walls. The palace was subsequently used as a prison in the time of the Palæologi, was utterly abandoned after the conquest of the city by the Turks, and is to-day a gaunt and empty ruin, some vaults among the massive grandeur of its foundations serving as a place where glass-blowing, after a very primitive and rude method, is carried on by ragged and miserable Jews. It is painful to add that the Hall of the Emperors, with its supporting columns and finely wrought capitals, sheltered, a few years ago, an active manufacture of lucifer matches, which perished in a grand conflagration. It left the columns calcined and blackened, but it procured freer access to the beautiful ruin.

Seen from within the wall, the western face of the building shows a hall surrounded by open arches, supported on columns with highly wrought capitals and fine work around the arch. On the first floor, the windows are of great height and width, then— above a broad band of ornamental brickwork between belts of marble—a second row of seven windows, equally high but narrow; two of these windows in the centre are filled up. The space between the lofty arch of the windows is ornamented with tesselated work of brick and marble, of great delicacy and varied design. On the sides of the palace facing the city and the Golden Horn, heavy projecting marble supports show where balconies and galleries added beauty and grace to the majestic proportions of the monument, and at the north-eastern angle, a projection like a square tower or gigantic buttress was crowned by a gallery on which (tradition says) that the Emperors used to present themselves to the people assembled in the space below.

On the side of Constantine's palace facing the Greek cemetery, great and cruel destruction has, within the last year or two, obliterated all trace of the beautiful vaulted archway that stood at a right angle with it, connecting the south wall with a heavy block of masonry pierced with windows and crowned with shrubs and flowering weeds. This also has now fallen beneath the merciless pick and crowbar, leaving a hideous gap of useless stones and rubbish.

The mention of stones and rubbish in connection with this historical ruin, recalls an anecdote given on good authority. It would seem that Justinian, during a stately progress between the palaces of the Acropolis and the Hebdomon, lost, from his imperial crown, a splendid jewel, a diamond of twenty-five carats; this occurred in the year 549 A.D. We must suppose that anxious search was made for the precious gem, but the diamond lay concealed, and so remained, while nine hundred years of political convulsion, of wars and bloodshed, the sack of the palace by the Christians, and the fall of the Greek Empire, swept over and desolated the spot. Then the diamond vouchsafed to come once more to light in the hands of a little shepherd lad : he picked it up among the ruins and loose rubbish, and found it doubtless, a pretty help in the sort of " chuck-farthing" game still in favour among Moslem children. The father, however, was a wise man ; he guessed something of the value of the shining toy, obtained an audience of the sultan, Mahomet Ghazi, and received in return for the almost priceless jewel, the post of chief shepherd of the imperial flocks ; the child was educated at the expense of the Padischah, and became in time a person of eminence. The diamond received the name of "Tchoban Tashy" (the Shepherd's Stone) and was placed among the most precious jewels of the sultan's treasury. This "Shepherd's Stone" is clearly a jewel with a destiny, for it comes once more into notice, helping, this time, not to make a poor lad's fortune, but to take a rich man's life. In the reign of Sultan Mahmoud I., the diamond, requiring to be reset, was confided to an aged Armenian jeweller of great renown. The old man was bending anxiously over his work, duly impressed with the importance of the occasion and of the fatal consequences of any accident to the stone, when his hand slipped, and there! before his terrified sight, appeared a thin line, seemingly a crack, crossing the precious jewel! The shock was too great, and the unfortunate jeweller, with an exclamation of despair, fell back and expired. Terror had blinded him to the fact that it was merely a hair from his eyebrow that, falling on the diamond, gave the appearance of a flaw.

X.

THE LAND-WALLS OF CONSTANTINOPLE.

NO. III.—FROM TEKFUR-SERAÏ TO THE SEA OF MARMORA.

Kerkoporta.—Useless Destruction.—View from the Top of the Wall.—Kachrié Djami.—The Land-Wall of Constantine.—The Adrianople Gate.—The Lycas.—The "Riven Tower."—An Ancient Burial-place of the Gothic Guard.—A Monster Cannon: its requirements, its vengeance and its fate.—Mevlaneh Capoussy.—Silivria Capoussy.—The Burial-place of Ali of Janina.—The Golden Gate.—A Railway Arch!—The last Tower of the Land-Walls.

The destruction of these magnificent walls is being carried on so ruthlessly that it is difficult now to trace the spot where, but a few years since, a very low walled up archway—the Kerkoporta—marked a site of sinister renown. It is buried under the heap of stones and mortar raised by the destruction of the wall on the east side of a massive ruin adjoining Tekfur-Seraï. On the side of the terrace at the foot of the walls, some slight indication of the low archway may be recognised from within the city.

For the history of this small and little known passage through the fortifications we must refer to the patriarch Constantius, who calls it "the famous gate of Kerkoporto;" says that it is mentioned by Cantamzène, and (quoting Michael Ducas on the subject of the great siege) continues: "Some of the older men, having knowledge of a small subterranean gate, which for many years had remained firmly shut up below the palace at the spot called now Tekfur-Seraï, they made it known to the Emperor, who gave orders for it to be opened, and from thence to visit the firmest portion of the walls, fighting from outside of them. This secret gate was called the Kerkoporta.

. . . . "Whilst all the Greeks, with the Emperor, resisted vigorously against the enemy, and made every possible effort to repulse them, and turn the assault from the side of the crumbled wall—now called Top Capoussy—the will of God led the enemy in by another route; for the Turks having found this gate open, penetrated there to the number of some fifty, mounted on the walls and killed the sentinels. . . . . The Greeks, who fought outside of the wall, having perceived the Turks behind them, took flight and retired into the city in great disorder and with a terrible struggle by the gate of the Karsia. . . . . It was thus that the little gate of Kerkoporta was one of the principal causes of the conquest of Constantinople."

The triple line of fortification is well seen from

this point, the great wall of Theodosius, the battlemented wall and towers on the terrace beneath, and the broad moat, also strengthened by a low wall with battlements, in most places now fallen away. The great gateways in the Theodosian wall (beginning at Tekfur-Seraï) are double, the most important being on the outer side, and a second, standing a few yards within towards the city.

The grassy terrace is shaded now by a stately growth of walnut, fig, and mastic trees, some rising sedately from the ground, others in wild entanglement among the towers and blocks of fallen masonry, tearing them asunder with mighty roots, while their waving branches overhead tenderly caress and deck the time-worn ruins.

For those who do not mind a scramble, it is not difficult to mount to the summit of this portion of the high wall, and even to walk along it for some distance by a narrow footway between thick hedges of broom and tufty shrubs. You look down into the yawning chasms of the great towers, and across the beautiful city with its mosque-crowned hills, over the sparkling Marmora, its islands floating in a violet haze, to the soft outline of the Asiatic mountains. Within the wall spreads out a wide expanse of thinly populated quarters, a wilderness of gardens and neglected orchards, of unused ground and space laid waste by fire, with here and there a line of closer building leading to some great mosque or central point. This great extent of apparently unneeded building ground within the limits of the city sufficiently proves the futility of the excuse often made for the reckless destruction of the walls, that Stamboul needs room to expand in this direction.

A short distance from the wall, you may see the Kachrié Djami, familiarly called the Mosque of the Mosaics, which has lately undergone the desecrating application of a coating of yellow wash; and, near the centre of the city, the great mosque of Sultan Mehemet—raised on the site of the Church of the Twelve Apostles—is a landmark by which some idea may be formed of the extent of the city of Constantine and of the great addition made to it when the Emperor Theodosius II., in the course of the fifth century, raised the boundary now crumbling to decay. The land-wall of Constantine is supposed to have crossed from the Sea of Marmora, at the part now called Vlanga Bostan, and, passing by the Church of the Twelve Apostles, to have reached the Golden Horn in the neighbourhood of the building known as Gul Djami.

On the summit of the hill crowned by this great church, there existed anciently a mortuary enclosure, or place of monuments and tombs of emperors and princes. The city gate leading from thence has been called Polyandrion and (in the opinion of Dr. Dethier) it is on this account that the corresponding gate in the wall of Theodosius received the same name of Polyandrion; it is now called Edirneh-Capou, or the Adrianople Gate; it leads to the old post road to Adrianople, and is the second gate open for use.

Near the wall, on the side of the city, stands the handsome mosque—built on the site of the church of St. George by Mir-i-Mah Sultana, the favourite daughter of Sultan Soliman I.; it rises superbly on this, perhaps, the highest point of Constantinople.

The gateway is wonderfully picturesque; the massive octagonal flanking towers are crowned with trees, and the old bridge with its ruined parapet looks down upon a grove of fig-trees and a long stretch of gardeners' ground, while on its other side stands an ill-built, irregular, native café, with its bewildering draperies of tattered sail-cloth and ragged matting, stretched out on poles for shade, and its tawny tiling peeping through a wild cascade of wandering vines. Near the wall a stonecutter's dilapidated shed serves as a framework for more wild garlands, and beyond the café, on the farther side, a lofty plane-tree casts a broad shadow over many-tinted, quiet groups, crouched on low stools as they smoke the thoughtful narghilé.

After passing the Adrianople Gate, the road descends into a broad valley, spans a tiny streamlet at the bottom, and climbs the opposite height of Top-Capou; always, as before, and onwards to the sea-shore, bordered on the left hand by the grey walls and battlemented towers that tell of fierce warfare raging around them in many a bloody siege, since first that line was traced and those foundations laid, more than fourteen centuries ago; on the right, by the long stretch of quiet graves in the deep shadows of a cypress grove. The broad moat begins here to be crossed by narrow water bridges, intended to flood it in times of danger from many reservoirs, both within and without the city, of which all traces have been lost, and it must be supposed that the insignificant rill that enters within the walls in the dip of the valley, and trickles through the long meadow called Yeni-Bagtcheh, had, under its ancient name of the "Lycus," some claim to be called a little river. Its chief use now is to localise the scene of Constantine's hopeless resistance and glorious death. It is always supposed that the last of the emperors, whose piety and heroism threw a bright gleam over the death throes of the lost Empire, fell in front of the great breach, not far from the northern border of the small stream. Near this spot two high towers defended a gateway, anciently closed up; one of these, commonly called the "Riven Tower," had been opened to its foundations by earthquake;

it fell a few years since, but sufficient of its ruin remains to identify it. The gate bears the inscription numbered 14 in Dr. Paspati's lectures on the walls, and is called by him the "Fifth Gate."

About half-way between the Adrianople Gate and the bottom of the valley, another walled-up archway, by others thought to have been anciently called Pemptos, was for hundreds of years concealed in thick foliage, until, in a fit of destruction during the winter of 1868, orders were given to convert these venerable ruins into building and road-making materials. They began upon some smaller towers of the lower line of fortification, and, unexpectedly, brought to light a Christian burial-place, with many slabs of white marble bearing inscriptions in ancient Greek and large crosses, some of them very large, as fresh and white as if just laid down. A few days later these interesting remains had been carried off to the Seraskierat, where the new War Office was being built; fine marble was required for cornices; it was found in the interior of these blocks after the inscriptions had been carefully chipped and chiselled off; some fragments, however, remained, bearing a Gothic name, and learned local authorities pronounced this to be a burial-place of the Gothic guard of the Greek emperors, called Fœderati.

The destruction of the small towers also brought to view a small white marble gateway, facing the main entrance, and showing, according to authorities, that this was a triumphal entry rather than an ordinary passage-way; as may be seen also at the further extremity of the walls, where the archway with green marble columns served as a first entrance leading to the great triumphal triple arch called the Golden Gate. The marble ruin at the Pemptos Gate remained for a while a desolate white spot amidst grey walls and heaps of rubbish, then passed away in ignominious utility.

Top-Capou (the Cannon Gate, formerly called the Gate of St. Romanus), is thus named from the immense cannon which was brought against it by Mohammed II. Wonderful accounts have been handed down to us of this monstrous engine of destruction, cast at Adrianople, for the Sultan, by a Hungarian named Orban. When finished, fifty pairs of oxen could scarcely make it move, and then it needed two hundred men on either side to keep it steady; the advance of the monster was heralded by fifty carpenters and two hundred pioneers to put the roads and bridges in order; it required two months to get over an ordinary two days' march; needed seven hundred men to serve it; took two hours to load; discharged stone bullets of "twelve palms in circumference," and of fabulous weight; and, finally, having in vain battered the gate and towers of St. Romanus, wound up its history and its exploits by bursting and shattering to pieces Orban, its unlucky founder. It left one of its monstrous stone balls on the ground, where it was seen some years ago, among the market gardens beyond the cemetery; it, doubtless, still reposes there undisturbed, amongst artichokes and peaceful cabbages. Two bombs of smaller calibre were also brought by the Turks against this main point of attack, and two cannon-balls were suspended within the gateway when it was repaired by the conquerors. The upper part of the gateway has been quite lately destroyed, and one of the balls may be seen in front of a little café across the road, at the foot of a gnarled and withered cypress. At Top-Capou, the recent destruction of the walls has stopped; onwards, until you reach the Seven Towers, the ruins are the natural results of time and earthquake, and the triple line of fortification increases in beauty as you proceed.

Mevlaneh Capoussy is named from the téké of the Mevlevi dervishes on the opposite side of the road. This gateway must have once been very handsome, as four columns of porphyry, with sculptured capitals, yet remain—two on either side; but the upper part of the archway has been filled up, and two fine shafts laid horizontally across the top of the square opening have, while going up rather than down in the world, greatly lost their fitness and dignity.

The next gate, Silivria Capoussy, rather resembles the gate of Adrianople with its octagonal flanking towers, its neglected bridge, its café, and its spreading trees beyond; but the bridge lies obliquely to the entrance, and the view which here opens out, the long vista of walls and towers, of green-embowered terraces, and dark cypress groves, ending in the soft distance of the Sea of Marmora, is the finest point in this unrivalled panorama.

Facing this gateway, on the edge of the cemetery, at the angle where the Silivria road plunges into the funereal gloom, stand, side by side, five tombstones, covering the head of Ali Pasha of Yanina and the remains of his three sons and of a grandson. The inscription on the celebrated Arnaout chieftain says—

"He alone is Eternal!

"The Governor of Yanina, who rendered himself independent during more than thirty years—the celebrated Ali Pacha—here is his head!"

White remarks that "no prayer is requested for his soul, he having been decapitated and his body interred elsewhere."

You pass onwards, and soon after may perceive a walled-up archway, so thickly buried by crowding trees that it would be difficult to trace, but for a grass-grown bridge at this point spanning the moat, but seemingly leading nowhere, and for the heavy towers standing closer here than at other parts of the line.

The gate of Yedi-koulé, contiguous to the fortress of the Seven Towers, is the last now open for use, but quite near to it you see the remains of the once magnificent triumphal entry, the Golden Gate—a smaller archway flanked by columns of green marble with Corinthian capitals bearing the Roman eagle—and, beyond, two immense towers of white marble, between which a triple archway, the centre arch of noble height, is now walled up.

As you pass on in the shadow of the cypresses, the beauty of the ruins increases at every step—the foliage is more luxuriant, the ivy-covered buttresses overhanging the moat more strongly defined; the turbaned gravestones more irregular; the cypresses more venerable; the contrasting purple shadows and golden light more effective—until you come unexpectedly upon a rough stony embankment. It has pierced the venerable walls by a railway arch of singularly bad form; a train flies shrieking through the opening; some workmen on the summit of the walls are picking down one of the strongest sections of it, and showers of dust and stones destroy all poetic associations. The ruined ivy-mantled towers, the battlements, the broad moat with its fantastic waterwheels, continue to border the narrow way. They end in a beautiful octagonal tower rising from the shore; but even here the railway company has laid its pitiless hand of destruction, and cast into the sea the hitherto uninjured battlements that so nobly crowned it, to make a rude landing-place for their working material.

This tower has an inscription on a band of white marble near the summit. In the whole length of the walls numerous inscriptions appear for the bewilderment or the triumph of the learned: some are on tablets, others on bands of stone or marble, and some again in ancient tilework.

XI.

BALOUKLI AND THE FESTIVAL OF THE FISHES.

Up the Golden Horn.—The Okmeïdan.—Aïwan-Seraï.—The Greek Burial-ground.—An Animated Scene.—Dancing Hamals.—Laborious Enjoyment.—Greek Dancing.—Solemn Gaieties.—Tchinganas.—A Funeral.—The Church of Baloukli.—The Miraculous Fishes.—The Fragments of a Festival.

To-day, of all days in the year, is the day for an excursion from Pera to Baloukli, by the road skirting the land-walls of Stamboul. The road from the Golden Horn to the Sea of Marmora is delightful at all times, but it is most attractive at this season of the Greek Easter. The old grey towers are now putting on their gayest draperies of fresh young foliage, for large trees have sprung, unchecked, from the cracks of the crumbling masonry; the judas-tree blushes and glows amidst wild vines, figs, and sycamores; the showering snows of cherry and apple blossom, so lately sprinkled over the broad moat, have passed away, and young green corn and stately artichokes, with sturdy beans and homely kitchen herbs, fill the deep hollow with a rich carpeting of verdure; the nightingales are in full song, and the whole face of the country is alive with holiday-makers.

This Easter Friday, old style, is the day especially devoted by the Christians of the Eastern Churches to visiting the sacred fountain and the miraculous fishes of Baloukli. Most visitors from Pera ride or drive round by the Valley of Sweet Waters and the suburb of Eyoub, to the broad road beyond the walls; humbler pilgrims go there partly by water, partly on foot. We will follow the latter, as the most interesting line of route, and descending the ladder-like pathway through the little burying-ground, gain the scala of Kassim Pasha, where a small flotilla of caïques waits at the wooden jetty. Before embarking, however, a brief contest with the "caidkjee" is a duty owed to society, but the bargain is soon struck, as there is great competition, and you are afloat, shooting past the Admiralty, and feeling bound to admire the bright-looking building that has taken the place of the old irregular deep-eaved wooden structure, which was, however, infinitely more picturesque.

The scene, as you row up the Golden Horn, is, probably, too familiar to excite much interest. The long range of the Arsenal workshops line the shore on the right hand, backed by the trees of an enclosure called the Sultan's garden. A fine palace, built by Soliman the Magnificent, formerly stood on this spot; at a later period, another Sultan added to the embellishments of the palace some Venetian mirrors, from which the name Aïnaly Kavak (the Mirrored Gully) has spread to the large village covering the slope of the hill until it reaches the Okmeïdan (the field of arrows), an ancient archery ground, where Sultans drew the long bow or had it drawn for them: tradition affirms that the marble columns, dotted about upon the grass, mark the spots where the imperial arrows were dexterously found by their courtiers.

Then you pass Haskeui, climbing, tier above tier, up the steep face of a second hill, towards the sad-looking burial-place of the Jews. No trees are planted in these cemeteries, and the vast bare extent of prostrate gravestones is inexpressibly dreary and forlorn. This burial-ground above Haskeui existed in the time of the Greek Empire.

The Stamboul side of the Horn wears a pleasanter aspect: konaks and gardens, mosques and minarets, cover the swelling hills with patches of red and grey, or vivid green, with flashing sunlight, amongst which rises conspicuously the graceful mosque of Sultan Selim, and the domes of the Fétiyé Djami—once the church of the Virgin—which held (amongst others of almost equal note) the tombs of Alexis Comnenus and of his daughter, Anna. Below this spreads the Phanar, with the

Patriarchate, the old Greek quarter stretching on until you come to Balata, given over to the Jews; and, looking up the hill again, you mark the Kachrié or Kahiré Djami, formerly dedicated to the Saviour.

But the caïque is nearing the scala of Aïwan-Seraï, and we see, standing in bold relief, the square mass of the ruined palace of Constantine, above the double line of walls and towers that mark the site of the Blackernæ.

Turning to the right on landing, the street leads past Odoun-Capoussy, the spot until lately spanned by a ruinous archway. And immediately beyond this, a fountain and a shady grove form the entrance to the picturesque and venerated suburb of Eyoub; on the left hand begins the far more venerable line of the land-walls of Constantinople.

Passing the fountain and little guard-house, the road winds through the grove, and skirting a belt of market-gardens, above which loom, grey and majestic, the Tower of Isaac Angelus and the ancient State prisons of Anemà, rises with a steep ascent, and passes the point where Eghri-Capou (the Crooked Gate) stands in an angle of the fortified wall. A few yards farther on the Taxim, or reservoir for the distribution of water throughout Constantinople, is covered by a low building of massive grey stone. Here, the view opens out, and reaching the Greek burial-ground at the foot of the ruined palace, Tekfour Seraï, you pause in the shade of green, rustling boughs.

It is a beautiful spot, although the unsightly wall which has arisen of late years has singularly destroyed the picturesque aspect of the approach, without being apparently of much real use. Instead of climbing the little hillock of rough earth fringed with bright green tufts and vagrant daisies, you pass through a gap of the already crumbling enclosure, and find the tomb-besprinkled sward sparkling with the intense freshness of the spring, so soon destroyed by the first summer heats. Flickering patches of sunlight and shadow play on the soft grass and on rough grey stone or marble slabs lying scattered here and there, as if to form convenient seats for the gaily-tinted groups that rest or wander or dance or flit about, making little rainbow spots all over the ground; shekerdjis, with their glittering sweetmeat trays, are doing a grand stroke of business with the children; a man in a pink cotton jacket, crouched on the ground, ladles out steaming pillaw from an immense cauldron; a seller of mohalibé wanders along with his gaudy platter poised on his head, the delicate creamy jelly covered with a damp cloth, and the row of bright-coloured saucers, the polished metal bowl, the arrow-headed spoons, and the bottle of rose-water, all sparkle and flash as he crosses a patch of vivid sunshine. Then there are semitdjis, with their yellow rings of sémits dangling on a long pole, and—in a very shady spot—a heap of fresh lettuces in water. "Bouz guiby! bouz guiby!"—it is water "like ice!" that is thus cried and offered about; and a cavedji has set up his steaming kettle on some stones, roughly put together to shelter the embers from the windy quarter. Behind all this glitter and movement, the solemn grey towers and battlemented walls frame in the laughing picture, while the rich bistre and sienna tones of Constantine's ruined palace rise, clear and vivid, against the intense blue of an Eastern summer sky.

After passing the Adrianople Gate, the road dips into a valley, rising again to Top-Capou. A few years since, the unbroken sweep of walls and towers, the triple line of defence, the moat and the water-bridges, viewed from either eminence, formed a perfect picture; now, aimless and senseless destruction has fallen on this matchless girdle of the ancient city, and left many of the venerable towers mere heaps of crumbled masonry.

But the stream of busy life is pouring onwards to the grove of the sacred fountain of Baloukli. Bright groups of Turkish women, gathered wherever a low parapet or a few stones on the edge of the road offer means of rest, are enjoying the day after their fashion, staring at the crowd and smoking tchibouks or cigarettes, according to age or fashion. Some jolt along in scarlet-tilted arabas, or in the gaudy, ricketty talika. There are horses also, and donkeys, all jogging forward on the same way, now with a man holding a couple of children before him, now with the little ones swinging contentedly in panniers.

Bands of Bulgars and Wallachs are filling the air with the plaintive melancholy strains of their untaught music; then some wild, discordant, shrieking notes proclaim a party of musicians heralding a dancing cluster of Armenians in their holiday garb: baggy white trousers, the material of which has been so lavishly gathered into superfluous folds in the bulk of the garment, that a painfully tight fit only has remained for the sturdy thigh, and nothing whatever to cover the knee. Lower down, covering begins again, in the form of a gaily-coloured stocking, bound round and crossed and swathed, like an ancient Roman sandal. A crimson scarf, rolled and twisted, circles the waist and wanders about the person, falling in a deep loop over one hip; a bright satin open waistcoat, a jacket of striped Damascus silk—gold-colour and purple, or crimson and pale green—with a fez almost hidden under a painted handkerchief, bound about it loosely, turban-wise, complete the fantastic, rarely-worn holiday adornment of the humble, hard-working Armenian hamal. His usual attire is brown felt and dirt, but to-day he is radiant, and he performs heavy prancing capers to the sound of the excruciating bagpipes with all the joyousness of a child Some demure middle-aged men go along holding each other's hands, or break into a *pas de deux*, grasping each a part of the friend's ample waistband.

There is no rioting, no quarrelling; the crowd thickens as we advance with the stream, and after passing the Mevlaneh-Capou on the left hand, and the pink and grey téké of the dervishes on the right, turn off the high road towards a rising ground shaded by the terebinth and plane trees that mark a Christian cemetery.

Here again the objectionable boundary walls have almost destroyed the sylvan beauty of this once charming spot, cutting the soft slopes of tender sward and foliage with their hard lines and dreary, barren surface. There is a long row of military tents, and farther on, other tents are full of cooks and cafédjis busy with their frizzling, and frying, and roasting, and boiling, under the trees; and far away, also, among the thickly strewn gravestones of the Armenian cemetery, the dancing, the piping, and the feasting are going on vigorously.

A brisk clapping of hands draws us to a ring of dancing hamals. The sounds that animate them are drawn from a drum and a fife, worked by two heated, ragged, and energetic musicians in the centre, the dancers labouring slowly round and round. They are not all young and in the spring of life and gaiety by any means: many grey-headed men combine to form a broken circle. The evolutions are conducted by a gaudy personage who steps on with an air of heavy responsibility, held lightly at arm's length by the next dancer, their little fingers only being twisted together, in order that the leader may be free to elaborate the ponderous fancies that are to guide the ring. The rest of the performers cling together, each one's hand upon his neighbour's shoulder. The leader waves a handkerchief with his disengaged right hand, and slowly, heavily, like a circle of treading elephants, the dancers—grave and serious—knead the ground: they turn the foot, they sway all together; they have made a little step; have they advanced? No, they have swayed heavily back again; but another step brings them slightly onward, and so, gradually, they work round, till the drops of perspiration stream from the brow; but still they toil on. They will go on and on for hours, and they feel, poor simple creatures, that they are mightily enjoying their brief holiday, with the mild dissipation of their treadmill exercise.

The Greek dance is more vivacious: there are sounds of quick music, and at a short distance a group is leaping and vaulting round a man who scrapes a little Turkish kit. In this ring the dancers hold each other more loosely, and the leader flourishes his large cotton handkerchief wildly, as he attitudinises and springs about, all following his not ungraceful movements with more or less success. Seeing strangers hovering near, the fiddler's scrape is brisker, the dancers' leap more energetic, until, from sheer exhaustion, they stop at last, mopping their flushed faces, while the musician goes round with a bowl to collect his scanty payment.

There are no women in these groups: Greek women sometimes join in the "romaïka," or form a circle by themselves, in quieter festivities; Armenian women never dance in public in Constantinople, though they do so in their own country.

Besides dancing, many other amusements are provided for the crowd: swings are in full play, and weighing-machines extremely popular. The swings are not at all considered as the exclusive property of supple youth: heavy men, with grave and perhaps anxious faces, wait their turn patiently, and swing as if fulfilling one of the serious duties of the day; and they are equally conscientious in the matter of the whirligigs and merry-go-rounds that occupy every convenient patch of open ground. They eat lettuces also between whiles. Every second person you meet carries a vivid spot of yellow-green about with him, touching up the effect of the poorest and dustiest attire; and he will wear the ornament all day long, for as soon as he has nibbled through the lettuce of the moment, he begins upon another, and so on, to the end of the day's pleasuring, excepting always the important pause during which he partakes of the heavier temptations so lavishly spread around. Throughout the grove there is an open-air cooking of kebabs, and frying of fish, and sale of greasy galettes, of ices, cakes, halwa, sweets of every kind, and, above all, of clear fresh water, which is carried about in casks, in skins, in bottles, in pitchers, always, if possible, covered with bunches of young walnut-leaves, and when that cannot be obtained, the vendor carries a bough in his hand; every one has somewhere about him, holding, or fixed in his headdress, or among his wares, great tufts of horse-chestnut blossom, lilac, judas-tree, or guelder rose.

There are solicitors of various kinds sprinkled through the crowd: men go about collecting money, supposed to be for the benefit of the church of Baloukli. One carries a plate nearly covered with flowers, while his companion sprinkles you with holy water from a metal bottle. There are also the cripples and beggars in indescribable rags and tatters, and the lean, miserable dogs, who gaze at first wistfully from a distance, fearing the familiar stone, but soon take courage and become importunate. But the most remarkable of all these beggars are the gipsy women, the "Tchinganas." They swarm at every festivity; such wild and picturesquely tattered creatures, tall and slender, with flashing eyes and wavy raven locks; their gaudy cotton garments flutter in the sunshine; a large rose or two is stuck in the greasy headgear; they come in troops of three or four, and sinking on their heels, with clapping of hands and swaying of the body, utter a hideous, screeching ditty, of which, doubtless, the less that is comprehended the better.

The festivities of Baloukli are not confined to the grove immediately surrounding the church, for, beyond the Greek burial-ground, the Armenian cemetery covers a slope shaded by spreading terebinth-trees, where the dancing and gaiety go on, amongst the graves, as merrily as below. A little apart from the throng a funeral is being quietly performed. Some women weep, the priests chant their inharmonious dirge, idlers look on—and the drums, the pipes, the fiddles, and the bagpipes squeak, and groan, and scrape, quite near the burial party; yet no one amongst them seems to feel that this rough intrusion on the solemn silence of the grave is terribly painful and unseemly.

The sun, fast dipping, is sending bright streams of light and trailing shadows across the trodden grass; the crowd is melting slowly and irregularly along the distant road, and the moment has arrived when a visit to the church may be undertaken with some hope of reaching the fountain of the miraculous fishes.

The church of Baloukli is a modern structure, reared on the site of similar buildings often destroyed and as often rebuilt. The first church of the Pegé Zoodochus was raised by Leo the Great, augmented and embellished by Justinian, destroyed, and again erected by Basil the Macedonian, who also built near the same spot a handsome palace, much frequented by subsequent Greek emperors in the spring season. The present church was raised about the middle of this century by the Greeks under the Patriarchate of the learned Constantius, from whose work, "Ancient and Modern Constantinople," these details are derived. The little chapel covering the sacred "Ayasma," which was formerly enclosed in an extensive monastery, dates back to the period of the Lower Empire, although this, also, has been recently restored and embellished.

A descent into the chapel of the fountain is by no means easily accomplished: the narrow flight of stone steps is thronged with devotees pushing their way upwards, their hair streaming with water. The steps are wet and slippery, the heat suffocating; and it is wiser for the present to content ourself with the gallery, which commands an excellent view of the whole scene.

The little chapel is comparatively quiet; the scuffling and the struggling that had been going on all day, after the manner of Eastern Christian worshippers at holy shrines, is subsiding, and the last stragglers of the crowd are performing their devotions in peace. Some drink the water of the holy spring; some pour it over their heads, their hands, their faces; then, bringing little candles, lighted, stick them, carefully arranged, on a turning stand. After this they go towards an aged priest, who stands before the altar holding a small cross, with which he touches the forehead twice, then the mouth of the worshipper, who kisses, first the cross, then the hand of the priest, making a small offering of money. Others of the people, who had completed their round of observances, are engaged in kissing all the pictures on the walls in succession, crossing themselves the while, and lifting up the little children for the same purpose. The people are not allowed to take the water from the "Ayasma;" it is supplied by an attendant, who keeps a range of wooden mugs always filled. Many of the devout bring bottles for carrying away a supply.

There are some gold and silver fishes floating in the basin of the holy fountain. They form the subject of a characteristic legend. It affirms that when the city fell into the hands of the Turks, a priest attached to the church on this spot was engaged in the homely occupation of frying fish for his dinner. A friend rushed in to announce that the enemy was within the gates. "It is impossible!" replied the priest. "I could as soon believe that these fish would leap alive from the frying-pan." Whereupon the fishes, constrained to bear testimony to the truth, leapt out, and have remained to this day with one side cooked to a fine red colour, the other side remaining silver white. How they got themselves into the fountain the legend sayeth not, but there they are, and can be seen by the believing any day. And why not? Gold and silver fishes are abundant and very thriving in all the ornamental pieces of water in the gardens of Constantinople.

Contiguous to the chapel, and within the wall of the enclosure, some buildings have been erected for the use of any persons wishing to reside for a time in retirement. The rooms are small, but very clean; they have no furniture, except a low divan and a square of matting, the temporary occupant providing for his own comfort. The remainder of the considerable mass of buildings is occupied by the clergy attached to the church.

Every one is now turning homewards. The day's holiday is ended; the scene of the late festivities, shortly before so full of life and movement, looks deserted and shabby; the fresh bright grass, all trampled and soiled, strewn with lettuce-leaves, broken egg-shells, faded branches, and limp, discoloured flowers; the few last hawkers and vendors are packing up their wares; folded tents are being heaved up on to the backs of patient horses; the bright little hearths of the coffee-sellers blink and flicker amongst smouldering ashes. Along the road people are dragging their slow steps, carrying the little ones of their party, and find themselves, perhaps, as they plod silently onwards, unconsciously joining company with two weary little bears and a tired ape, all three, as well as their wild Asiatic proprietors, utterly worn out with their day's exertions for the amusement of an appreciative public.

XII.

VILLAGE LIFE IN TURKEY

Round the Meïdan.—The Meïdan.—The Grey Wooden House.—The Imâm's House and the Battle of the Broomsticks.—Ibrahim.—The Rose-Coloured House.—The Ruined House.—The Yellow Konak.—Two Cottages.

In one of the secluded villages that overhang the Bosphorus I found opportunity to become acquainted with the simple histories and daily lives of the inhabitants of a small cluster of houses and cottages, and, wishing to render faithfully both the lights and shadows of the following slight sketches, I endeavour to trace them, without choice or preference, exactly as the dwellings stand surrounding the meïdan, or village green.

Every village in Turkey has some central spot corresponding to our village green in England. On this meïdan—a grass-grown, irregular space, shaded by a cypress, with a few small acacias and sycamores—is found the public pump, the stone mortar for crushing corn, the raised oblong stone slab on which coffins are rested outside the mosque, and the horse-trough with the fountain for the ablutions of the faithful before entering their place of prayer.

The mosque itself, standing on one side of the space, is extremely small, and with its minaret, which shows a great patch of brown brickwork where the plaster has fallen away, does not certainly wear an aspect of luxurious prosperity. At the foot of the mosque two or three aged turbaned tombstones nod crookedly at each other across a patch of tangled weeds; the horse-trough is broken, and the fountain has run dry; the stone mortar has long been unused, but the oblong rest for the "taboot" is as needful now as when first erected—a silent witness to the one event of our lives that times and fashions leave unchanged, unchangeable. It was but the other day that a woman's bier was laid upon that stone, and the chant of the imām, repeated again and again—"May God give her hope!" was answered by the murmured "Amīn," of the surrounding crowd.

On a line with the mosque, and partly built on to it, stands the house of the imām; a very modest little house—we should call it a cottage. It is painted dark red; outside the trellis-work blinds (the cafesses) of the upper windows, hang two bird-cages, with some bottles of vinegar, put to ripen in the sunshine. Nothing can be simpler or more devoid of architectural beauty than this little group of buildings, yet the charm of the sunny East is over it all—in the rich tone of the woodwork, the sun-painted glow on the old whitened minaret, in the patch of pure azure between the branches of the dark foliage beyond, and in the fresh brightness of the springing grass and weeds that fringe the crumbling walls.

Let us take the houses as we see them, without moving from this spot, and learn something of the inhabitants of each of them in turn. Besides the imām's house, there is the yellow stone konak; the rose-coloured house, at the entrance of the lane in front; the grey wooden house, a short distance up that lane, and the ruined house that faces it. We can distinguish the roof of a cottage above the edge of bay-trees; one or two other roofs dimly seen among the cypresses on the right hand, also interest us. We will begin with the grey wooden house.

A wooden house, painted grey, standing in a little garden. Above the wall the upper floor projects, and is supported on slanting beams. Simple white curtains give the place an air of neatness and comfort, and a few garlands of bright-leaved vines, wandering about the grey planks and fluttering in the golden sunlight, convert it into a picture.

This house belongs to a respectable, elderly widow, Fatma Hanum, a Circassian by birth. The tale of her life is not a romance; her career has been that of most of her countrywomen, in its adventurous, unsettled childhood, and the tranquil existence of later years; many a Circassian, in the harems of Stamboul, might relate her experiences in nearly the same words as those in which Fatma tells her simple story.

In her childhood she was called Ayesha; the recollections of her Circassian home are faint and uncertain, but she knows that her father was a Beyzadeh, a small notability in the Caucasus.

Fatma's first vivid impressions of life date from the time when she was carried off with her little brother Ahmed by a foraging party of Russians. The wild scamper across the border, the transfer of the children to a Russian family living near the southern frontier, the early days of her childish servitude, pass across her mind like a troubled dream. She remembers to have been gently and kindly treated, and not to have been separated from her brother; but this quiet time was of short duration, and her recollections become more circumstantial as the trials of her young life began once more.

The Beyzadeh, who was not of that class of Tcherkess who habitually sell their children, was overwhelmed with grief at the loss of the little son and daughter. He set on foot the most searching inquiries, and learning that the children had been carried into Russia, commissioned a friend, who had access to that part of the country, to find out the place of their captivity, and to use every means to bring them back to their home.

Mehemed Agha set out, and after many wanderings suddenly, one day, discovered the lost children in a field a short distance off; they were helping the servants of the Russian family to set out the dinner under a tent, for it was warm summer-time.

Mehemed, checking his horse, led him under the shelter of a high bank, and through an opening in the hedge watched his opportunity. To dart forward, catch up the little ones, mount them before him, and disappear, was a feat that experience had rendered easy to the wily Tcherkess. His intentions may have been honest when he undertook the quest at the prayer of the bereaved parents, but little Ayesha's blue eyes and soft chestnut curls were too much for his integrity. Such a child was far too valuable to be simply restored to her native village. What profit might he not make by the sale of such a sweet little maiden! But he could not keep the girl and restore the boy; both must go together. And so, as the tired horse plodded along the desolate mountain track, it seemed to the bewildered children that the country looked less and less like the surroundings of their old home, and when at length he stopped at a small town on the sea-coast, and Mehemed handed them over to the custody of an evil-looking man, Ahmed and Ayesha, young as they were, knew the fate that had befallen them, and that they were in the house of a slave-dealer.

Here Fatma's recollections became again confused. Was it weeks or months—was it a year or two—that passed over while the children dragged out the weary time of their captivity in the heavy air of the unwholesome town, so different from the pure breezes of their mountain village? She cannot say; but she clearly recalls the day when, as she sat with Ahmed sad and listless as usual among a group of slaves, the master entered the enclosure, and, making a general inspection of his property, spoke to the children. "A man is coming here," he said, " to look at you all, but you two must hold your heads down and not speak one word; disobey me, and I shall punish you severely." The slave-master was cruel, and the threat was well understood. Someone came in; the frightened children, crouching in a corner of the courtyard, held their breath and dared not raise their eyes to see who it was that spoke in a voice they seemed to recognise. The stranger passed carefully round, but seeing nothing in the crouching ragged forms that would recall those he was seeking, turned away: in later years they knew that it was their elder brother.

Soon after this Ahmed and Ayesha, still together, became the property of an Armenian merchant of Trebizond. As a Christian he could not legally purchase them, but he gave in exchange a stipulated amount of goods. Who can say how many pieces of Manchester print and of Sheffield ware, guns, knives, or what not, represented the value of the little Circassians? The transfer was a fortunate one for them, for the Armenian merchant, a lonely man, had taken them chiefly out of pity for their friendlessness; he treated them with the greatest tenderness, and Fatma Hanum speaks with gratitude of his fatherly care during those early years.

Ayesha was a tall and blooming girl when business at length brought the old Armenian to Stamboul, where she was able to render him great service by displaying his goods in the harems, into which he could not himself penetrate. One of his best customers was the wife of a high official of the palace, and Ayesha's sweet face and winning manners so took the fancy of this lady that she proposed to take the girl as her personal attendant. It was a hard struggle for the poor old man to part with his adopted daughter; but, trade was bad, his business was decreasing yearly; he knew that Ayesha would be kindly cared for in her new home, and so he let her go. On the occasion of her installation in the pasha's house she was for the first time called Fatma, in accordance with a Turkish custom, frequently followed, of re-naming a newly-acquired slave.

Fatma was happy. Providence had placed her in one of those respectable, old-fashioned Turkish families who treat their dependents with the kindness most likely to insure their zealous and faithful service. Being the property of the lady, her duties consisted at first in attendance upon her mistress; but, after some time of careful training, through her intelligence and general steadiness of conduct, she was promoted to the office of bash calpha, or chief superintendent, all household matters concerning the female portion of the family being under her control. Fatma Calpha was equal to the occasion; no harem in that neighbourhood could show rooms more daintily neat and clean than those inhabited by the pasha's wife; no table was better served, no house more quiet and orderly than that over which Fatma held a watchful supervision. The tchamashir, or wash, fluttering on lines in the harem garden of that konak, was always spotless; the linen more delicately embroidered, the sheets more neatly worked at the border, than those that any other harem could show; and also—to the credit of the calpha be it said—in no house was the amount of debt incurred by the younger slaves for little articles of finery so small as in this konak at Tash-Déressi.

When Fatma was about five-and-twenty the pasha and his wife began to think it time to recompense her eight or nine years of dutiful service. There is no law which can oblige an owner to release a slave at any given time, but adet (custom), often as powerful as law, rules that a just, God-fearing Mussulman householder shall consider that a well-conducted halaïk has, by so many years of useful work, gained her right to freedom.

The lady was terribly unwilling to lose the attendance and care on which she had for so long depended for the orderly comfort of her home; but she was a just woman, and when the Pasha proposed, as a husband for her bash calpha, Ali Bey, a clerk in his office much valued for his steady conduct, the lady at once saw the matter in its right light, spoke to Fatma on the subject, and began to occupy herself actively with the preparations for the marriage.

The presents made to the bride-elect were numerous and costly; the friends of the family brought offerings that proved their goodwill and esteem, while household furniture, dresses and linen, ornaments, and even diamonds and jewellery of some value, were the contributions of the master and mistress. But their crowning gift was the grey wooden house, built expressly for the young couple. The title-deed of the little property was presented at the ceremony of the nighiah (betrothal), at the time of the signing of the marriage contract. Fatma also received on that occasion her "paper of liberty," and became at once by that act Fatma Hanum.

The marriage was a happy one, but there were no children to enliven the quiet household; so the husband and wife spent much of their time—the winter months especially—in the konak of those whom they still called their "Effendis," coming in the summer to their own little place in the country, where Fatma made a small profit by the sale of eggs, goats' milk, and fruit.

Ali Bey was a man of very regular habits. Each evening, on his return from town, he would stop to smoke a quiet narghilé with some friends, seated on low stools outside the village café. He would discuss the news of the day, sigh over the deplorable state of things in general, say "bacalum!" to every suggestion or expressed hope of active reform, and then wind his way homeward, not disdaining, in spite of his neatly buttoned-up coat and respectable appearance, to carry with him, dangling by a string, the fresh fish or vegetables that were to figure at the evening repast. During the Ramazan he regularly provided himself with a supply of simits—ring-shaped biscuits garnished with sesame seed—bought from a baker renowned for the perfection of his Ramazan cakes.

Ali Bey died two years ago, and his widow has her home with the worthy family to whom she chiefly owes this modest competence; but she has unexpectedly recovered the long-lost traces of her own family, has been to visit her relatives in Circassia, and has received them in the grey wooden house. The discovery came about in a curious way. Fatma, at that time about sixty years of age, was one day crossing the bridge of Stamboul, when the sight of a party of newly-arrived Circassians made her think of Ahmed, the companion of her childish adventures. She had lost all trace of him since that early time. These Circassians were from her own part of the Caucasus; the dress, the once familiar dialect, the homelike look of the party, raised a crowd of memories. If Ahmed still lived he might be like one of these; perhaps like that old man who is looking at her so intently, and with an expression so strangely familiar. The recognition was mutual, and people hurrying across the bridge stopped to gaze and wonder at the unusual spectacle of the fond public greeting between an aged Turkish woman and an equally venerable Circassian emigrant.

The Imām's House.

The door of the imām's house is slightly open, and you may see Muniré Hanum, the imām's wife, hard at work at the washtub, stopping now and then to take a hurried look into the earthen pan in which dinner is bubbling over a small brazier in the background.

Her dress is a sort of brown wrapper, very vague in form and independent of fastenings; on her head she wears a bright yellow handkerchief, which is, as usual, all awry with energy, for she is a wonderfully brisk little woman, as brown as a berry and as active as a grasshopper; when she speaks, eyes and hands are in constant motion to accentuate the expression of her acute, clever remarks.

That half-open door of hers is a point of great vantage; it not only overlooks the meïdan, with the five or six little lanes that meet on that spot, but it commands both the front and back entrances to the yellow house opposite, the home of her especial enemy the kiatib's wife. While Muniré rubs her linen she can note all that passes up and down that part of the village. She is the centre of local news and gossip; but, unlike such characters in general, she is exceedingly industrious and a good warm-hearted little body, very grateful for benefits received, and ready to do a hand's turn for anyone who may need it.

Muniré Hanum is a peasant woman from a village in Anatolia, not far from Angora. She came to Stamboul as servant in the household of some pasha's wife, who subsequently "wishing," as she said, "to do something meritorious for the good of her soul," gave Muniré in marriage to the imām. The husband himself is a meek, effaced member of the humble household. A visitor to Muniré may have a perception of a white turban and a cotton dressing-gown somewhere in the background, which soon melts away behind a door-curtain and is seen no more, unless, on leaving the cottage, you may chance to perceive him flitting round the gallery of his little minaret.

The imām and his wife have two children, boys; they can keep no servant, for they are very poor, the official salary being only about five shillings a month. And for this miserable sum, paid by the Evcaf, the poor man has to travel all the way to Eyoub, at the head of the Golden Horn, and often in vain. They are at present several months in arrears, not having even received the trifling allowance always made for the lighting of the mosque during Ramazan.

There are no fees for religious offices among the Mussulmans, and the services of the imām, when required in marriage contracts, naming of infants, funerals, &c., are given gratuitously; but it is customary for people who have the means to do so to make some small present in money or in kind on these occasions. In most of the ceremonies above-named the imām is present not in his religious character as leader of public worship, but in a civil capacity, as a sort of district magistrate. An imām, also, has generally the charge of the school attached to his mosque, where a small payment is made for each child. But he makes the best part of his gains by following some handicraft or trade.

Our imām, however, does not appear to possess any industrial capacities, and the gratuities of the villagers amount to very little, for the village is not rich; the war and the burden of refugees has distressed the people sorely, and were it not for the industry of Muniré and for the help given by some well-wishers, it is hard to see how these poor people would contrive to live.

But the imām's wife has had to deal with worse troubles than the arrears of payment and scanty resources. A few years back, and while her little Mustapha was a child in arms, these same presents of sympathising friends raised such a storm of jealousy in some of the surrounding harems, that a conspiracy was formed amongst them to get her divorced from her husband, and sent away from the village. These kind neighbours undertook at the same time to provide the imām with another wife from their own circle.

Poor Muniré was in dire distress at this cabal against her; she wept incessantly; friends took up her cause, and the storm blew over. But she was not likely to forget the intended injury, and the mutual ill-feeling culminated one bright summer's day in the Battle of the Broomsticks.

The immediate cause of war was the pump-handle! Some one had broken that useful appendage to the village pump on the meïdan, and no one would plead guilty and repair the damage. On that eventful morning, as the imām's wife was standing within her doorway, her feelings at boiling point from the lack of water for a heavy wash, the servant boy of Hamdi Bey (who lives in the small konak to the right) came sauntering down the lane. There was an aggressive twist in the set of his fez, and a general air of defiance about him that looked singularly suspicious. *That* was the aggressor! Muniré saw the truth at once. She caught up her yashmak, gave it a vigorous twist round her brown face, and rushed at him with the accusation, and a demand for the instant repair of the damage.

"You idle, useless, mischievous fellow!" says she. "You ghiaour!"

"Ghiaour indeed!" returns the lad; "ghiaour yourself, Muniré Hanum; there is no bigger ghiaour than you in all this country part. Colaï (easy) is it, you say? Colaï! molaï! what is that to me? Do you think I will mend the pump-handle at the bidding of such as you?"

Then follow stronger epithets, the noise of the dispute bringing Hamdi Bey's wife upon the scene. She supports the cause of her servant, and the two ladies interchange sentiments which grow in force of expression until Muniré, beside herself with rage, dashes into her dwelling, to reappear immediately armed with her broomstick, with which she falls upon the offending lad. But Hamdi Bey's wife has a similar weapon also close at hand; she rushes at her adversary, and the battle rages in earnest. A circle of women has gathered at the sounds of strife. Their veils and general attire are more or less dishevelled; they scream at the combatants and to each other; they call on the Prophet to stop the combat, and shout for a zaptié, who is not forthcoming; but no one ventures to get in the way of the showers of blows, until the imām and the bey appearing on the scene, drag their respective wives back into their own harems. The crowd, after much chattering, gradually disperses. Being in Turkey, the pump-handle has not been repaired, and as to the hanums, they have ever since maintained towards each other a dignified attitude of "armed observation."

A second similar battle took place on the same spot, and I grieve to have to record that our Muniré was again one of the combatants; but she had great provocation.

We have mentioned the wife of the kiatib living in the yellow konak opposite to the mosque: this woman is Muniré's chief enemy in the village, for the imām's wife steadily refuses to salute her by the title of Hanum Effendi and to kiss the hem of her dress, an act of homage which the proud woman is not entitled to exact; but the quarrel ripened to open hostilities in the following manner:—

A piece of land adjoining the garden of the konak had been purchased by an individual who had duly fenced it round and sunk a well, thus establishing his rights. Unfortunately he died without a will, and the land was claimed by the Evcaf as wacouf, or mosque property. As such, the imām's wife considered that they had some right to the fruits of the little orchard as long as it remained untenanted: at any rate, her eldest boy was one day seen there by the inmates of the yellow konak, quietly plucking the figs, which are of a particularly fine quality. This outrageous conduct on the part of the poor imām's son was not to be tolerated. The hanum sallied forth and proceeded at once to bodily chastisement; but Muniré, drawn from her house by the screams of her child, met the enemy on the little green, and sticks were wielded as lustily as the broomhandles had been a while before. In this encounter poor Muniré was worsted, and retired crestfallen and lamenting within the shelter of her little house. How many anathemas she hurled through the cafesses at the flaunting figure of the triumphant adversary, how fervently she doomed her and all her family to "Gehenna," history does not record.

The village is now much quieter, but we must relate yet one other combat of which the meïdan was also the theatre, as it brings fresh actors on the scene, in an animated encounter beween Ibrahim's sister and his wife. And who is Ibrahim?

Ibrahim is a "saka" or water-carrier; a poor, hardworking, saving, honest man. Formerly he lived—contented and cheerful—upon gains that seemed scarcely sufficient to keep body and soul together. But, patience! if the bread of one day's earnings was hard and insufficient, the next might bring him the chance of a bowl of curdled milk or a portion of goats' cheese; perhaps a few bits of mutton ham or a hot mess of pillaw cooked in strong Russian butter, which is euphonistic for modified tallow; at any rate, lamp oil and vinegar, flavoured with fennel and bitter herbs, was often obtainable with the bread, and so he got along. He even began to save money, and might have continued to prosper but for a small inheritance which devolved to him on the death of his parents; they left him a half share of their house, conjointly with his only sister. This legacy proved the ruin of Ibrahim the water-carrier. He grew ambitious; not satisfied with possessing only the half of a dwelling, he dreamed of becoming a builder and sole proprietor. He collected his savings, and land being very cheap in this secluded village, he managed to purchase a small plot of ground. After some delay he began to raise the new dwelling, but it was the "old, old story" in the matter of house-building; the outlay exceeded the estimate, and, striving to complete the work, he borrowed at ruinous interest.

On this followed a more serious misfortune; Ibrahim married. Had he taken a good, hardworking girl, such as Refika, the fisherman's daughter, or Yildiz, the halaïk of the Pasha's wife, he might have done well yet and worked away the debt; but poor Ibrahim made an unhappy choice, or rather it was made for him, for what could he know about these young girls, though they were his immediate neighbours? He had never seen them except veiled, far less had he entered into friendly conversation, or been able in any way to learn for himself their feelings or dispositions. Such a scandalous amount of intimacy had never entered into his mind as possible, so there was nothing to be done but to leave the choice of the bride to an old woman who undertook the commission, and who speedily married him to the daughter of Dèli (or mad) Hafuza, a woman in the village half crazy and wholly bad.

Ibrahim's sister lived with the newly married couple. She was herself a married woman, but her husband being at work at some distance from Constantinople, she continued to inhabit the paternal mansion, the half of which, as we have seen, belonged to her. Nessibé, the new wife, conceived a strong dislike to her sister-in-law, whose quiet, homely ways ill accorded with the flighty tendencies of the daughter of Dèli Hafuza. She determined to get rid of her, and bent all her energies to raise up ill-feeling and disagreement between the brother and sister, who had hitherto lived in perfect harmony. The poor woman for a long while bore these troubles uncomplainingly, till one day, driven to bay and provoked beyond endurance, she struck at Nessibé with the tongs of the mangal. They were standing on the meïdan; the affront was public, and soon the village was in commotion. Dèli Hafuza flew to the defence of her unworthy child, and had the offender arrested and marched off by the zaptiés to be tried at the police-court of Galata Seraï. Poor Ibrahim bravely accompanied his sister, and stood by her during the short trial; she was condemned to pay a lira and released, but she quitted her brother's house, and now lives in great tranquillity with the wife of Yussuf, the Albanian gardener.

Ibrahim, broken-hearted at these domestic storms, left his wife for a time, but he has at length taken her back. They live quietly though very poorly, for the new house is untenanted, work is very slack in the village; and the dry bread of Ibrahim's present poverty has a bitter flavour which was unknown in his happier days of hope and cheerful toil.

Yussuf's wife, with whom Ibrahim's sister has taken refuge, is the niece of our vivacious friend Muniré, who, thinking to advance her fortunes, brought the young girl up from their native place in Asia Minor, begged the marriage trousseau all round the village, and married her to Yussuf of Scodra, who was supposed to possess a small independence. This Yussuf had been gardener and factotum to an old lady, who, at her death, left him her little property; but he fell into the same pitfall that had led his friend Ibrahim to ruin: he began to build a house with his newly acquired wealth, found it insufficient, borrowed at 50 per cent., and is now burdened with a heavy debt which there seems not the slightest chance of his ever paying off.

Yussuf is a kind and careful husband, but he has brought from his Albanian home rules of conduct regarding the inferiority and needful subjection of women that are far more stringent than those in favour here. He keeps his wife very closely at home "to mind the house and do her work." At Scodra, he says, a woman, if she meet a man in the public highway, must cross the road, to leave his passage unimpeded. Yussuf and his wife have a baby girl, a very pretty little creature, of whom the young mother is immensely proud. Their little cottage is poor and miserable-looking, and forms a great contrast to the next house on our visiting list.

The Rose-coloured House.

This is next door to Yussuf's dilapidated dwelling, and is the prettiest and most attractive-looking house of the cluster that we have undertaken to examine. It belongs to a Government official, Nouri Effendi, who, happily, is possessed of sufficient means to live respectably and to keep his property in order.

This is such a very quiet, well-ordered household that there are no startling adventures to relate about any of its members, but it is worth describing as offering an excellent type of the harem of a respectable middle-class Turkish family—a subject so ill-understood by strangers, or indeed by the greater number of those differing from them in faith, who pass their lives beside them, and yet remain in profound ignorance on the matter.

Nouri Effendi has only one wife, who is the mother of his three daughters and two sons, but the harem is rather numerous, for it comprises, besides the buyuk hanum and two of her daughters, a married sister of the effendi, an old aunt or two, and more or less female relations, always to be found there on a long visit. There are very few slaves, but the number of the feminine portion of the household is this year increased by several miserable widows and orphan girls, victims of the late cruel war, who are sheltered, fed, and clothed as a pious and undeniable duty.

The family of Nouri Effendi pass their quiet uneventful lives between the house in town and the rose-coloured dwelling in the country, which last is decidedly the favourite residence. The eldest daughter is married away from home. A year or two ago she was a fine blooming young woman, as fresh as a rose and as gay as a bird; now she is pale, thin, and languid. The neighbours surmise that the removal from the cheerful family circle in which she grew up—with a good deal of the freedom of country life, in which the young people spent the greater part of the year—to the restraints of her present home in the city, has not been an advantageous change for poor Besmé Hanum; but the principal cause of pining seems to be that in some complicated way she has to bear the infliction of three mothers-in-law, so austere and rigid in their rule that her life is made a burden for her, and she would gladly return to the gentle loving home from which she has been too early removed.

Warned by the pale looks and saddened life of the eldest daughter, her sister Faika, although fully sixteen, is as yet unmarried. The parents have determined that they will not allow her to leave them, and friends are now actively engaged in seeking a suitable husband, and one who will consent to live in his father-in-law's house. This is a condition very frequently made when marriages are negotiated. The family tie, which is strong in all Turkish homes, is especially so in the circle of the rose-coloured house; and in the konak, in Stamboul, a handsome room is always considered as belonging to the eldest daughter whenever she may come on a visit.

Faika Hanum is a modest-looking, gentle-mannered girl; her quiet self-possession and unaffected dignity on welcoming a stranger are quite charming. She wore a simple skirt and jacket of pale grey stuff, her only ornament being a small natural sprig of verbena placed on one side upon her soft nut-brown hair. She is a fairly good musician, and seems eager to improve herself if there were opportunity of doing so.

In close proximity to the orderly rose-coloured dwelling of Nouri Effendi, we find a habitation which is popularly known as

The Ruined House.

Those who visit Refika Hanum must not be of a nervous temperament, or in any way infirm, for she lives in a sort of cobweb of a house, so old, so dilapidated, such a ruined assemblage of trembling planks and yawning gaps, of walls out of balance, and of incohesive stairs, that it is hard to imagine how any human being can make a home there. And yet that was once a beautiful dwelling, a family mansion, which has passed from father to son, and which a moderate amount of care might have preserved. It was worth preserving. When you have contrived—almost in peril of life or limb—to reach the ruined chambers of the upper floor, you find the remains of decorations of great beauty.

In the principal rooms the ceilings are formed of an intricate and delicately worked panelling; the walls, the doorposts, the window-frames—indeed, all parts and corners of the chamber—are covered, either with panels curiously worked and painted, or with stucco, upon which flowers and designs in the most delicate arabesque are painted in slight relief; over the doorway leading into the chief room of the harem some Arabic verses ornament the woodwork. These decorations are more than a hundred years old. In some parts the colours have faded, in others the stucco has fallen away, while a few of the compartments in the more sheltered corners of the rooms are still as fresh and clear as when first executed; but the doom of Refika's paternal halls has gone forth; there is little doubt but that "the ruined house" will fall entirely to pieces in the course of the ensuing winter, after which, as the land is for sale and the situation good, something very bright and new, and utterly uninteresting, will arise in its place.

These richly and tastefully decorated dwellings of the olden time are now very rarely to be found in Constantinople or its neighbourhood. Little care is taken to preserve them, as they are considered old-fashioned, out of date; and their loss is the more to be deplored, that the modern style of building at present in favour is quite devoid of any attempt at taste or beauty of outline.

Refika's parents, notwithstanding the faded splendours of their home, are very poor people now; the father is simply a fisherman, and the mother is afflicted with a lawsuit, which absorbs the greater part of her time and all the money that she can scrape together, and both are spent utterly in vain; hence arise frightful quarrels. The fisherman, who is addicted to raki, beats his wife, because, returning hungry and weary from his day's toil, he finds no hanum in the house and no dinner ready. The hanum shrieks, and carries on a fierce war of words, and then proceeds to vent her anger and vexation on her unfortunate daughter, who clearly deserves a better fate. The sounds of this domestic strife are most alarming when heard for the first time. "Oh, Abraham! what are those dreadful screams?" I had said to an intelligent Jewish lad, who was very proud of his knowledge of the English language. "That noise?" he replies; "why, there's bad man there; he drink raki, and then he plenty smack his madama!"

One gets used to everything, and no one now much notices the quarrels in the ruined house; but her friends and wellwishers would like to see poor Refika Hanum transplanted into some better and more congenial home. In the meantime Refika's presence and handy services are in great request amongst the neighbours, and this necessity for continual employment, with the consciousness of being useful, help to keep up her spirits, in despite of the unhappy circumstances of her life, and she is usually bright and cheerful, although she confided to us her solemn conviction that some of her young companions, jealous of her industry, had given her the evil eye, and that nothing she might undertake could succeed.

Refika is not the only child of her parents. She has an elder sister, married to a yorghandji or quiltmaker. There is a young brother also, an idle, drunken vagabond, who is a continual source of trouble and annoyance to the neighbours.

Refika herself is a handsome, intelligent girl, with a modest propriety of demeanour that, considering her disadvantages, is quite remarkable. She is also exceedingly industrious, and contrives to support herself by her honest labour. She used formerly to act as guardian to the little children of the quarter on their way to the school of the village, which is on the opposite side of the valley, collecting them at their homes, and bringing them in safety back again. For these services she received a small remuneration. At present her chief occupation is painting handkerchiefs. When this work fails she knits socks or does crochet-work for sale, or helps the neighbouring harems if there happens to be some festivity or unusual amount of work on hand. She makes dresses also very neatly and prettily.

We went to see her at work upon her handkerchiefs. She was a pretty subject for a picture, as she sat on the ground, bending her clearly-cut, regular features and soft, dark eyes over the rude frame; her rich chestnut hair, that fell in long waves over her shoulders, was ornamented with a spray of red roses, placed on one side. The frame was of the most primitive construction—four pieces of wood nailed in a square, and supported on either side by an old stool and a broken box. Refika held her colour in an ancient pomatum pot, and dabbed at her flowers on the muslin with a miserable little brush in the last stage of baldness; but her implements seemed to suit her, at any rate. Poor girl! she knew of none better or more convenient. The method of working is as follows: a square of thin white muslin, with a pattern previously traced in black, is stretched on the frame. The worker begins by wetting with liquid alum all the parts that are to be reserved. She then colours the ground with a piece of wadding dipped in dye, and the muslin is boiled, after which the flowers are coloured with the brush, and the muslin washed a second time. This is a common style of handkerchief. A better sort is made by first painting the flowers, then covering them with gum, and boiling the handkerchief so prepared in the dye of the groundwork.

A great many Greek and Armenian women find employment in the painting of these handkerchiefs. Those who live near the Bosphorus wash their work in the sea-water, and hang it on lines to dry in the sun; this is supposed to set the colours.

The Yellow Konak.

There is little to relate about the inmates of this house, and that little cannot be told in words of praise, but we have promised to give in these slight sketches of village life and character the simple uncoloured truth, the sombre shadows as well as the bright and the softer lights, and therefore we must speak of Djémilé Hanum, wife of the kïatib, and the imperious mistress of the yellow konak.

To be called Hanum Effendi by her poorer neighbours, to see them bend to kiss the hem of her dress, is one great aim and desire of her life; it is an ambition not often gratified, for she is not a favourite in the village, and, as we have seen, Muniré, the imām's wife, whom more than all the haughty Djémilé has endeavoured to subdue, especially rebels against this claim to superiority.

Many sad things are said about Djémilé Hanum, and her arrogance is the mildest of her faults; but her husband is away from home all day, and she rules the household and her own conduct exactly as it may please her.

Djémilé is of Rayah origin, from some town on the borders of Thessaly; how she became a Mussulman the village chronicle does not explain, but it is certain that her thoughts often turn with regret to life in her native place, and when a countryman passes by, she will talk over old friends and acquaintances, and, forgetting for the time that she is Djémilé Hanum, will call on the name of the Virgin and wish she were in the home of her childhood once more. Her partiality for her countrymen is even carried so far that neighbours shake their heads, and sun themselves in the conviction that "*they* at least know how to behave and to live respectably, though they may *not* expect folks to kiss the hem of their antary. Hanum Effendi, indeed! Yes; a nice, proper sort of hanum, who as soon as the poor kïatib's back is turned, has nothing better to do all day than to chatter to every stranger; and then, not even keeping behind the chink of the door, but showing her bold face quite plainly, the shameless creature! She might as well walk straight out into the road without her yashmak! And that tall Albanian who is always in and out of the house! Yes; we know how to hold our tongues, and not to talk scandal; but let such hanums look at home, and mend their ways, before they attempt to rule over their neighbours. And that graceless son of hers! When people have sons who are the terror and plague of the village and the ruin of all the lads of the place, they need not hold their heads so high, and try to walk solemnly in state, with their feràdjies trailing the ground and a train of women behind them."

There was a wedding one day at the yellow konak; as might be expected, the company was not of the choicest. Indeed, so free and bold were the young ladies who had gathered in the central hall, that the bridegroom—a son of the kïatib by a former wife, a shy, timid sort of man—dared not venture through the midst of them to fetch away his bride according to custom. The poor girl waited in all her oppressive bridal finery: the heavy diamonds on her head, cheeks, forehead, and chin; the gold embroidered velvet antary, the streaming threads of gold falling on either side of her face, and the glittering dark gauze veil that completely concealed her features. She waited trembling and ready to faint from heat and agitation, but the bridegroom still hung back, and shrank from the laughter and riotous jesting of the unruly band. What was to be done? Djémilé Hanum had a luminous idea; she collected all their slippers, left at the foot of the staircase, flung them into the garden, and fairly turned them all out of the house.

The Cottage among the Bay-Trees.

There are many branches of the family whose ancestors dwelt in the now "ruined house" scattered about the village and its neighbourhood. Some are rather wealthy, others live humbly and poorly. Amongst these last may be reckoned a small household living in a cottage in the fields; its roof may be seen peeping out from the dark foliage of a tall hedge of bay-trees. The owner of the place, Hussein Agha, cultivates a large piece of ground in fruit and vegetables; he has also a few beehives.

It is a charming spot; but what is not charming on these lovely slopes, under the flickering lights and shadows of overarching boughs, swayed by the lime-scented breezes, with the hum of insects among the flowers, and the drip of falling water somewhere in the rustic garden?

Our visit was paid outside the door of the cottage, and seated on low stools among the flower-beds. Hussein Agha and his wife are quiet, respectable, elderly people. He has but this one wife, and the three children are hers, but at present the domestic circle is increased by some young "mouhadjirs," or refugees taken in from charity.

The good old people, however, are not happy in their children, who are all grown up and married. One son in particular is a cause of bitter grief, and it is no wonder that the gentle, faded face of Hussein Agha's aged wife wears a sad anxious look. Life is in truth very hard and bitter for this worthy couple, and it is piteous to think that they have no Christian hope to cheer them in sorrow, and to brighten the dark hours of declining life.

Two Cottages.

Two little cottages, standing nearly side by side on the border of the Turkish burying-ground. They command one of the most beautiful points of view in all this part of the Bosphorus; but I do not think their inhabitants reflect much upon the view. Their chief preoccupation is cows.

Both the cottages belong to widows; one is a woman from Lazistan. She had married in her own country a certain Mehemed who had been taken there as an infant from the massacre of Schio. Laz Mehemed, as he was called, had had his freedom given him at the time of his marriage, and came with his wife to settle here. Having been careful and under a good master, he had managed to put by money, so he bought first the tiny cottage, then two or three cows, and made considerable profit by the sale of the milk and of the fruit of his garden— the figs especially were in great demand. In process of time he invested in another house, and was beginning to feel himself a man of substance, when death overtook poor Laz Mehemed, and he left his cottages and his cows, his vines and his fig-trees, to his Laz wife Eminé, and to their two children, a son and a daughter.

The daughter married a tradesman, but she was not his first wife; there was a hanum with prior rights who had been "left lamenting" at Eyoub, and to whom he, after a while, returned. For the daughter of Laz Mehemed proved to be of a capricious turn of mind, thought she should like to try a different home, found a pretext for obtaining a divorce, and married a dependent of a rich family in the neighbourhood. The second venture, however, was not at all successful; the new husband had been accustomed to an easy life, and probably was hard to please; the laborious tradesman had been contented and docile; decidedly it would be better to have him back again.

The mother settled it all; the divorced couple were married over again, and once more the deserted first wife is alone—but not for very long; her successor and rival is seriously ill, and it is probable that in a few weeks or months she will have ceased to be a cause of grief and heartburning in the home at Eyoub.

The second cottage is the dwelling of Hadgia Hanum, who was also one of the Schio captives; her Greek name was Haïdée. She was quite a little child when first brought here as the property of the wife of a pasha, and was educated in the harem as waiting-woman. Her mistress treated her kindly and, when she was grown up, gave her, according to the custom in most good families, her liberty and a husband and settled her in the world.

Her husband died many years ago, but Hadgia is a clever industrious woman. She also had contrived to put by money, built for herself the little cottage, and, like her neighbour the Laz, kept cows. The milk she sold was the purest and the most creamy that could be obtained in the village; her yaourt, or curdled milk, the sweetest and freshest that could be met with anywhere; her caïmak, or clotted cream, unrivalled; in short, Hadgia was a treasure of a milkwoman, and became in her humble way so prosperous that, though then elderly, she was sought in marriage by a widower with one daughter. After a few years the widower reposed in the picturesque cemetery on the slope of the hill, but the daughter remained. She was on the point of marriage with a zaptié or policeman, when, at the time of the betrothal, on which occasion the marriage contract is signed and all money arrangements stipulated, it was found that, with the wife, the zaptié had expected to receive the house and the cows. Hadgia very naturally declined to despoil herself of her little property and only means of support, and the policeman departed.

Bad times followed, and Hadgia found herself under the sad necessity of selling the cows. The purchaser could not pay the money down; he obtained long credit, but before the delay expired the cows had all died, and then payment was refused altogether. Hadgia sued her debtor, but the decision was given against her, and the defrauded woman, after all her years of hard but successful labour, remains now poor and destitute. She need not so remain, but that old habit is too strong for her. She has a brother and two sisters—Christians from Schio—who are in comfortable circumstances. They visit her from time to time and do their best to persuade Hadgia to return to Christianity and to make her home with them; but she cannot bring herself to contemplate as yet this important and, in every way, desirable change.

XIII.

THE TURKISH GIRLS' SCHOOL.

The Normal School of Yéré Batān.—Opening Ceremonies.—A small "Medjliss."—The Drawing Class Room.—A First Lesson.—Art Students, their Ways and Manners.—Discord. —A "Tender Infant."—Practice better than Precept.— "Yavash."—Cracked Konaks.—Djénab.—Déli Fatima.— Working for the "Imtihan."—Eminé.—Fetiyé and Muniré. —A Circassian Mother.—Djémilé and Her Work.—Camma, the Abyssinian.—The Examinations.—A Visit to the Home of Djénab.—Black Coffee and Gossip.—The Marriage-maker. —Anarchy.—The Poor Old Mudir.

An effort in the cause of female education was made a few years since in Stamboul by the establishment of a normal school for women, with a view to train Mussulman teachers for girls' schools as well as for the harems.

Most little girls of the humbler class attend—together with the boys—the school of the "mahal," or quarter in which they live, until they are old enough to adopt the yashmak and feràdjé; they are then withdrawn, and it was in order to continue in a better manner these early-checked attempts at education that the normal school was founded by Savfet Pasha, at that time Minister of Public Instruction.

It was established in a house situated in the Yéré Batān quarter, close to the mosque of St. Sophia, a board over the door bearing the name in large Arabic characters being the only distinguishing mark.

The instruction was not only offered gratuitously, but a small monthly payment was made to the pupils to cover their expenses, as many came from distant suburbs of the city, and to encourage their attendance. This plan is often pursued in the beginnings of native schools in the East. The scheme of education consisted of simple studies, especially those connected with their own language —the Arabic and Persian—Turkish writing, both common and ornamental, geography, arithmetic, drawing, and needlework : music and French to be added at a later time.

The school was formally opened in the spring of 1870 by the Minister and by Munif Effendi, President of the Council, with some of its members, and a few mollahs and imāms. Forty pupils assembled on the occasion, and the rooms were soon filled with veiled women, the young girls accompanied by their mothers, or some other female relation. Every one remained standing, the members of the Council and the mollahs in front, the women arranged in rows behind.

The names of all those inscribed on the list having been called over, the Minister read a speech, in which the advantages of education for women were set forth, particularly as enabling them to maintain themselves through their own labour and talents; and he brought before them as worthy of imitation the industry and acquirements that render so many Frank women self-dependent.

The rules and regulations of the school were next read out at some length, in a trembling voice, by a white-haired and venerable effendi, the Director of the new establishment. He was evidently "quite unaccustomed to public" reading, but he got through it at last, and ended with a smile of ineffable relief; after which prayers for the Sultan and for the prosperity of the undertaking were made, each one finishing with "Amīn," repeated by all with clasped hands. Finally, each pupil was presented with a packet of school-books, and the ceremony was over, Savfet Pasha, as he left, addressing a few words of kindly encouragement and goodwill to all concerned.

To picture the working of this new scheme of the Turkish normal school for girls, and to render truthfully the little characteristic incidents connected with it, I must extract some pages from a journal very carefully kept, as, on the foundation of the school I had consented to take the direction of the drawing class, which I continued for two years, with the hope of effecting some good in aid of an institution in which I felt much interest, whilst I should be able to gain an insight—otherwise unattainable—into the life and feelings of middle and lower class Turkish women. Drawing was taught with the especial object of improving the designs used by the women for various works, such as the painting of muslin handkerchiefs and embroideries of several kinds.

May, 1870.—Just returned from Stamboul. I had gone to Yéré Batān in order to make arrangements about the classes, and was received by Emin Effendi (called indifferently the Mudir Effendi or the Reïs Effendi, both terms being equivalent to Director). I found him in company with another " venerable ; " but business was not inaugurated until the arrival of a third personage, slightly less venerable, but still sufficiently imposing from the gravity and dignity that seemed to exhale from his snow-white turban. The last comer—a member of the great Medjliss or Council—was forthwith seated in the place of honour, and having been served with coffee and a long tchibouk, the other members of this little " Medjliss " had their coffee also, and most of them their tchibouks; after which the business of the meeting is entered upon. In this they are all very considerate towards the ghiaour lady, and ascertain the hours most convenient for the drawing class before arranging those of the other professors, two more of whom had by this time arrived.

I find that the wearer of a green turban (an emir, or descendant of the Prophet) is the teacher of Arabic and of ornamental writing. Another turbaned *confrère* is Ismail Effendi, the professor of arithmetic, geography, the use of the globes, &c. He is an imām attached to the mosque of Beshiktash.

The first drawing-class at the school of Yéré Batān. The house is situated exactly in front of the entrance to the great cistern of Constantine, called Yéré Batān Seraï (the underground palace), which gives its name to the quarter. From the windows on the first floor you may look down into the courtyard of the old wooden konak; the entrance of the cistern is through a sort of dry well or hole in the centre of the court.

A few words will describe the class-room, a moderate-sized apartment : a row of windows closely set on the side of the street are furnished with the indispensable cafesses—the trellised blinds—indicating a harem. A large map of the Turkisk Empire nearly covers one end of the room, whilst on the two sides narrow mattresses are laid against the walls, and, in front of them, a long low table in painted wood. The teacher's place is established between the windows, so as to command the two lines of pupils; it is raised, forming a sort of humble throne a few feet above the ground, and has a cushion on which he is supposed to crouch. It is furnished with a movable plank, to serve, when rested on the two arms, as a table.

The whole of this arrangement is utterly unpropitious for the study of drawing: we must gently get it all changed, and substitute tables and chairs; but everything of this sort is slow and difficult of accomplishment. No man can enter these rooms (the harem) whilst the women are there, excepting the professor, who gives his lessons in the sala, for which the pupils present themselves with a semblance of veil twisted about the head, and a cotton over-gown, worn in common in preference to the heavy feràdjé: if a workman, or even the old porter, is obliged to enter the harem precincts, the women must all veil themselves before he can be admitted.

The forty girls are assembled; some, indeed, may be called women of mature age. All seem eager for the novelty; they crouch on their mattresses or kneel against the low desk, handling their new "kurshun kalem" (lead pencils), and making fearful "breaks" in their pieces of drawing-paper. They are very good-humoured but rather inclined to be riotous.

Some few are of a superior class, quiet and ladylike. They exert themselves to subdue the effervescing spirits of the others, whilst I endeavour to write down the names. Such soft Oriental names! Fatima, Zeheïra, Hàtidjé, Ruveida, Djémilé, Eminé, and many others—the names of free women, never given to halaïks or slaves. Three of the pupils are Jewesses, sisters; there is an attendant, an Abyssinian, who is called Camma. She has lived in Algeria, and speaks excellent French.

I now find that I am expected to cut forty pencils, not one of the "art students" having the faintest idea on the subject; but their notions of the rights of a professor seem more developed. They ask if I am going to beat them with a stick if they do not work well, seem to consider it my recognised privilege, and are rather disappointed to find that I do not take kindly to the idea.

Very simple models are given out, and the work begins, accompanied by a chorus of little exclamations, as—

"Amān! amān! my black pen will not work! See, now its nose has come off!"

"Look this way, madama! my lamb madama! diamond madama! See! see! I have done a little stroke!"

"Wallah! wallah! it is *too* difficult."

"Ouf! I wish I had a cigarette."

"Djémilé, you pushed my elbow; now the black marks have run all over the paper! Vaï! vaï!"

And so on: the more refined amongst the pupils keeping very quiet and making their little attempts with patience. I construct new noses for the wounded pencils, and heartily wish that there were a directress to keep order.

A week or two later.

The class is more orderly now; most of the pupils have become steady, and are beginning to make a little progress. I also begin to know them better. There is Lutfiyeh, a very young widow from Adrianople. She now lives near two sisters who come regularly—Djénab and Hourié—daughters of a clerk at the Porte; all three, as neighbours, are close friends and arrive together.

Kerem Hanum is a very gentle ladylike-looking person; she thinks a great deal of herself as the grand-daughter of a Caziasker. She is very handsome, with a delicately soft complexion and beautiful dark eyes. Almost all the pupils have small, well-shaped hands. They belong principally to the class of inferior Government clerks; there are one or two slave-girls amongst them.

In the midst of the lesson a young slave of Lutfiyeh's brings her in a cigarette, from which she takes a puff or two, in defiance of rules; and there is a strong suspicion of other contraband proceedings in the startling correctness of some of the outlines; but it is difficult to detect the misdemeanour of tracing, all being crouched at the back of the desks. No tables as yet.

In the sala adjoining, the arithmetical mollah is

haranguing his class. He wears a loose open-sleeved cotton dress and a white turban. He sits up upon the divan beneath the windows, with his Turkish divit or writing-tube stuck in his shawl girdle; a bottle of ink and some reed pens are placed beside him.

The pupils, partly veiled, are seated on the ground in a semicircle. The lesson is given with the help of a blackboard and chalk, the women and girls working out their calculations in turns. All are very quiet and orderly in their behaviour.

There is trouble at the school. The Italian work-mistress, whose premises are on the lower floor, cannot succeed in establishing order. She complains of a want of respect, and especially of the domineering conduct of the three Jewesses, whose father has some inferior post about the Medjliss, which gives the young ladies an exalted idea of their own importance. I decline to interfere, but shortly afterwards I am told that the mudir wishes to speak to me.

In the small reception-room the old gentleman and the caligraphical mollah are solemnly seated, cross-legged, on the divan. Old Emin Effendi, who is slightly afflicted with palsy, makes a little complimentary speech; gratifying, but I wait for some more practical communication. Then it appears that every one is displeased with Madame Elise. Rose, the Jewess, explains that she scolds and screams at them as if they were children. The poor woman lodged the same complaint against Mademoiselle Rose, asking piteously, What was she to do with so many unruly beings? Then the Reïs Effendi: "Yavash! yavash! things must go on gently and softly. The school is yet young and tender—an infant, only just rising, as it were, from the sea. We must gently draw and attract the scholars, not repel them. There should be no difference between Mussulman, Christian, or Jewess."

To the reply, "We are all cardash" (sisters), the fez and the turban bow stately approval.

These are beautiful sentiments, but a more competent direction than that of the poor old patriarch, and a better organisation, would do more than sentiment to insure order. The improvement is much needed, for many pupils have already left.

In this flush of brotherly feeling, however, I seize the propitious moment to remember that the table in the drawing class-room (there are tables, now, and chairs) which should have been cut down long ago, according to promise, is still in its first long-legged condition. Had it not better be lowered immediately? Ah, yes, certainly; it shall be done. Yavash! yavash!

This word "yavash" (slowly, gently, all in good time), is it not, with its twin-brother "backshish," the very key-note of Turkish misrule and Turkish ruin? But in the case of the little school quarrel, the old man was right.

The class is looking up again. The Jewesses have left, and there are several new pupils. One woman is from the Caucasus; she has with her a sweet, bright little girl, who comes after the lesson to chatter with charming *naïveté*. She greatly admires some outlines which her mamma has perpetrated in her own home, and exhibits as the result of supererogatory industry: "My mother has done her drawing; she did it so" (raising her tiny hands), "against the window, you know; it is so beautiful! And we have got such nice new 'ghiaour' books!"

Many of the pupils show remarkable aptitude (not against the window), for many work honestly and with great painstaking. Djénab, Hourié, and Hafuz Ruveïda are the most promising pupils. A young Syrian girl from Beyrout has just joined. She is greatly bejewelled, and apparently feels much contempt for the undisciplined members of the class, having herself already had some training in the excellent missionary schools which have flourished for many years in her own country.

Simple landscape studies are in vogue at present—bits of cottages, ends of ruins, and other picturesque outlines that exercise the Eastern mind considerably. "For why," say they, "are all the konaks and kiosks in Europe cracked and spoilt?"

Some of the girls, in a burst of artistic enthusiasm, break out into sketches from nature. Lutfiyeh brings me an outline of St. Sophia, with a neighbouring konak, as seen from her window. Sheïkhoura also has a konak, and wild Fatima a crooked vase filled with the drollest little flowers. Perspective is utterly ignored, but the mere attempt to do these things shows progress and comprehension.

Djénab is most industrious. Over and over again she will begin the same subject until it is copied correctly. Wild Fatima is a strange being—a female dervish. She works with fitful diligence, is often very rebellious, and delights in uttering slow, solemn jokes that convulse her companions with laughter. I do not understand much of what she says, which is doubtless fortunate, for the older women cry out, "Ayb! ghyunah!" (a shame, a sin!), and she is made to understand that recitations from " Nasr' eddin Khowadja " are not suitable to the solemnity of a drawing-class. She affects to pout, bears no ill-will, and soon after produces a nicely done sketch as propitiation.

She is such a remarkable type this Fatima: they call her "déli," or mad, in the class, on account of her eccentricities. She has a preference for strong black leather Blucher boots, worn without socks or stockings, her dress at the same time being of very draggled faded muslin, with an elaborate steel chain meandering about her throat and shoulders. A Turkish pen-case is stuck into her girdle, and she wears a dervish's felt cap cut low and bound with a black handkerchief; a little flower frequently adorns the headdress, but does not suffice to soften the general wildness of her appearance. Western innovations have not, as yet, in her case quenched the picturesqueness of the Asiatic. For a long time I thought her a native of the far east of the empire, but she one day hunted out her birthplace on the map; it was only, after all, Angora, in Asia Minor.

Looking round the table over which the pupils are bending, it may be remarked that although several of them keep on their yashmaks, they are not over the face, but loosened and thrown back in graceful folds upon the shoulders; the elderly and plainer women are always the most closely and carefully muffled up.

The time of the "Imtihan," or school examinations, is drawing near; the pupils are stimulated by it and working well; very slowly and with much rubbing out some have the patience to vanquish the difficulties of their tasks. Vere Forster's series of models have just arrived, a present from Lady Hobart; they are in great demand. Everyone wants them at once, but I often hear from different parts of the table, "Amân! yapamam!" (alas! I cannot do it!).

Eminé, a Circassian, is fond of the outlines of animals. She says all women ride in her country, and she bravely undertakes to copy the skeleton of a horse that happens to be amongst the rest. This model causes some astonishment. "Vaï! vaï! what strange ugly horses you have in your country! Madama djim, are all the horses in Franghistan made like that?"

There is a poor old body among the pupils, Fetiyé Hanum, a native of Broussa. She is very industrious, for she has great need of her work as a means of livelihood, and she hopes to obtain a place as teacher in one of the small schools. She has no talent, but she plods on, always seated beside her friend Muniré, who is also far from young, and with even less taste for art; but both of them, by dint of great pains and trouble, have at length made some progress. They are very quiet and teachable, and they show such innocent pride in their work when the much thumbed, much berubbed pencil drawing has reached completion, that I have a very kindly feeling for these two simple, unpretending women.

Djénab Hanum, although by no means the oldest, is looked up to as the leading pupil in all the classes; her progress in general knowledge is astonishing. She is a Stamboulie, about two-and-twenty, and was married ten years ago, her husband, now a lieutenant in the army, being at the time of his marriage a lad of fourteen. He appears to take an interest in his wife's drawing. Any work of hers prettier than usual is carefully borne home to be shown to her effendi.

Eminé shows great natural talent; she is very silent and docile, rarely looking up from her drawing. Many of these Eastern women touch with great delicacy, their small hands and taper fingers seeming especially formed for light and minute work.

The elder sister of Eminé is the mother of the pretty little black-eyed child. "What a sweet little girl you have," I had said one day to the woman, who was lounging idly about as usual.

"Oh yes," was the reply; "she is very pretty, and she is for sale, you know. Can you tell me of anyone who wants a nice little girl?"

Now, I find, that not having yet succeeded in her unnatural commerce, she is trying to make the best bargain she can out of poor Eminé, suggesting that if all the fine education that is being given her does not result in gaining her a good husband, at least she might be sold to advantage!

Poor Eminé! she is not pretty but she has an honest gentle face. She hangs her head at this. Camma tells me she is very poor. She is evidently despised by her fellow-pupils because she is only a Tcherkesse. Eminé is often sad and tearful, and her cruel sister is very harsh to her.

But in describing the most striking figures in the class I must not forget Djémilé, the little daughter of the writing-master, the stately green-turbaned "emir." Djémilé is the untameable sprite of the school—the very spirit of mischief and insubordination embodied in a fairylike form. I am going round the table. Little Djémilé, at the farther extremity, is apparently intent upon her task. I reach her in course of time, to find blank crumpled paper, the relics of pistachio nuts, and the sound of that most unpleasant of all Eastern diversions, the vigorous chewing of mastic.

Severe Professor: "Now, Djémilé, I certainly shall let your Baba Effendi know how very badly you behave. I am so much displeased at such idleness and inattention, that, really———"

Djémilé—suddenly stroking my cheek with henna-stained fingers: "Now, madama djim! now then! don't say anything more! I am going to be *so* busy. Why, I am working for the Imtihan! And I am doing a cracked seraï—there's the top of a chimney almost finished!"

While speaking she has contrived to pin my dress to her antary, to purloin her neighbour's india-rubber, and to produce a convulsion at that end of the table which makes all the pencils play strange freaks. But the mite looks so provoking, yet so bewitching, with her lovely dark eyes turned up to me, her faded pink antary, and the bewildering twist in her scrap of green gauze perched above a cascade of bright chestnut curls, that I hardly know, for the moment, whether to regret that weakly abandoned stick of discipline, or to set her in a good light and—take her portrait.

Djémilé is light-fingered also, but *too* light-fingered—a weakness that she shares with many of her age and standing. It was necessary to keep careful watch over the colours, and most especially over the cake of carmine. Long experience had proved that all the varieties of rosy pigments had a strange tendency to disappear, while simultaneously with the loss a peachy bloom would glow on the youthful cheeks of the younger inmates of the harem in which the ill-fated colours had gone astray.

I hear, one day, high words and angry tones—a rare sound here, indeed. Camma Calfa and the wife of the porter are quarrelling over a certain gilt-edged glass, in search of which the latter had invaded the domains of the Abyssinian. In order, at length, to still the noise, the portress is gently put out of the room, and Camma is told to continue her energetic oratory elsewhere. She was very picturesque during this outburst; her wavy hair, very long and fine, and literally raven black, had escaped from her bright handkerchief and fallen over her shoulders in ripples of jetty lustre; her skin, the colour of new copper, is fine and soft as an infant's, her eyes like brilliant velvet, nose and mouth small and shapely. These Abyssinian women are sometimes beautiful.

As has been already noticed, there is no matron or class superintendent in this school, and I constantly urge the necessity of putting some competent, respectable Mussulman woman in the post, to insure regularity of attendance and general order; but the old mudir does not see matters in the same light. He thinks that his presence is all-sufficient, although when wanted to settle any matter of business he is generally making his "namaz," or taking his siesta. He rarely comes into the class-rooms, but is satisfied with sending messages, and so "the tender infant, risen from the sea," is growing up an ungainly, ill-conditioned child, quite unconscious of rules or order. At the time and place for which I am responsible, my pupils (in Turkish "Shaghird," the disciples, the faithful) are kept within bounds; the turban, beard, and fine voice and manner of Ismaïl Effendi awe into attention the students of his classes; but for the rest anarchy prevails, and I see the signs of premature decay in the institution, which has not yet attained its full growth.

It is the day of the Imtihan (the examinations) before breaking up for the holidays. I find the girls in a state of flutter and excitement, going over their lessons to each other; Djénab, in yashmak and feràdjé, very pale, and trembling with nervousness.

Savfet Pasha, the Minister, arrives with the examiners; they take their places on the divan in the central hall; the pupils, veiled, crouch on cushions at the farther end. They are called up in turns. Zeheïra is first on the list: she sits on her heels, her hands folded, in front of the principal examiner, an old mollah, who is very careful and attentive, going through a long examination in Arabic and Persian. This is followed by questions on arithmetic, and the pupil, rising, executes a sum on the blackboard, the bit of chalk trembling a good deal; then, with a wand, on the great map, she goes through a course of the geography of Europe in great detail, explains something of the use of the globes, and repeats an ethnological lesson. The examination ends with Turkish writing of two kinds.

Some of the pupils answer briskly, delighted at the opportunity of a little display; others are very timid. Djénab, who was to have done especial honour to her instructor, declines, at the last moment, to come forward, making her escape into the inner room, from which she looks round the opening of the door, singularly picturesque with her floating veil of snowy muslin. The examinations are very satisfactory; certainly Ismaïl Effendi, the Beshiktash imām, is a most efficient teacher. Lady Elliot, our excellent ambassadress, Lady Hobart, and other English ladies who, at my request, visited the school about this time, were much surprised and pleased at the amount of instruction so rapidly acquired by these Turkish women.

The verbal examinations finished, the drawings are passed in review and pronounced highly creditable; the girls are pleased, and crowd round me as the whole party moves downwards to the lower floor, where they have made a very fair display of work of many kinds: dressmaking, crochet-work, tapestry, and other styles, both useful and ornamental. Some of the workers have combined to produce a large "séjjadé," or prayer-carpet, in tapestry, intended as a present for the new mosque that is being built by the Validé Sultana in Ak Seraï.

During the holidays that followed the examinations I paid, with a friend, a visit to Djénab and Hourié at their own home, finding with difficulty the house, which is behind the rounded end of the Hippodrome.

Both the sisters receive us at the head of the stairs; they are very simply dressed. The house is scantily furnished but beautifully clean, and in the upper room, to which we are conducted, the prospect over the Sea of Marmora, towards the mountains of Asia, is magnificent.

After a long delay the buyuk hanum, the mother of the family, makes her appearance: a strange-looking little woman, who must have been singularly handsome in her youth; a black gauze handkerchief is tightly bound round her head, with one very large and bright artificial flower placed exactly in front. She is a lively person, with a decided judgment on men and things in general. I quickly learn from her that all the pupils of the school are quite good-for-nothing: that they pass their time wandering from house to house, neglect their domestic duties, and behave giddily on their way backwards and forwards. The old lady is severe; she declares that if matters do not mend she cannot permit her daughters to continue to attend the classes.

It seems to me that this very correct matron, whose faded cheeks betray a strong touch of rouge, and whose black eyes gleam in the shadow of that flaunting rose above her brow, might perhaps also, in her own young days, have been a little inclined to laugh and saunter out of season; but I refrain from expressing the sentiment. One by one I mention those pupils of the school whose conduct seems quiet and orderly, and finally prove undeniably that the sweeping condemnation so unsparingly pronounced is not merited. We are very merry as I make this censorious hanum retract her verdict in almost every instance. It is not unworthy of remark that gossip and scandal are as natural an accompaniment to the black coffee and tobacco of Eastern matrons as they are declared to be to the traditional cup of tea of the ancient maidens of the West.

The younger women in Mussulman society, especially if unmarried, rarely speak in the presence of their elders unless directly addressed, so that their views and sentiments are not easily ascertained by a visitor. In the present instance the buyuk hanum maintained the conversation, Djénab, as eldest and long-married daughter, joining in from time to time; while Hourié, a well-conducted girl, although sixteen or eighteen years of age, scarcely opened her lips during the visit.

I remarked that in this simple family all small points of etiquette were as carefully observed as in those of a higher rank; the daughters offered the refreshments instead of an attendant, the elder sister handing the coffee on our arrival, the younger the cup of delicious sherbet before our departure. The rules of politeness were also carefully followed in the adieux. The hanum received our farewell compliments standing in the middle of the floor; Djénab took leave of us at the door of the outer room, Hourié at the head of the stairs; all said they hoped we should come again—an indispensable phrase never omitted.

Work has been resumed at the school of Yéré Batān, after a month of holiday. During the time of the lesson a veiled woman came silently into the room, and without a word to anyone walked round the table of the elder class, looking searchingly at all the girls. I ask Djénab who she is, and why she has come. "Kiz bakar" (she looks at the girls), is the answer. I don't understand, but no more is said until the stranger, having stared hard at the best-looking amongst them, and particularly at Hourié and Sheikhoura, has left the room. Then Djénab explains: "She came to look at the girls, in order to choose a wife for somebody." So that is it; I comprehend now; the class has served for the time as a kind of market, and I see the reason of Hourié's unusual splendour of attire—the light-coloured gauze dress with gaudy trimmings, a gold watch and chain, and a fantastic headdress, all worn with a twittering sort of look and a general airiness of manner!

I noticed to-day, on my way to the school, a little incident worthy of remembrance. The road was extremely dirty, and a poor ragged little old woman, in attempting to cross, had stuck in the mud, bewildered. A cleanly-dressed man, picking his steps carefully along the side, sees the difficulty, and without a moment's hesitation crosses to the rescue, takes the shabby bundle gently out of the hand of the poor old creature, and helps her along until stopped by a great lake of mud near the kerbstone. There is another pause, but a very handsomely dressed negro, passing at that moment, instantly gives his aid, and between them they jump the old lady over, one of them picking up and carrying her yellow slippers, the bundle is put into her hand again, and each one goes on his way, quite simply. I am afraid the old woman did not even thank her rescuers; it was all taken as a matter of course. And I also went my way, revolving in my mind the question, "Would well-dressed people step into the mud for a thankless old beggar-woman quite so readily elsewhere?"

The elder pupils at Yéré Batān are beginning to paint flowers in water colour; they even attempt some from nature. The class is much excited about this; everyone is eager to leave off the "black" drawing and to get at the brushes and daubing. Eminé, good, quiet girl, has been patiently plodding on at a branch of cyclamen, conscientiously sketching each detail before indulging in colour. Fétiyé Hanum and her friend Muniré have both brightened up considerably under the fascination of flowers and paintings.

I hear that the old mudir is taking the writing class, and that there is a professor the less on the staff of the school. I strongly suspect the old gentleman of having effected this change in order to add the professor's small salary to his own immoderately high pay. There are many intrigues of this sort always going on; they are very prejudicial to the wellbeing of the undertaking.

The attendance has become very irregular, and the school is sadly falling off. Every festival or unusual occurrence serves as a pretext for idleness and the " promenade." During the Ramazan it is necessary to be indulgent on this point, as the severe fast, not only enjoined, but practised at that time, makes study or close occupation almost impossible. But the Ramazan and the Baïram holidays are over, and yet we are constantly told that two or three of the best pupils are absent—gone to the baths or the bazaars, or even "quezmeyeh quitmek" (to take a walk!)

Again, I hear that two or three of the women have gone to mosque. This, if true, is praiseworthy, but one cannot but feel that the time chosen is unfortunate. A few are scrupulous in performing (on the premises) their "namaz" at the call of the muezzim—a devotion which I always respect, regretting only that the revolving method of calculating time in Turkey should place it, during some seasons, in the midst of the hour allotted to the drawing class.

To-day it is the morrow of a "kandil guisdjessy"

(one of the seven holy nights), and lessons are hurried over that the pupils may join the women who are crowding into St. Sophia, which will be full, they say, as men are excluded from that mosque for the day.

I close my notes here. After two years of very earnest effort I gave up my charge, partly for personal reasons, partly because wearied out by the unnecessary fatigue caused by the want of a competent person to superintend the conduct of the pupils and the regularity of the classes.

The intention of this school was excellent: under a very careful and strict management it might have been made a source of great benefit to a large class of women. It struggled on, being supported by Government money, for a few years; but this endeavour to introduce a better sort of popular education for women has at length failed. Stay! *has* it so utterly failed? The school once opened under such good auspices, was provisionally closed the other day. The pupils have returned doubtless to their indolent Eastern life; but who shall say that no good result may endure—latent, perhaps, but yet unextinguished—and that, in better and happier times, a renewed effort may not bear more hopeful and abundant fruit, if not in this elder generation, yet surely in the one which is now springing up.

Some of the pupils have already reaped a slight material benefit from their studies; amongst others, old Fétiyé of Broussa and her friend Muniré, were both eventually placed in the employment for which they had worked so patiently, as teachers in a girls' school of the quarter; and if their teaching might not, perhaps, be of the brightest order, it was, at least for them, a success, and an encouragement to the efforts of others. I met them unexpectedly one day in Pera, and I do not know whether the "ousta" or the "schaghirdlar" had the greater pleasure in the meeting.

Hourié, who had not evidently suited the taste of the official match-maker, was finally married to an officer in the army.

Scheikhoura disappeared from the scene. Hard things were said of her, poor girl! I never learnt the truth.

Camma, the clever, bright-eyed Abyssinian calfa, went to Teheran with her husband.

Eminé I lost sight of, although I incidentally heard that her ignorant, scheming sister was giving lessons in Turkish A B C, and as much more as she could pretend to undertake, at a salary of nearly £5 a month! But gentle Eminé? I would give much to learn her fate.

And what of the poor old mudir? I met him a few weeks since, near his house overhanging the Bosphorus. He was greatly pleased to see me, and hoped that I should pay the school once more a visit. A few days later I heard that he was dead, suddenly, in a fit of apoplexy.

The school has at length been reopened in other premises. It is struggling on, and it may be hoped that the direction and organisation of the classes has improved.

XIV.

THE IFTAR.

Turkish Society.—Ramazan.—The Iftar.—Djémilé and Zeheïra.—How to sit round a Dining-table.—"Bouyouroun."—A Varied Repast.—"Aschourah."—The Young Hanums.—Sabiha and the Little Boys.—Neighbourly Visits.—Hospitality.

SOCIETY in the sense in which we understand the term, the social and friendly intercourse between men and women, must be impossible in Turkey so long as the yashmak and the seclusion of Mussulman women continue in full force, and (in spite of the enthusiastic declarations of superficial travellers, that the regeneration of that unhappy country depends upon the speedy tearing off of the veil of her women) they must so continue for at least another generation, until education shall have gradually and safely prepared the way for the change; but society, as it is understood amongst the harems of Stamboul, in the form of a perpetual and ceremonious interchange of visits, is carried out to quite an alarming extent—visits in person and visits by proxy; visits of polite inquiry and visits of inspection; visits of salutation, of congratulation, of condolence; visits on every festive occasion, public, private, and religious; and especially visits during the evenings of the months of Ramazan, the only period of the year in which Turkish women are accustomed to go out on foot into the streets at night. They avail themselves freely of the privilege. At that time, cloaked and yashmaked groups, preceded by an aiwass (messenger) carrying a paper lantern, flit about the usually silent streets and lanes of the Mussulman city; some are on the way to make their evening namaz at the mosque; others to join in the festivities of a friendly neighbouring harem; all prepared to profit to the utmost by the liberty permitted by the season, and to enjoy the hours of festivity as a counterbalance to the hours of fasting.

It is well known that the month of Ramazan is kept by all good Mussulmans as a period of the strictest fast during the day, from sunrise to sunset. They abstain not only from food of any kind whatever, but even from liquids, taking no drop of water during that time; they suspend also the enjoyment of tobacco, which is scarcely less indispensable to their daily life. As a compensation for these rigorous privations, the night is partly devoted to feasting. For the rich and idle, who pass in sleep the greater part of their days of penitence, the suffering is considerably lessened; but for the poorer classes, for workmen and servants, the Ramazan, when it falls during the long days of the hot summer months, is cruelly severe; and it is to be remarked that precisely these hard-working and labouring "faithful" are those who hold the most strictly to their religious observances. Aged people and children are not required to keep the fast of Ramazan; and women in delicate health are also freed from the obligation for the time, but they are expected to make up the required number of penitential days before its recurrence in the ensuing year; and the ill-advised visitor who may risk a visit to a harem as that season is drawing near is sure to find several of the inmates undergoing their days of "pèrhiz" (abstinence), and consequently pale, weary, and slightly out of humour.

The fifteenth day of Ramazan, on which devout Mohammedans go in crowds to salute the "hirkaï schérif" (the holy jacket) and other relics of their Prophet, is a sort of Mid-Lent; the fast of the daylight hours is in no wise relaxed, but the evening is regarded as a time of special rejoicing, for which invitations to strangers are reserved. It is a time for family gatherings also. Married sons and daughters revisit their parents' homes, bringing their children to kiss the hand of the "Buyuk Baba Effendi" and of the "Hanum Niné" (the lady mother); brothers and sisters meet and exchange complimentary greetings; inferiors pay visits of respect; and the men of the family, and relatives who are not admitted within the harem, send polite messages of inquiry after the health of the elder ladies and of such as are above themselves in rank. This interchange of visits and "compliments of the season" takes place upon all the occasions set apart as festivals, and the etiquette which regulates them is minutely and rigorously observed by all well-ordered families.

"Iftar" is the name given during the Ramazan to the repast which breaks the abstinence of the day, and the exact moment of the setting of the sun is announced by cannon all over the city. It was formerly the custom to keep open house for the iftar during the entire month; people came to dine without invitation; but the gradual changes of custom, and especially the impoverishment of the country, have forced upon householders the necessity for withholding this too lavish hospitality, which is now only maintained in the case of the poor. Every evening crowds of mendicants assemble before the gates of the palaces and of the richer houses; they are served in turn (a certain number at a time) to an ample meal of pillaw and stewed meat and vegetables, and each individual on leaving receives a silver coin, and frequently some new article of dress.

In the highest classes of Ottoman society the invitation to the iftar is an obligatory politeness, and the local papers never fail to announce the fact, interesting only to local readers, that the ambassador of one or other of the Powers has made the iftar of the preceding evening with the Grand Vizier. The labours of politeness which devolve on this high functionary during the month are arduous; the etiquette of his invitations is most strictly regulated, and each evening a number of such as are entitled to the attention surround his board in order, according to rank and precedence, from the highest officer and minister of state down to the simple clerk in the offices of the Porte.

Having accepted an invitation to take the iftar of the fifteenth day of Ramazan with the ladies of the family of A—— Pasha, in Stamboul, I paid them a visit in the course of the preceding week, in order to ascertain the precise date of the festival, Europeans being subject to mistakes of calculation, owing to the Oriental custom of reckoning the day from sunset.

I found that Djémilé Hanum, the first wife of the Pasha, had gone to the neighbouring mosque to hear a celebrated preacher. Turkish women are in the habit of attending the Friday prayers and sermons throughout the year in any of the mosques of the city, but during the month of Ramazan, when these edifices are crowded, certain of them are reserved for the especial use of the harems; the list is published in advance, and the Nour' Osmanieh, the large and beautiful building standing near an entrance to the bazaars, is one of those most frequently selected for the devotions of the veiled worshippers. In great and wealthy houses the Ramazan prayers are recited by the imām of the establishment in a large central hall of the konak, the harem or female portion of the family taking part in the ceremony from behind grated screens placed there for the occasion.

Zeheïra Hanum, the younger wife of the Pasha, was within on the occasion of my visit, very busy with her household cares and surrounded by a tribe of children; but she came forward to greet me with great cordiality, and was especially anxious that there should be no mistake as to the time for which their invitation had been made.

On the appointed day, no carriage being procurable on account of the festival, I left Pera on foot, accompanied by a friend; we hastened through the badly paved streets of Stamboul, dreading at each moment to hear the boom of the sunset gun before reaching the konak. To be behind time under the circumstances would be a more than ordinary failure in good manners; but by great exertion we gained the large gateway while still some rays of sunshine lingered in the sky, and, quickly admitted by the porter—a warlike-looking individual wearing a monstrous black turban—crossed the courtyard, and tapped at a modest wooden door sheltered from the outer court by a rough screen. The door of the harem was opened by a tall negress, whose shining ebony features gleamed with smiles, and some young slaves advancing, assisted us up the broad easy staircase in a manner intended to show especial deference and respect. On occasions of ceremony it is the custom for the slaves to place themselves one on each side of the new arrival, and, thus carefully supported from the elbow, the Mussulman lady allows herself to be slowly and laboriously escorted upwards. To a " Frank " this constrained movement is, to say the least of it, unpleasant ; but as a mark of great attention it has to be endured, and the slight infliction is soon ended, the reception-rooms of the family being rarely higher than the first floor.

A slave raising a heavy curtain of camels' hair embroidered with gold, we find Zeheïra Hanum waiting to bid us welcome, and to assist a hurried change of dress ; for the sunset signal is now rolling over Stamboul from each of its numerous batteries, the guests and children are already seated, spoon in hand, a slim Circassian girl waits to pour water over the hands from a ewer of richly ornamented silver, while another holds the soft towel embroidered with gold thread, which we take with us to the table, and in a few minutes we are in the places of honour reserved for the stranger ladies.

Two tables had been arranged on the matting of the " sofa " (the central hall). They are formed of disks of burnished brass, about four feet in diameter, placed on a low stool ; beneath this is spread a large square, which is often of silk woven with gold threads, and soft cushions are laid around. In some rich houses these dining-disks, called " tepessy," are made of solid silver.

An Eastern woman taking her place at the tepessy (scarcely a foot and a half above the ground) sinks upon her cushion in the most graceful manner imaginable, but the feat is by no means so easy of accomplishment by a " Frank." It is necessary to be so placed as to leave the right arm free to reach with ease the dish in the centre of the table; you endeavour, perhaps, to kneel in an easy way, but the cushion is soft and yielding, and there is danger of an unexpected over-balance amongst the saucers of pickle and sweetmeat ; you sit back, but your spoon makes vague and useless advances towards the distant soup-bowl ; you turn sideways, to find that you are scarcely showing due politeness to the mistress of the house, upon whom you have deliberately turned your back. It is bewildering. At length a pitying calfa brings forward a little stool, and with infinite precaution your feet are slipped beneath the low tray; and there they are condemned to remain, immovable, until the end of the repast, as an ill-advised movement might easily overturn the banquet. It is needless to expatiate on the torture which is sometimes thus silently endured, but it is undeniable that the ease of position conferred by prosaic tables and chairs more than counterbalances the picturesque effect and Oriental charm of crouching round a Turkish tepessy. This method of dining almost on the ground and of eating with the fingers is rarely now adopted, all "civilised" Oriental families taking kindly to our Western customs in this respect; but even the most Europeanised amongst them return, during the month of Ramazan, to the primitive habits of their ancestors, which they regard as more orthodox.

Our dinner-table at A—— Pasha's was presided over by his sister-in-law, Besmè Hanum, an elderly woman, very amiable and attentive to her guests. I am placed beside her; my friend, the eldest daughter of the family, a niece, a young bride, the elder wife, and a Turkish visitor, complete the circle. Zeheïra Hanum keeps order amongst the children at a second dinner-table which had been set up within a short distance.

There is no tablecloth, but everything is neatly arranged upon the polished metal. Before each guest is a piece of ordinary bread—a flap of unleavened dough slightly baked and looking like mottled leather—and two spoons, one of them in box or horn, and the other, more delicate, in tortoiseshell, the handle ornamented with coral and inlaid mother-of-pearl. Sometimes these spoons have a little crooked branch of coral at the tip to avert the evil eye. Each person is provided with a small ring-shaped cake called "sémitt," some pieces of which are always taken before the Ramazan dinner, as well as a small quantity of condiments, such as caviar, olives, salted and dried mutton, cheese, or pickle. At the table which I am describing these "hors d'œuvre" were spread about in abundance, surrounding a handsome silver stand, holding covered cups filled with lemonade, of which each guest partook; and then, the stand being removed, a stout negress deposited in its place, with an air of triumph, a large tureen filled with a delicate white soup.

The spoons are raised in expectation; it is Besmè Hanum who resolutely tucks up her right sleeve above the elbow, and, as mistress of the ceremonies, is the first to dip into the tureen, murmuring the customary invitation, "bouyouroun," at which all the spoons join company; and after a few minutes of silence, well employed, the soup is borne away, to make room for a turkey stuffed with rice, currants, fir-nuts, and spices. Very little is taken from each dish, as their number and variety are infinite, but each one is tasted, and little excursions are made between whiles amongst the saucers—a pinch of salad from one, a preserved fruit from another, then a morsel torn as delicately as possible from the centre dish of fowl, taking in passing a dip into the curdled milk or a flavour of pickle or red pepper; then back again to the middle of the table, which exhibits probably by this time a mound of luscious pastry.

Vegetables form an important part of the Turkish culinary system; you may frequently count a dozen varieties at the same time, besides many herbs and plants of which we have no knowledge on our Western tables. They use, according to the season, marshmallow leaves, cucumbers, vine leaves, cabbage, or even the half-open bud of the gourd or melon, to form the "dolmas" stuffed with rice and chopped meat, which never fail to make their appearance at every repast.

In serving a dinner, it is considered the right thing to alternate the sweet and the savoury; thus our turkey is followed by "baclawa," a rich pastry composed of flour, butter, and pounded almonds soaked in honey; after this the "tcheurek"—puff paste filled with cheese and herbs; a dish of fried fish yields the place of honour to the "ekmekkadaïf," or thin pancakes interlarded with lumps of clotted cream; and to this again succeeds a mound of artichokes dressed in oil. The "aschourah," a sweet porridge which makes its appearance upon most festive occasions, deserves a few words of explanation, as this preparation has a legendary origin. Aschourah is composed of Indian wheat, barley, wheat, dried raisins, nuts, almonds, walnuts, pistachio nuts, and even dry Windsor and haricot beans, boiled and sweetened, ten ingredients in all; a remembrance, says the legend, of Noah's residence in the Ark, "into which the water must have penetrated at length, and produced an unexpected soup amongst the remnants of his dry stores." Aschourah is made in great quantities in all respectable houses during the first ten days of the month Mouharem (the first month of the year) to be sent about to friends and to be liberally distributed to the poor; at this period, any persons presenting themselves at the door of a konak receive without question a bowl of aschourah.

Our iftar was concluded by sherbet accompanying the pillaw, and then each guest rose with little ceremony, to wash her hands over the handsome silver basins held by the attendant slaves, or at the marble fountain let into the wall of the "sofa."

The custom of eating with the fingers, very

repugnant though it may be to our sense of cleanliness, is not so repulsive as might be imagined in the case of well-educated Turkish ladies, whose hands are invariably small and delicate. Politeness forbids excursions into a neighbour's field of labour; each takes from the portion of the dish placed in the front; and it would be difficult to realise, without witnessing the feat, the dexterity with which the most dangerous-looking morsels travel from the centre of the table to the mouth, sustained by two fingers and the thumb of the right hand, aided by a piece of the flat bread, without marking its passage across the board. The left hand is never used.

We follow Besmè Hanum into the reception-room of the harem, and rest at length upon a couch of French manufacture; the Turkish ladies place themselves according to their age and taste, the elders very much at their ease upon the broad divan; whilst the younger hanums, anxious to give proof of "civilisation," endure the infliction of upright chairs. While the coffee is being served in the tiny porcelain cups, held in "zarfs" of silver filigree, we have leisure to note the appearance and dress of our fair neighbours. The eldest daughter of the Pasha, a young wife and mother, is seated opposite to us, holding her fat rosy-cheeked baby boy upon her lap. This young hanum is very pretty, and has exquisite little hands, but her figure is short and already alarmingly stout. Her cousin, seated beside her, has no beauty of feature, but the vivacity of her countenance and the sparkle of her fine dark eyes cause you to forget the irregularity in the outline of the face. She wears an aigrette coquettishly arranged in her headdress, with a French paletot in black cloth, which claims to make its wearer appear "à la frança;" for she disdains the easy grace which should be natural to her, and sits perfectly upright upon the straight-backed chair, quite " comme il faut," and evidently most uncomfortable. On the next chair sits the young bride equally " à la frança," and consequently ill at ease; she is a tall and fine blonde, with an exquisite complexion and a decidedly ladylike appearance; her clear blue eyes have a soft good-tempered expression, and the rich masses of her bright chestnut hair are well seen beneath a small velvet toque trimmed with a bird of paradise; her antary and schalwars are of pale green silk. The ladies of the house are very simply attired in printed cottons, and the little boys wear quilted cotton pelisses, clean, warm, and inelegant. These children, four or five in number, wander about softly, for little Turkish children are brought up to habits of submission; they are, in fact, almost too quiet.

After the coffee the ladies begin to smoke; Besmè Hanum is provided with a tchibouk of formidable dimensions, the younger ladies are satisfied with cigarettes, of which immense numbers are consumed in the harems.

The conversation, sustained with great difficulty with our imperfect Turkish, begins quickly to flag: the subject of the weather is soon exhausted; the bad state of the streets, the distance from Pera, the hope of a fine summer, are not subjects adapted to lengthened discussion; we praise the children, but that opening also is soon worked out. What *can* one find to converse about with women, however good and amiable they may be, who scarcely ever leave the circle of their home duties, who never travel, do not read, have seen nothing, know nothing of all that interests us most? Shall we talk of housekeeping and servants—the last feeble resource of a feminine mind in despair of a subject? It is impossible—households and servitude with them are on such a strangely different footing.

Suddenly Sabiha, a pretty little girl about ten years old, has the bright idea of exhibiting her work—slippers which she is embroidering for the " Baba Effendi." Our loudly expressed admiration encourages the young boys of four and five to show their learning also; they bring in books of geography, some pictures of natural history, and, finally, a Turkish edition of " Robinson Crusoe!" Upon this we make friends immediately; the children, charmed to discover that their "Djuma" (Friday) is a mutual acquaintance, begin to chatter over their pictures and to relate with great animation a recent visit to a menagerie, to which their father had taken them. The witty niece, joining them in the conversation, gives an amusing account of her interview with a giraffe newly arrived, who saw for the first time a woman veiled in white, declaring that visitor and visited were equally alarmed at the unusual apparition.

In the midst of our conversation a clapping of hands is heard from behind the camels' hair curtain which falls before the doorway. It is the Pasha who is coming. A slave enters quickly and begs the bride to withdraw—she is not a near relation, and the Pasha may not see her unveiled face; she consequently rises and retires with a slow and majestic step, whilst the aged sister-in-law folds about her head a muslin scarf to represent a yashmak; the two wives, the daughter, and the niece remain, but all rise respectfully as the master of the house enters the room.

The visit of A—— Pasha, a cultivated man, speaking with facility several languages, formed an agreeable change in the programme of the evening; he conversed with all in turn. To ourselves he expressed the pleasure with which he remembered a somewhat lengthened stay in England, some years previously, and professed a very deep appreciation of roast beef and plum pudding; with the ladies of his family he discussed the news of the neighbourhood, and entered into a lively argument with his witty niece on the subject of the name which should be given to some newly-born infant relative—a nephew's child, I think it was; they finally agreed that it would not be inappropriate to call the baby "Ramazan." The conversation was in full flow: suddenly the Pasha rose and darted from the room, leaving us rather wondering at this unceremonious exit, when a murmuring sound of voices from the direction of the staircase explained it—some fresh visitors had arrived for the harem, of whose presence the master of the house was supposed to be unconscious as he hurried through the central hall, where they waited to be divested of their yashmaks and feredjés by the attendants. They proved to be a Turkish lady and her young daughter, living in one of the opposite houses, who, in their quality of "comshoular" (neighbours), had dropped in to spend an hour or two in friendly chat; for a good deal of friendliness and sociability is exercised between "neighbours;" and though it was quietly hinted to us that in this instance the visitors were not so welcome as some others might have been, these hanums being considered "fast," yet, as neighbours, they must be received with politeness.

Coffee having been served to the new arrivals, the mother accepted a tchibouk and the daughter a cigarette, and, while slowly enjoying the perfumed tobacco, they put us through the usual examination as to our ages and social condition, and at length, that oftworn subject exhausted, turned to their Mussulman friends, entering on a lively recital of their last adventures and experiences at the promenade of the Sweet Waters.

Djémilé and Zeheïra listened quietly, but without, as it seemed to us, much response. They know little or nothing of the world beyond their own family circle; with the exception of some rare occasion, such as the marriage of a relation, or other equally obligatory reason, they scarcely leave their home, living in great retirement; the chief excitements of the year being the periodical changes between town and country—the konak in Stamboul and the yali on the Bosphorus—with an occasional picnic party amongst themselves, when, with children and attendants, they wander to some favourite spot, and spend the long summer day in shady glades or near a rustic fountain.

Djémilé and Zeheïra are the two wives—yes, alas! the two wives of one husband. Many a hidden jealousy, many a bitter feeling, must inevitably colour their otherwise tranquil lives, but they dwell together in apparent amity and concord; their tenderness and care are equal for all the children, and their lives are modest and blameless. We recoil, and naturally so, from the idea of polygamy, and of multiplied household ties legalised by religion and by law, and English homes in the East have for years rejoiced in the conviction that no better or higher type of Christian family life could have been offered to the observation of Mussulman society than that which was most prominently before them in the family and domestic circle of the representative of our people, Sir Henry Elliot, and that the gentle lesson of example has done much to influence and rectify the judgment of many a harem on the subject of our Christian homes; but it would be well indeed if all Christian families dwelling in the East could point to their rendering of our higher and purer standard of domestic obligations and duties as a model on which to reform the harems of Stamboul.

The supper to which we were shortly summoned was spread upon a table covered with a white cloth, and chairs had been provided. In the centre of the table was placed a silver epergne loaded with bonbons; around a profusion of apples, pears, dates, nuts, pomegranates, pistachio, and dried figs; there were plates also with a knife and a table-napkin for each person; at either end of the table a plate holding little squares of Broussa towelling, wetted, soaped, and neatly folded, offered a substitute for finger-glasses.

The supper passed off very gaily, our amiable entertainers vieing with each other in showing every possible attention to the strangers, and, in defiance of excessive fatigue, we found ourselves obliged to return with them into the reception-room, when the *soirée* recommenced, varied shortly after by a barbaric concert which had been organised by means of some wandering musicians, who, passing through the streets, had been pressed into the service of the harem entertainment, and installed in a large room communicating with the " selamlik." A movable lattice screen drawn across the room permitted the women to be present without being themselves seen.

Turkish music is for the most part unmitigated suffering for European ears, but the hanums seemed to enjoy it intensely, and it was quite late at night when we at length accomplished a retreat to the chamber prepared for us. Djémilé Hanum conducted us there, carefully inspected all the preparations made for our comfort, sprinkled lightly some drops of perfume upon the embroidered pillows, and left us with the most polite and friendly expressions of good-will.

An hour before the dawn the sound of a small drum beaten up and down the street gave notice to the Mussulmans that it was time for them to take their last meal before the rising of the sun. In many houses this last repast is almost as comprehensive as the dinner, though served in an informal manner. It is very customary to sit up all night, and to retire to rest as the hours of fasting draw near.

A nicely arranged breakfast was served for our benefit on the following morning: a great effort of politeness on the part of our hostesses, as it is usually exceedingly difficult for Christians in Stamboul, during Ramazan, to procure refreshment of any sort at other than the regulated hours. But in this hospitable harem all the ladies paid us little visits of farewell, and grouped themselves about the head of the staircase, offering the usual graceful compliments as we took leave, pleased with our visit and touched by the cordiality of our reception—a cordiality, I may observe, which this simple and hospitable people never fail to exercise towards those who meet them frankly with feelings of kindness and good-will.

This little family party which I have endeavoured to describe, the patriarchal usages and customs which are met with in simple middle-class respectable houses, are very far from realising our Western notions of the indolent luxury of the daily life of the harem; and yet this existence, monotonous and colourless without doubt, but simple and unpretending, is the mode of life of the great mass of the Mussulman population. I should remark, however, that polygamy is now the rare exception, and not as formerly the established custom; and that it is very unusual to meet with more than one wife in the home of a Turkish gentleman of moderate fortune. Lavish extravagance and culpable disorder may be found in the great houses, whose inmates are striving to introduce what they imagine to be the domestic usages of the centres of civilisation; but for each one of these families, whose follies and whose failings are known to the world, there are hundreds, thousands perhaps, of quiet, sober, respectable households, amongst which still linger the primitive usages and traditions of the shepherd Turcomans, their nomad ancestors.

XV.

THE GREAT BURIAL-GROUND OF SCUTARI.

The Rustic "Café."—Dreamy Influences.—The "Mézarlik."—Three Little Donkeys and their Driver.—Ali Baba's Wife.—The Oil Jars.—Copper Mangals and Metal Lamps.—Allah-edeen.—Alnaschar's Eggs.—A Dream rudely broken.—A Turbé, Tombs, and Shrines.—Reverence.—Beautiful Epitaphs.—The Tomb of a Horse.—Its Extraordinary Efficacy.—The Use of a Long "Tesbih."—Gloomy Depths.—Lingering Rays.

THE aim of the excursion had been the téké of the Howling Dervishes; but, on reaching the little wicket, we found that it wanted yet two hours to the time of opening. What was to be done? To rest in the first place. The only resource in the matter of rest and refreshment in these old-fashioned neighbourhoods is the open-air café, where you are, at least, sure of finding shade, as the humble " iskemlé " (the straw-stool) can be shifted about to follow the travels of the shadow cast by a friendly bough, and you may also hope for good black coffee, with the chance of arresting some passing dealer in simits, Damascus pistachio nuts, and halva, made with sesamé seeds, that celebrated grain, whose name must always awake in the echoes of youthful memories the story of its mysterious power and of the tragic fate of the Forty Thieves.

The secluded outskirt of the Asiatic suburb of Constantinople is so thoroughly Oriental-looking, so world-forgotten, that as you sit watching the quiet life of the little street in front of the café, you are carried back, by the feeblest effort of imagination, into the midst of scenes and personages of familiar story that take life again under the dreamy influence of the rustling leaves and the soft trickle of the wayside fountain. The upper end of the street passes away into the deep gloom of the cypresses of the great "mézarlik" (the burial-ground); near us, a plane-tree, beside the broken marble fountain, spreads its gigantic arms across the road, casting a chequered shade upon the uneven stones; then there is a broad patch of sunlight, blazing on a rose-coloured house and on its draperies of vine-wreaths; more houses, up and down, in and out, irregular, with broken lattices, projecting windows, roofs out of all rule or order, and deep rich masses of purple shadows. A humble chandler's shop, a bakal's, forms the corner of a narrow lane, and then the street dips into a soft grey mist from which a minaret rises into the glowing light, and more rebellious vine branches, waving, catch bright sparkles of the golden rays. A little clattering sound breaks the stillness of the cypress grove; three donkeys come tottering out of the deep shadow: they are very small, with slender legs and hoofs, but they bear their heavy loads of wood bravely. The driver, a Persian, wears a faded blue gown, gathered in at the waist, and a greasy skull cap; he walks barefoot, and it is evident (for surely this is Ali Baba in person) that he has not yet pronounced the "open sesamé!" which is to end his poverty. But we are easy on his account; his wife is waiting at home, for have we not just seen her enter the old pink house in a long blue checked shroud with a black gauze over her face? We know also that inevitable fate is preparing the due punishment of the "thieves," for in that bakal's shop lies one of the great oil jars which, later, will play such an important part in the tragedy. Morgiana, the acute slave, is standing before the shop. She is shrouded also, but very audible as she wrangles over the purchase of a piastre's worth of tallow dips. Beyond the bakal's, under a broken shed, a man in an old green turban sits among his wares—copper mangals, rusty iron pots, and a few metal hand-lamps. A youth, rather jauntily dressed, with a rose stuck over his right ear, is gazing idly at the lamps; he takes one up to examine it, and softly rubs away a stain of dirt. It is Allah-edeen! We hear the rustle of genii wings amongst the trembling leaves

VOL. I. T

of the plane-tree overhead. At the foot of this tree, and near the fountain, a barber is busy on the head of a dervish who has lost an eye, and, a little apart, on one of the great knobs of the roots, sits Alnaschar with a basket of eggs just brought in from a tchiftlik beyond Tchamlidja. "Youmourtah! tazé youmourtah!" (fresh eggs) cries he, rather absently, for he is evidently in a day-dream: the basket is hazardously poised on an uneven stone, and———. The shriek of a railway train pierces the dreamy stillness; the vision is rudely broken; the fancy has melted away. Let us stroll into the solemn burial-field before we take the steamer back to town.

There is a small mosque at the entrance of the road, beside it a modest wooden building; the ground floor is a turbé, full of tombs, which are inlaid with mother-o'-pearl, and partly covered with splendid Cashmere shawls. Close by, we see the tomb of some venerated saint; it is surrounded by a railing, and a great bush of box-wood, growing up from the centre, is covered with fluttering votive rags. Before the shrine, something like a birdcage suspended from a pole is full of little tallow candles, to be lighted at sunset. The bits of dirty faded rags so often seen fastened to the railings or other available spot about tombs that have a reputation for sanctity, are pieces taken from the garments of sick persons. In the low wall of the cemetery, as in many other walls and nooks, may be seen crumpled pieces of paper stuck into the cracks and crevices—little torn, discoloured bits, thrust in without order or method: they have been picked up from the ground by devout Mussulmans and put where they cannot be trodden on, lest the name of the Almighty might be found on them and so dishonoured. Near at hand some people are filling in two graves. One bier is lying on the ground, covered with a beautiful veil of yellow Broussa gauze; the mourners, still lingering, chat cheerfully with the imāms and a few idlers who have sauntered to the spot. Some children racing noisily about are checked only when too near the open graves.

Many of the epitaphs on Mussulman tombstones are beautiful in their poetic feeling and tenderness, and it may be observed that those on the graves of women completely dispose of the absurd theory, so prevalent in the West, that Mussulman females are held by their own people to be without souls. Translations of many of the most remarkable epitaphs are given in White's admirable work on Constantinople, from which the following are extracted. All funeral inscriptions are headed by an invocation to the Almighty, the most usual form being, "God only is Eternal!"

(*On the tomb of an infant son of Saliha Sultana, in the cemetery of Eyoub.*)

"A flower that had scarcely bloomed was prematurely torn from its stem. It has been removed to those bowers where roses never languish. Its parents' tears will supply refreshing moisture. Say a "fateha" for its beatitude!"

(*On a young lady.*)

"He, the Immortal!

"The chilling blast of fate caused this nightingale to wing its course to heaven. It has there found merited enjoyment. Lababa wrote this inscription, and offered up a humble prayer for Zeïneb. But weep not for her; she has become a sojourner in the Gardens of Paradise."

In the Scutari cemetery. (*Upon a lady who died in childbirth.*)

"He alone is Eternal!

"From this perishable to a better world, the young and excellent Seïla Hanum departed, while depositing her burden. Tree and fruit were both transported to the gardens of Paradise. Rivers of tears cannot efface the dear heart's image from the memory of her husband, Osman Agha, son of Ismail Reïs. A prayer for their souls!"

(*On a child's tomb.*)

"God only is Eternal!

"Here below I was but a frail rosebud. The bitter wind of destiny blew upon my stem, and I was transplanted from the garden of this world to bloom in Paradise."

(*A mother's lament for her young daughter.*)

"God only is Eternal!

"The bird of my heart has flown from my soul towards the gardens of Paradise. It was the decree of fate that my daughter should live but thirteen years, and death has taken all from her mother in taking her. Alas! that her bed of rest should now be one of stone!"

(*On a man's tomb*).

"Traveller, I ask of thee a prayer! If to-day it is needed for myself, to-morrow it will be required for thee! Recite, O passer-by, the first verses of the Koran for the soul of Ali, the master tailor!"

Towards the south-western limit of the great Scutari burial-ground, and almost hidden among moss-grown graves, rank weeds, and cypress stems, you come upon a venerable monument—a stone vaulted roof, supported on columns, that covers nothing but a plain surface of trodden earth, with a small upright stone marking the headplace of the occupant. The people of the neighbourhood call it the tomb of a horse, and point to another burial-place enclosed in a railing, heavily trimmed with votive rags, as the grave of a saintly man, the owner of the much-honoured steed. This monument, which is wonderfully picturesque, with bird-sown sprigs of cypress shooting from the cracks of the worn grey stone, is very similar to the tomb erected to commemorate the horse of Mohammed the Conqueror, this latter in the cemetery of Eyoub, on the summit of the hill called Sandjakdjilar, the "standard-bearer." A curious superstition connected with this graveless monument in the Scutari burial-ground lends at least probability to its supposed origin. The horse is the emblem of strength, and this spot is endowed, they affirm, with the miraculous power of giving firmness and strength to the legs of weakly, crippled children. The application of the charm takes place on Fridays, in the afternoon.

A very dilapidated imām officiated on the day of our visit there; two or three women of the humbler class had assembled, holding their sickly babies very tenderly and anxiously. Each party brought a new whisk broom, with which the officiating priest swept carefully round the area three times; then, taking the child under the arms, proceeded to drag it round backwards, so that its legs should come as much as possible in contact with the strength-giving earth.

This was done three times, with a pause at the head of the grave, when the little limbs were flapped down—also three times. A penny was the charge for this inexpensive if ineffectual remedy, and the mother bore away her child, taking great care not to turn her head as she departed, lest the charm should be broken. On leaving the horse's grave the patient is carried to a small building near at hand, that contains, under one roof, the tomb of a Turkish saint and a Christian ayasma, or holy well. An old woman, singularly alive to the merits of backshish, presides over the fountain, at which both Mussulman and Christian drink, after which the ancient lady produces a monstrous chaplet—a tesbih—of large dark beads, which she passes three times over the head of the visitor and down to the feet—like a skipping-rope. As this operation is paid for, any one that pleases may enjoy the privilege; in the case of the children who had been dragged round the horse's grave it is a necessary and completing part of the cure.

A high road leads through the nearer part of this vast cemetery; the low, streaming rays of sunset gleam through the rare openings in the dark arcades of tombstones and cypress, to touch here a venerable turban, mossy and weather-worn, there a simple upright slab, with coloured clusters of the vine or blossoms and twining branches—a woman's resting-place. At one spot a grave has fallen in, and bones and rubbish and decayed wood half fill the yawning chasm. Beside it an ancient stone, regilt and beautified, bright with the graceful tracery of its Arabic inscription, tells of the unforgotten dead, and of the pious care of his descendants. Then you pass a family burial-place surrounded by a railing, farther on a cluster of imāms' turbans, and in a more ancient part the light flickers on a gaunt assemblage of roughly hewn upright masses of grey stone, without ornament or symbol; then, striking a red gleam from a new fez-capped monument, wanders in emerald sparkles along the grass, and melts in the impenetrable depths of gloom beyond, a gloom that no living, joyous ray can ever pierce—a sombre region of long-forgotten graves, where the gnarled and whitening limbs of the neglected trees groan with a weird, unearthly sound at the touch of the breeze which may not freshen the heavy vapours; where a silence "that can be felt" is rarely broken by the stir of human life; a very region of hopeless sadness, depths on whose brink you might seem to leave for ever "ogni speranza!"

It is not good to pause in the dark, chill atmosphere; pass out from the shadow of the cypresses into the warm sunshine that streams in level rays across the open ground of Haïdar-pasha. It gilds the lofty towers of the Selimieh barracks, and plays lightly with the vapour of the boat just steaming into the quiet bay; it flashes from the crosses of the new church of old Chalcédon; it casts a joyous, rippling band across the Sea of Marmora; it sparkles on the Princes' Islands; and, touching with a softened radiance the swelling hills that bound the Gulf of Ismidt, lastly, and most tenderly—as all beneath sinks into pearly grey—it lingers with a blushing glow, and dies upon the snow-clad summits of Bithynia.

XVI.

THE HOWLING DERVISHES.

The Téké.—A Venerable Scheïk and his Little Son.—Discriminate Salutations.—Devotees.—Growing Excitement.—A Pause.—Infant "Faithful."—Frantic Devotion.—A Holy Santon.

THE téké of the "Howling Dervishes" at Scutari is an unpretending building standing on the outskirts of the town, and at the entrance of a road leading through a corner of the great cemetery. The chapel, an oblong room or hall, has a gallery supported on pilasters running round three of its sides. This gallery is screened in one part by latticework (cafesses) for the use of Mussulman women; the broad space beneath, divided from the floor of the chapel by a railing, being devoted to visitors. Strangers are freely admitted to witness the ceremonies in the chapels of the dervishes' convents, being merely required to take off their outer shoes before entering and to stand during the performance.

At the principal end of the chapel there is neither gallery nor railing, but a slight recess—the mihrab—occupied by a copy of the Koran placed on a stand, covered with a gold-embroidered velvet cloth; above this, in large gold letters, an inscription in which the name of the founder, Ahmed Rufaï, may be easily deciphered. A horse-tail standard is reared against the wall, and around the mihrab hang instruments of torture of appalling aspect: daggers, with balls and chains, larding-needles, thongs of leather, swords, and iron hooks; round the front of the gallery are suspended small kettle-drums and tambourines. The floor is partly covered with skins of the Angora sheep, some dyed red or blue, others in their native creamy white. On one of these the scheïk takes his place; but when engaged in prayer he makes his prostrations, not on the sheepskin, but on a sejjadé, or prayer-carpet.

The chief of this téké is an elderly man, pale and serious, with flowing, grizzled locks and beard. His bearing is peculiarly dignified and in harmony with the fine lines of his dress—a dark green pelisse with large open sleeves, and an ample muslin turban wound round a felt cap. A very small boy, of five or six years, a perfect miniature of the scheïk, dressed in a red and yellow gown and a little fez, comes solemnly forward, salutes his father with intense gravity, kissing his hand and putting it to his forehead, and then takes his place beside him, sitting back upon his heels.

Several prayer-carpets have been spread upon the centre of the floor. People are assembling; they are not all dressed as dervishes, for many wear the common dress of the country; each person reverently salutes the scheïk before passing to his place. There is a very careful distinction observed in the manner in which these salutations are returned: those of, apparently, the highest religious rank receive a kiss on either cheek; for such as wear the green turban round their felt cap the scheïk touches that also with his lips; of others, again, he merely receives the salutation.

The service opens with a low chant, the worshippers kneeling and going through the positions required by Mussulman prayer, the little boy following every movement with the gravest decorum; they stroke their beards, he strokes his tiny chin, and shows no sign of weariness or insubordination; he sits back, as before, when the prayers are ended, gravely watching throughout the whole proceedings.

Then the prayer-carpets and sheepskins are folded in heaps on two sides of the chapel, and an elderly man, gifted with wonderful lungs, sitting crouched on one of the heaps, leads another chant, accompanied by a performer on a small native violin. The devotees, standing in a row opposite to the scheïk, begin to cry out all together the name of the Almighty, with a few words accompanying each cry. Then they hold hands and sway in a mass, shoulder to shoulder, now sideways, now forwards. The murmur, at first gentle, soon increases in vehemence; they become heated; a dervish goes round the circle with cool linen caps for such as wish to cast off the turban, or felt "kulah," or fez; then they begin to throw off their warm upper clothing, for the exercise is growing fast and furious; many strip all but the shirt, from the waist upwards, not intermitting for one moment the swaying and the groaning shout, "Allah! illah Allah! Allah! illah Allah!"

Meanwhile the scheïk has passed behind the chanters, attended by a black dervish, who lifts off his master's turban, kisses it, and lays it reverently down beside the others, then puts on him also the linen skull-cap.

Many well-dressed Mussulmans have by this time glided into the chapel and stationed themselves behind the sheepskin seat of the chief; several small boys and girls come in without any disturbance, and sit on their heels on a line with the little son.

There is a pause in the shouting; the scheïk returns to his sheepskin and begins to bless bottles of water, brought for that purpose; he murmurs a short prayer or invocation over each bottle as he blows into it; it is then handed back to the owner, supposed to be endowed with healing virtue.

Some babies are next brought forward by the black dervish, who is very energetic. He lays them, three or four in a row, on their faces, and is particularly careful to straighten their little limbs, holding them gently down; but there is no sign of resistance from these infant devotees, as the scheïk, first passing his right foot softly down the body, walks over them, carefully stepping on the upper part of the leg and supported on each side by an attendant; the pressure, though momentary, must be considerable for such tender forms, yet, strange to say, the little ones seem to enjoy it; there is not a cry or murmur from any one of the children. Many have gone of their own accord to undergo the sacred trampling, and laid themselves down as if it were a customary observance, jumping up afterwards quite briskly and kissing the hand of the scheïk, who, in return, presses his two hands gently on either side of their little faces, murmurs a prayer, and blows upon them, after which, well pleased and feeling all the better for it, they regain their places without the least confusion.

Amongst these children, a sweet-looking little girl, with long fair hair streaming over her faded pink cotton antary, came and knelt down before the venerable man. It was a lovely picture, the delicate child placing her slender hands between his broad palms, the light falling strongly on the fair head with its pale green twist of gauze for adornment, and on the venerable beard and sober-toned cloak of the dervish. The background, a sombre depth marked here and there by glimmering touches of light reflected from the implements of torture.

Some of the infants, after undergoing the tread and receiving the blessing, are carried round by their mothers to be blown upon by the most saintly among the worshippers.

The row of "howlers" has formed again during these proceedings. They hold each other closer now, the arms entwined and the hands on the shoulder, so that it is in a compact mass that they sway altogether. The stamping and howling becomes every moment wilder, as the excitement increases. The voices have grown harsh and hoarse. The recurring cry, "Allah! hou hou! Allah! hou hou!" loses at length all semblance of words; it gathers into a roar like the wild howl of some savage beast. Perspiration streams from the faces, the veins of the head swell; you expect to see them fall into convulsions, but still the swaying, and the stamp, and the groaning "Allah! hou!" go on ever stronger and fiercer. It is a cry of raging demoniacs; nature cannot longer endure the strain. Suddenly the measure changes to a rapid jump for the space of a minute or two, then ceases. The maniacs are instantaneously calm and apparently little fatigued. The performance was over, having lasted for upwards of two hours, during which time the scheïk, calm and dignified, had never once looked towards the group of strangers stationed within a few feet of him.

I had visited this téké a few years since, and on that occasion saw something of the wild use of the sinister-looking weapons and implements that are now suspended on the walls, rusty and covered with dust. They lay, then, about upon the ground, tossed among leopards' skins, Santon's wallets, and other strange-looking objects. The order of the ceremonies had been the same as that just described till, in the height of the swaying and excitement, three men darted from the circle, seized each a long skewer, and presented themselves before the scheïk. He prayed and blew upon them, then, with his finger in the open mouth of the enthusiast, pressed the cheeks very firmly, passing at the same time the long thin larding needle quite through across the mouth and out at the other cheek. Thus larded, the men walked off, and placing themselves in a row, stood for half an hour looking very placid and comfortable under the circumstances. The cheeks were again pressed on the withdrawal of the skewers by the scheïk; there was no apparent wound, a single drop of blood alone marked the spot.

Such evidences of misguided fervour, though mild as compared with the self-torture of Hindoo devotees, are yet sometimes to be met with here in a manner sufficiently elaborated to be terribly ghastly. A vision of this sort once startled the writer in the bazaars of Broussa. In addition to the skewer, which looked like a fixture, the holy Santon (his religious rank must have been elevated) wore a larding needle in the flesh of either temple and two heavy iron plates woven into the shoulder and into the right arm, with which he fiercely presented his begging dish to the gaping crowd.

But to return to the téké. Besides the three skewered worshippers, other fanatics put themselves to a test even more severe. A man stripped to the waist laid himself down on his back and seizing one of the short thick daggers, held the point of it upon his breast; the scheik, a heavy man, with only one supporter, mounted calmly on the ball which topped the handle of the dagger, and stepped across. After this, the excitement becoming fiercer, men rushed about the chapel seizing the weapons, cutting and slashing themselves with frantic gestures. One of these enthusiasts soon made his appearance in the outer room to which most of the spectators had retreated, with a bleeding sword-gash across his naked breast.

This display of wild and terrible fanaticism is not now, or is at least very rarely, permitted at the dervishes' tékés, but similar exhibitions of misdirected zeal and courage take place among Persian worshippers in the Validé Khan on the tenth night of the month Mouharem.

XVII.

A STEP EASTWARDS.

NO. I.

On the Road to Nicomedia.—In search of the Tomb of Hannibal.—Church of St. Euphemia.—Elastic Railway Arrangements.—The Bay of Kalamitza.—Ayasma of St. John Chrysostom.—Fanaraki.— A Summer Palace of Justinian.— " Kaïsh Dagh."—Maltépé.—Tomato Paste.—Cartal.—Pendik.—The Gulf of Ismid.—Station of Guebseh.

ONE short step : hitherto an ill-made, unsuccessful, single line of rail, skirting the Gulf of Ismidt and leading, so to speak, to nowhere in particular ; but who shall deny that, once in competent hands, with sufficient capital and honest management, it may prove the one "step in the right direction" that shall open out the mighty highway between East and West ? This railway follows in great measure the line of the old Roman road to Nicomedia (Ismidt); the town of Guebseh, lying half way, was formerly the first station for the caravans of pilgrims leaving Constantinople for Mecca, before steam arose to simplify the holy pilgrimage.

One bright morning our small party undertook a

little pilgrimage of another kind : a visit to the tomb of Hannibal. According to Pliny and authorities of his time, as well as local legends, the celebrated Carthagenian was buried in the neighbourhood of Lybissa, now Guebissé or Guebseh, for which place there is a station on the Ismidt line. The terminus is at Haïdar-Pasha, near the seashore, at the extremity of the large and thriving village of Kadikeui.

From the very starting-point all around is fraught with recollections of a famous past. On that rising ground to the left of the station stood the celebrated church of Saint Euphemia, built by Constantine on the site of a temple of Apollo ; the church in which the fourth Œcumenical Synod was held, so widely known as the Council of Chalcédon. The edifice was demolished after the fall of Constantinople, and the materials subsequently used to embellish the mosque of Sultan Soliman, but an ancient ayasma, supposed to have been connected with the church, and called the Holy Fountain of St. Euphemia, remained shaded by venerable plane-trees, until engulfed within the buildings of the terminus. It is difficult to find under these changed conditions, but it exists still ; ayasmas, as much respected by the Turks as by the Christians, are never destroyed.

The bell rings, and we are soon seated ; but at

the last moment an enthusiastic geologist, eager to test the rich mineral treasures known to abound in these parts, discovers that he has left his hammer in the caïque! The train waits for the signal to start, time is up; but there is a charming ease and elasticity in Oriental railway arrangements. "Don't let it distress you," said the good-natured conductor, preparing to light a cigarette, "fetch your bag; we can wait, but do not be longer than necessary." We begin slowly to cross the green meadows of Haïdar-Pasha; then, taking a strong curve to the right, see presently, in a deep cutting, remains of ancient work and masonry, cut through diagonally by the rails; it bears the stamp of having been hastily done; a narrow passage, about six or eight feet high, formed of rough stones and vaulted with tiles, apparently thrust into the earth from beneath: it takes the direction of the ancient city of Chalcédon.

This place, which sustained many sieges, was taken in the seventh century by the Persians, by means of a subterranean passage leading from their camp, on the neighbouring slope, to the market-place of the besieged town; and it is probable that the railway works, cutting deep into the earth for the first time since that remote date, have brought to light this passage, forgotten since the days of Heraclius. But we are long past the cutting, and the slackening train stops at the little station of

Kizil-Toprak, in the midst of vineyards and orchards, the first renowned for their "thaousch" vines (the supposed ancestors of the Fontainebleau "chasselas"), the latter for their cherries, which are scarcely less esteemed here.

What a soft and graceful picture it is, bathed in a flood of golden light, that opens before the rustic station! In the midst of the gardens, the great water-wheels, with their complicated bewilderment of spokes and shafts, turn slowly, surrounded by red and bronze garlands of the vine; a narrow, shady lane winds down towards the bay of Kalamitza, where, beneath a group of gigantic planes, we see the ancient chapel and Holy Well of St. John Chrysostom; the calm waters and the headland of Moda Bournou, with its fine avenue of terebinths and olives; beyond this, again, the blue Marmora, with the islets of Oxeia and Platé backed by the pale shadowy range of mountains bordering the gulf.

We pass at the head of the cypress-covered promontory known as Fanaraki, from the "fanar," or lighthouse, at its point. A summer palace of Justinian covered this beautiful tongue of land, and the crumbling earth-cliff and the beach beyond the point are full of old remains: pieces of rich marble and little cubes of the mosaic work are found in abundance among the stones and pebbles. It was a favourite resort of the Greek emperors, and, in their time, churches, baths, and cisterns spread over the ground at the head of the promontory. It was near Faranaki that the unfortunate Emperor Maurice, his wife, and eight of their children, were assassinated by order of the usurper Phocas.

As we roll on, in place of the dark cypress, we see the bright chaplet of the Princes' Islands, sparkling like jewels, as gay villas, and châlets, and sunny slopes dance again in the liquid mirror at their feet; but the eye, soon weary of so much brilliancy, turns for relief to the soothing quiet of the other side of the line—an uncared-for stretch of rough ground, softly flecked with wild flowers; then grey rocks rising among shrubs and brambles, which gently melt into the blue and tender colouring of the crags and crevices of Kaish-Dagh (Mount Auxentius). On that summit—the highest in the neighbourhood of Constantinople, and the last of a line of fire-beacons that stretched across Bithynia to the capital—there existed, under the Greek Empire, a church and a celebrated monastery; fragments of mosaic and other remains may be now found there.

There is a pause at Erenkeui, an insignificant station, that happens at the moment to be garlanded with sausages hung to dry; as in Savoy and elsewhere, the cottages are festooned with maize or tobacco. Soon afterwards we pass the old bridge at Bostandji-Keupru. Some interesting ruins remained until lately at this spot, but a squadron of Croats have been actively engaged in breaking them up for road-making purposes.

Maltépé is a rendezvous for sportsmen, and the hotel at the station puts forth great pretensions to elegance and civilisation, but the tourist will prefer to contemplate the picturesque houses and minarets of the village beyond, gleaming white amidst cypress and walnut-trees. Here is a ruined fountain shaded by a plane-tree also falling to decay; there a grove of olives, grey and dusky, relieved against a hillside glowing with the bloom of heather and lavender; splashes of bright red also, for much of this land is given up to the cultivation of tomatos and the fabrication of tomato paste. On every side you see piles of the fiery balls and sacks of the same hue under pressure of great stones; it is strange, even pleasing to the eye, but the odour arising from the heaps of decaying matter is sickening.

Cartal is a large village principally inhabited by Mussulmans; on the neighbouring slopes of Yakadjik many rich Turks possess property, to which they come in the spring and at the season of the vintage. There is no visible attraction in the spot, which looks bare and shadeless, but it enjoys air of great purity, and springs of water esteemed the best in all that part of the country. This has given occasion for one among the numerous acts of munificent charity for which the Egyptian Princess Zeïneb Hanoum is so justly celebrated. The town of Cartal suffered terribly from fever, occasioned by bad and insufficient water, and this lady, who owns the finest property at Yakadjik, had fountains erected and the waters of the much-esteemed springs conveyed to the town at her expense. In this neighbourhood, Justinian's famous general, Belisarius, possessed vast fields and vineyards.

At Pendik we stop for a short while to allow of the passage of the train from Ismidt, which creeps slowly by, showing in each third-class compartment a group of wondering turbaned heads. They are conscripts coming from the interior, to whom this miraculous passage across country must be a source of inexhaustible wonderment. The old guard at the station, dressed in a faded pink cotton robe and light blue petticoat trousers, who is carelessly waving a tattered green flag as a signal, while he jokes with some friend in the train, seems a figure singularly in harmony with the general *laissez aller* of the arrangements.

As you advance towards the head of the Gulf of Ismidt the scenery improves in beauty; on all sides thickets and woodland glades with openings rich with tufts of heath and ilex, cistus and myrtle, some marshy lands in which mighty reeds wave majestically. On the other side small islets covered with pine-trees are mirrored in the clear water that gives back every line and cordage of the great mahonas lying at anchor for their freight of charcoal from the neighbouring forest.

At Touzla, we find the rustic station in the midst of a grove of oaks speckled with white tents, and we pass through fields of flowering tobacco, and then some highly cultivated land, reaching at length the station of Guebseh—but nothing but the station! No sign of town or village; only a few pack-horses and two feeble donkeys, waiting to show that there is, somewhere about, a locality to which travellers and baggage have to be conveyed. We ask, "Does any one here know of the tomb of Hannibal, a great man of the old, old times?" "Yes, tchelebi, but it is not a tomb; the burial-place is up there, a *long* way off, at the top of that last hill there, where you see the two cypresses." This is unattainable; we make another attempt. "The old ruined castle that you call Eski-Hissar, where is that, then?"

"Oh yes! the old castle of the Djinns. It is down there, *ever* so far at the end of the great valley: you can see the tops of the towers against the water."

"Well, then, where is Guebseh?"

"Mashallah! our Guebseh! but certainly: it is quite easy; this is the road; it winds and winds among the hills, and in half an hour you are there. It is altogether in another direction."

How could the short limit of time before the return train admit of visiting these three interesting places on three different horizons? The best plan is to aim at the most visible attraction, and taking as guide the ruined battlements on the shore of the gulf, we plunge resolutely into the valley on the right hand of the great viaduct.

A STEP EASTWARDS.

NO. II.—GUEBSEH.

The Ruins of Eski-Hissar.—The Baths of Yalova.—Crusaders.—The Baths of Pythia.—The Turkish Peasant.—Guebseh.—Beautiful Mosque.—The "Mezarlik."—A Hanum of the Good Old Time.—A Native Repast.—The Camel Stables.

Down into the valley: a beautiful wilderness, where chestnut, walnut, fig and mulberry, medlar and olive-trees flourish in that rich soil and sheltered spot, almost without care or cultivation; here and there a patch of maize or a rough vineyard testify to some labour bestowed, while many a dry and broken fountain show how careless and shortsighted has that labour been, and, as if in stern reproof, the grey ruins of ancient water-towers, seen amongst the foliage, tell us that in long past times great works were carried out for the supply of water throughout the valley, and to the distant palace on the seashore.

A walk of half an hour brings you to the ruins, for which no more distinctive name can be obtained than Eski-Hissar (the old castle). It is a vast enclosure of battlemented walls, strong towers, and vaulted entrance gates surrounding a massive square building of much older date. On the side towards the water the precipitous face of the cliff is formed into a series of terraces down to the level of the beach. The noble proportions of the central building; the height and size of the interior halls; the remains of handsome columns of marble, porphyry, and red granite that still cling to the walls or lie about amongst the ruins, and the lofty arch of the windows, give to this place the appearance of a princely residence rather than that of the dungeon-keep of a fortress; and it is difficult to deny the strong probability that this may be the palace to which Constantine the Great in his last illness caused himself to be carried, here that he was baptised, and here died. The distance of this place, however, from Nicomedia, near to which city historians place that event, must leave the matter in some doubt.

There is a delightful resting-place within the shadow of a ruined gateway, and we pause for a time in the company of some harmless lizards and of a grass-green praying mantis, which seems to supplicate for its frail life, joining its slender forefeet in a manner irresistibly absurd. The view from this point is magnificent: gleaming through the azure veil cast by distance on the mountain slopes you distinguish, sometimes faintly, sometimes with bright sparkles or curling wreaths of vapour, villages, hamlets, and homesteads, most thickly sprinkled about their base; a soft and tranquil landscape, but one that has its place in the annals of the country and in the sanguinary history of the first Crusade. Directly in front lies Yalova, formerly Hélénopolis, famed for its mineral baths, erected by St. Helena, the mother of Constantine. Seven centuries later, the Crusaders, led by Peter the Hermit, spread over all that part of the country, and ere long a pyramid of bones in the neighbourhood of Yalova marked the tragic fate of that horde of undisciplined enthusiasts.

Other thermal waters near to Eski-Hissar—the baths of Pythia or Polopythia—were used by Constantine in his last illness, by Theodora, the wife of Justinian, and by many of the Greek emperors. At an earlier date, Pythia had been favoured by an oracle of Apollo, consulted by the Argonauts on their famous voyage in search of the Golden Fleece.

A few days later we are again at the station of Guebseh, with the determination of visiting the town, which contains a celebrated mosque. Not forgetting the quest for the resting-place of the Carthaginian hero, one of the party mounts a pack-horse in order to secure his owner as guide, and we are soon winding through the leafy lanes, meeting now and again a white-turbaned Ottoman trotting slowly along on a tranquil donkey; for here unpicturesque "frank" fashions have not, as yet, modified the Oriental type; you find the genuine Turkish peasantry, with its ignorance, its simple usages and superstitions, and its true and solid virtues: courageous and patient under unmerited misfortune; honest, sober, and charitable; respectful to the aged, tender to little children, hospitable to all—a simple race, that asks but a place in the sunshine, a handful of bread or rice, to thank God and be content. And yet what misery, famine, and decay are now blighting this beautiful and fertile land of Anatolia—a land teeming with riches, that needs but security and honest, well-directed labour, to give its treasures back a thousand-fold!

We have reached Guebseh, anciently Lybissa, where Hannibal perished by his own hand. Under the Ottoman rule, at the time when the caravans rested here on their road to Mecca, vast camel stables were erected which still remind the traveller of its past greatness. The fine mosque built in the reign of Selim I. is the chief attraction of the place; and our guide condescends to remember the strangers he has undertaken to conduct, and leads us, through many a winding narrow alley, to the market-place in the centre of the little town. We cause a sensation, for travellers are now almost unknown here. It is Ramazan; and the inhabitants, having nothing to do, do nothing but stare at us persistently, although, in spite of the severe fast which is supposed disagreeably to affect the temper and manners, they are perfectly well intentioned. Two or three of the younger loungers volunteer as showmen of the great mosque. It is a beautiful building, surrounded by all that constitutes a "pious foundation" of the highest order. Above the great gateway leading into the interior court, a square and very solid building, is the library, containing, they say, many manuscripts. To the right, on entering, you find a long range of low vaulted stone rooms; the imaret, or place of reception, and soup-kitchen for the poor, where a distribution of soup and pillaff takes place each day; on the other side is the khan for travellers, with stables for their animals; and, beyond this, the medresseh, or college, and cells for students.

In the centre of the court is the fountain of ablutions. Shaded by tall cypress and plane trees, that cast soft waves of shadow on the beautiful façade of the mosque, on the columns of the portico, on the many-tinted marbles that ornament the fine curve of the arches, and on the garland of wreathed Arabic letters which surround the principal entrance. A murmur of voices draws us to this door: within, an imām seated on the ground is reading in a grave, sonorous voice to a group of the "faithful" crouching in a half circle before him; they are listening with deep attention, that the unusual apparition of strangers does not in the least disturb. The inside of the mosque is handsomely ornamented with mosaic work and varied marbles, and with inscriptions in Persian tiling, the pattern raised in white on a pale green or blue ground. The mimbar, or pulpit, for the Friday discourse, is sculptured in arabesque, and the mihrab, the niche in which the Koran is placed, is surrounded by a rich and graceful design. This interior slightly recalls the celebrated Green Mosque at Broussa.

In the court of the medresseh everything looks poor and neglected; two or three softas are crossing the patches of rank weeds that should have been a garden, or standing at the door of their little cell, and an aged imām drags his great crimson papushes towards us with a friendly air. We enter on a perfectly safe and harmonious understanding as to the state of the weather, the appearance of the crops, and the hopes of the vintage, after which, our staff of guides having greatly increased by this time, we are borne off to see some stones "with writing" in the old cemetery; and, in truth, you find there, as in most similar situations, vestiges of Christian buildings, such as broken shafts of columns, now serving as tombstones; some blocks of marble marked with the cross, and one large slab bearing a long Greek inscription—all half buried in bramble bush and creepers, in a grove of gnarled and venerable cypresses. A large tomb with a domed roof supported on half-broken arches attracts especial notice; it is the mesar, or burial-place, of forty daughters of one mother—a hanum of the good old time, so says the legend. Two mounds of earth side by side in this remarkable turbé contain this marvellously fine family, twenty beneath each mound!

The shadows are lengthening over the rank grass and creeping up the grey moss-grown monuments; we return to the village café, where in the open street, and in the shadow of an old fig-tree, a collation, *à la turca,* is quickly laid out and disposed of, to the high satisfaction of a numerous and admiring circle of spectators. A metal disc placed on a low stool held thin slices of salted and dried mutton, native cheese, and flaps of unleavened bread, but the dish of honour is a huge bowl full of tomatoes, onions, and raw sardines, steeped in oil and vinegar. The long walk, the keen air of the hills, and a general disposition to be pleased with the well-meant attentions of our admiring friends, induced some of our party to take what was set before them.

All rested in the calm of the summer evening; then, as the rosy glow melted into faint purple tones, we took a friendly leave of the worthy villagers, and wound our way once more along the thyme-scented paths towards the station, pausing, however, on the outskirts to look at the long row of camel stables, so necessary when the caravan for Mecca formerly made its first station at this spot.

And what of the tomb of Hannibal? Alas! we never reached the lonely hill-top where tradition says that he has rested for more than twenty centuries. Perhaps some day a keener spirit of investigation may yet learn the truth about that desolate grave.

XVIII.

IN THE SERAÏ.

NO. II.

Once more in the Seraï.—A Pretty Scene.—In the Visitors' Room.—Neat Needlework.—Souvenirs of former Gaieties.—The invasion of Crinoline.—Art under Difficulties.—The Pocket Sketch-book.—The old Negress and the Sud'na.—Peaceful Pictures.—The Call to Prayer.—The Sejjadé.—The Namaz.—The Prescribed Hours.—The Tessbih.—A Dying Halaïk.—Marriage of the Ibrikdar Ousta.—Prosperous Servitude and Undesirable Freedom.—Ghevhéri.

Some years have rolled on with their inexorable changes, and I am summoned once more to the seraï of Zeïneb Sultana, now in her winter palace near Stamboul. I am glad to renew the old friendly relations with that harem, and to learn the fate of many of my former friends.

A cloud has passed over the house since the days of the military band and of the "bandanas." With the death of the indulgent father of the Princess, the glory of the establishment has been greatly dimmed, and the harem now numbers many fewer occupants.

I am stopped and questioned at the gate by the harem kapoudji. A few words suffice to establish my right of entry, and I am passed on to a group of lallas in the caveh odjak, and by one of them am conveyed within the "sacred enclosure."

In the vast sofa (the central hall) two or three girls are lounging near the garden steps, watching some of their companions busily engaged in hanging out their "wash" to dry in the sunbeams. They are all tightly bound in the picturesque striped bathing-towel, and their bare feet thrust into nàlin, or bathing-clogs. It is a pretty scene as they flit about from sunlight to shadow among the flapping folds of bright-coloured draperies; some tall cypresses and the white minaret of a neighbouring mosque standing out upon a sky of the purest azure, fill in the upper part of the picture.

I cross the hall, and raising a perdeh, or door-curtain, pass into the visitors' reception-room: it is the apartment of the Ibrikdar Ousta, very handsomely furnished with satin couches and curtains, rugs and padded quilts on the floor. Two girls are seated on the ground at work; one a gentle, auburn-haired girl, in a pale green muslin dress and brown handkerchief, is busy, with her work-box beside her, making an antary; the other is hemming a sheet of striped Broussa stuff. In one corner of the divan Djeïlan (the antelope) is arranging the hair of a little halaïk in a wonderful curly wig, "à la frança," while near the mangal or brasier, that stands in the centre of the room, a tall black agha is warming his hands. He is seated on a low stool, and talks quietly and gravely with an old negress who crouches on her heels. The poor old woman is ugly as an ape, but she has a good, kind, faithful face: they are both, I think, retainers of the house on a visit.

I have a long time to wait, and I watch the two girls as they work. Their progress is far less rapid, but infinitely more minute and accurate, than it would be with us; the ordinary hem, which in England is considered as quite sufficiently neat for common stuffs, is replaced by Eastern women— even with coarse cloths and garments—by a careful needlework edging in white silk; threads are drawn upon all possible occasions, for the sake of perfect measurement. There is an extreme of finish in these small matters that often makes our Western handiwork look slight and hasty in comparison.

Whilst I speculate on these little characteristic differences, the perdeh is raised from without, and a black slave enters with a great heap of gown stuffs, which she deposits on the floor. The women and girls gather round and begin to turn them over; they have been sent in for distribution among the halaïks. One particularly pretty print is admired by two of them ; both cannot have it, and presently it disappears from the heap—the "antelope" has slipped it under the skirt of her antary as the ousta enters the room to preside at the distribution.

And what has become of all the old friends of former days—of the military band, the performers of pantomime, the tumblers, and the would-be elegant ball-room beauties ? Ah! the gaieties are sobered, and many of the girls are gone from the seraï; some are married, more are dead. The military band was fatal to several of the performers, predisposed as these Circassians always are to consumption. Dilber comes to sit beside me, and we talk over the past times. She herself has long since given up the flute, and is recovering her health, but the clarionet player, and many others have been less fortunate. Souzy-Dil, the beautiful Georgian, was one of three balaïks given by the Princess as attendants in the great seraglio. After two or three years Souzy-Dil was married to an officer; she has lost her beauty, they say, and grown thin. Ta'asnevin, the pretty blue-eyed little halaïk, is now a tall ungainly girl, very affected in manner and tawdry in attire. The classical folds and draperies have almost disappeared from the scene to give place to skirts hideously distended over crinoline.

Wandering through the rooms in search of familiar faces, I find the Bash Djambaz (chief tumbler), who has renounced tumbling and the tight-rope and taken up literature, for she drags a crumpled volume from beneath a cushion and begins to read, with great show of facility, some lines from the " Bin-bir Guidjeh " ("The Thousand and One Nights"), seeking to astonish me by the wonders of the " djin " of the lamp. This, which is a slave's own room, is furnished with Brussels carpeting, satin hangings, a chest of drawers, vases of French artificial flowers, handsome porcelain cups, and other ornaments.

When I at length see Zeïneb Sultana I find her little changed. She is very simply dressed in the French style. I learn that she wishes me to *re*paint the dress of her portrait according to a new fashion-book just received from Paris—a strange undertaking, as the large canvas was varnished and considered finished years ago ; but, wishing to see something more of the inmates of that palace, I agree to do my best to make her picture "fashionable."

We speak of the old khasnadar, who has been long married. "Ah! yes," said the Sultana, " I was very fond of that khasnadar ; I have known her all my life, but her eyes got weak, she could no longer see clearly to keep the accounts, so I found her a husband. She has a very comfortable home of her own."

After this interview I went several times to the

palace. Upon one occasion the ousta charged with my well-being showed herself unusually anxious to ascertain the contents of my little hand-bag.

"What a pretty little bag you have, madama; let me take it upstairs for you. What do you bring in it? A book? No? What have you in that roll? The brushes? Ah! yes—but, madama, is there not a little book somewhere? a lead-pencil book?"

I now understand the drift of the questioning. I have been reported to the Sultana as having made some drawings in a pocket sketch-book. I produce the offender, which is borne off immediately to the "Effendimiz" (our lady).

There are sounds of distant laughter, and some time passes. At length the ousta reappears, returning the little book with, alas! one of the most cherished sketches of the "classical draperies" scored all over with pencil marks and nearly torn away, and a polite message from the Sultana, who begs that I will not do any more pictures of her women in their morning dresses, "with their robes all twisted about them; it is ugly, and the Franks will think her harem very ill-dressed." I may, if I please, draw them in their best clothes—meaning plenty of starch and crinoline. The proposal does not tempt me to further efforts.

One day in the guest-room, I find the former nurse (sud'na) of the Princess—a ladylike woman, who is often in the seraï on a visit. She is preparing to leave, and is carefully folding her yashmak about her head, kneeling as she does so on the ground, before a hand-mirror that is set up against the back of a couch. The old negress before mentioned comes into the room, and there is a joyous greeting between the two, producing rather a droll though touching little picture, for the nurse is still kneeling, so the poor old black sinks on her heels in front of her, and the lady in the intervals of pinning her muslin veil presses the withered black face and head between her hands with a gesture of great affection.

There are other pictures round about for those who may care to look for them. The windows of this room are on the garden side of the house, and you may see a pretty group of young girls under a tall cypress-tree, near the brink of a marble fountain. Nourmayan is seated on the grass, reading a book which is open on her lap; two others, with bunches of hyacinth in their hair, are playing a rapid game of backgammon, while a negress looks on admiringly, her yellow antary and scarlet headdress making a rich bit of colour, softened by the deep shadow in which she stands. In the background a cluster of children have gathered round an intensely ugly black agha, who is seated on the border of the fountain; one little girl he holds on his knee; he is evidently a great favourite with all the youthful party.

Some halaïks are walking in twos and threes along the gravel paths, and in one corner of a shady court-yard, beyond the flower-garden, you may just see a swing in great request. The girls are not veiled as they saunter in this garden, which is protected by immensely high walls from the gaze of strangers; for the same reason the latticed gratings on this side can be raised, unless the gardeners may be at work below.

As I look at this quiet scene and reflect on the different aspects and conditions of "slavery" in different lands, the call of the muezzim is heard from a neighbouring minaret. Hafiza, a young calfa, rises from the cushion on which she has been lounging, and leaves the room to perform the prescribed ablutions before beginning the namaz (prayer), viz., to wash the hands and arms to above the elbow, and the feet to above the ankles. She returns and proceeds to unfold her prayer-carpet, called a "sejjadé." This is an oblong rug, the pattern of which runs at one end in a niche-like form, leaving a space of simple colour, on which the forehead touches in the prostrations, thus—as a proof of humility—avoiding resting the head, at that time, on ornamental work and golden embellishments.

Hafiza carefully spreads her sejjadé, with this

pointed end of the pattern in the direction of Mecca; she next unloosens the long tails of her antary, which are usually worn draped up and fastened into the girdle; finally, she opens out a large muslin veil, which she throws over her head and shoulders, and begins her namaz, murmuring the words in a low voice, and going conscientiously through all the required changes of position: at one time standing with her hands held together before her; at another prostrated, and touching the ground with her forehead; then she sits back, with her hands slightly spread on her knees; again she rises, all in one movement, and stands. The varying postures continue until the whole series have been repeated three or four times in their regular order. The prayer finished, Hafiza folds up her carpet, places it away behind a cushion of the divan, and sinking into her lounging attitude once more, takes up the thread of her interrupted conversation, almost at the point at which it had been broken off.

Some of her companions have also responded to the call of the muezzim, others have let it pass unheeded; but the old fiction that Mussulmans deny that their women have souls is sufficiently refuted by the scrupulous care with which many amongst the inmates of a harem seek to ensure their future spiritual welfare by rigid observance of the appointed times of prayer, by obedience to the precept of frequent almsgiving, and by a strict observance of the very severe fast of Ramazan, never failing to make up before the Ramazan of the following year for any days during which, for reasons of health, they may have been obliged to break the abstinence.

As a further proof of the respect in which religious observances are held by many Turkish women —even when, perhaps, carelessly practised—may be mentioned the regard paid to the religious observances of others; the most exacting of hanums who may have chanced to fix upon a Sunday for any work about which she is particularly anxious, will yield without a murmur to the objection that the day is our "djuma," on which no work may be done. This reason is unanswerable: during my long experience I have never met with a hesitation on this point.

A few words on the subject of the namaz may not be out of place here. The call to prayer is made by the muezzim from the minarets of the mosques, five times in the course of the day: the first a little after sunset, the second at nightfall, the third at daybreak, the fourth a little after noon, and the fifth mid-time between noon and nightfall. There are also two other stated times at which namaz are sometimes made; but these are not obligatory, and are not called from the mosques. The hours are a little past midnight, and about an hour before daybreak.

The namaz enjoined on all Mussulmans at the prescribed periods are, strictly speaking, not prayers. They consist of ejaculatory sentences of praise and belief, combined with symbolical changes of position. When the namaz has been duly performed, a devout person will add a short private prayer, looking the while at the palms of the hands as if reading from a book.

The tessbih, or chaplet of beads, is, at times, used as an aid to devotional exercises; it is formed of ninety-nine beads, each one recalling a divine attribute of the Almighty. The tessbih is divided—by a larger bead or some ornamental mark—into three parts of thirty-three beads each. It is made of sandalwood, aloes, scented seeds, pearls, coral, or amber. These last are much esteemed, and when found of a pure pale lemon colour, they bear a very high price. The tessbih is in constant use by men of all classes and denominations as an occupation for the fingers; they are as indispensable to Easterns as the pipe or cigarette. Travellers buy them as ornaments.

Arriving at the seraï one morning, as usual, I find the halaïks sitting about, silent and melancholy: everything is hushed, and I learn that a dying woman is in the house—the poor Georgian, whose room I had formerly occupied. She had long ago forgiven the invasion, and I grieved sincerely for her hard fate. She is to be taken away, with a young Circassian, also very ill, in order that they may not die in the palace: they go to a harem in the neighbourhood, the house of one of the numerous dependents of the Sultana.

Through a lady intimately acquainted with the details of life in this harem, I subsequently learn that the stately, fair Circassian, whom I had known as the Ibrikdar Ousta, had been lately married.

"From the palace?"

"No; she went from there previously."

"But how could she go at will? Was she not a slave?"

"Yes, certainly; she was a halaïk, but she had more than given the customary time of service. She had been kept at her duties a long time, for she was an excellent manager; rather severe towards the young girls in her department, but keeping everything in the most perfect order. She is no longer young, and she wished, at length, for change. You know that the slaves of princely harems are never sold again. If the women here have a disagreement, or insist upon leaving, the Sultana does not seek to detain them."

"But what can they do, without relatives to receive them—alone in the world?"

"Oh, they are not at all alone or uncared for; their connection with the palace is sure to have made them acquainted with numbers of people, and amongst them there are some good friends who take them in and find husbands for them; for they *must* be married—what other permanent resource can they have? They cannot take service in a house; they have no means of gaining a livelihood."

"I do not see Djesbounour here—a gentle, quiet girl, formerly the Cavedji Ousta; you remember? Where is she?"

"Ah! poor thing, she is dead. She also left the palace by her own desire, but she did not find a comfortable home; she wandered from one house to another, and did not seem to settle anywhere. They said, however, that she was at length betrothed, and to-day I hear that she is dead."

"But who did the Ibrikdar Ousta marry?" I urge, wishing to learn as much as possible of the later lives of halaïks. "She married, you say; she was a very handsome woman."

"Yes, she was very handsome; I fancy I can see her now, as she used to look in the musical class-room, playing her flute, with a muslin veil all floating about her shoulders. She was fair and fresh then, but she has gone off frightfully, for her marriage is not at all a happy one. Her husband is a kiatib (scribe), a widower, and very well off, but terribly avaricious; and then, of course, a wife who comes from a great harem can never find in her new home the luxury that she has been accustomed to, probably from childhood."

"Poor Ibrikdar Ousta! Does she look very miserable?"

"Oh dear, no!" answered my friend. "She tries to make a great show of contentment before the world, but people say—everything is known, you see, in the harems—that the husband makes her wash and work, and do a great part of the drudgery of the house; she must feel it bitterly hard, for here, in the palace, she had two or three young girls to wait upon her."

"But what, then, made the ousta marry this man? She must have heard something of his character. Was his first wife as badly used?"

"Well, the first wife of the kiatib belonged to an old family of the Dereh-Beys. These families are now poor and down in the world, yet people still pay them a good deal of respect and consideration. So the first wife was not put to hard work, but she had a bad time of it all the same. This hanum possessed a little fortune of 30,000 piastres, her money, of course, according to the law, being absolutely her own, at her disposal. A husband is bound to maintain his wife in a style suitable to her rank, and she is not expected to contribute anything towards the expenses of the household. After a time the kiatib resolved to rebuild his house, and with great difficulty persuaded his wife to put her money in the undertaking. The konak was built, but the hanum afterwards endeavoured in vain to obtain the legal papers establishing her half-proprietorship in it. At last the poor woman, seeing herself defrauded, and being worn out with her anxieties, fell seriously ill. Her last words on her deathbed were, 'Give me, oh! give me my papers or my piastres!' It was again his covetousness that made the kiatib marry the ousta—only a Circassian slave, it is true, but the slaves of superior rank in these great harems can put by a nice sum of money if they are careful. They need have few expenses, and have no relations looking to them for help. They receive rich presents of dress and jewellery, and the sums left for distribution by the crowds of wealthy visitors who flock there on all festive occasions must mount up considerably by the end of the year. The elder women get, of course, the largest share of these windfalls."

"Have there been many other changes here during the past few years?"

"Yes, a few; but I think they were mostly after your time. Let me think! Ah! *who* do you imagine it is that has taken the Sultan's fancy? You would never guess; it seems so strange and improbable."

"Not Ta'asnevin?"

"No, not Ta'asnevin or any of the beauties of the harem. It is—you *will* be surprised!—it is actually that little crippled, sickly child, Ghevhéri. You remember what a poor little creature she was; but she grew up—not handsome, certainly, only with splendid eyes; but so intelligent, bright, and witty, that the Sultan was quite charmed with her. She was taken into the great seraglio, where she reigns as supreme favourite; all others are neglected for her sake."

Enquiring as to the fate of a widow of a former Sultan, I heard that she lived in great retirement with her little Shahzadeh (Prince), the only survivor of her three children. These widows of a Sultan are not permitted to marry again; the reigning Padishah provides for their maintenance. The widower of a Sultana is also forbidden to marry after her death, unless he may succeed in obtaining a second time the hand of an Imperial Princess.

XIX.

THE MIDDLE BRIDGE.

An Unfashionable Lounge.—Shores of the Golden Horn.—Churches and Church Mosques.—Black Sea Boats.—Caïques and Mahones.—A Pasha's "Five-pair."—Sandals.—A Man-of-War's Boat.—The Bazaar Caïque.

For those unfortunate people, condemned by adverse fate to pass the long summer months in the stifling atmosphere of Pera, there is a sad deficiency of "outlet" in which to breathe "a mouthful of fresh air" away from the dust, and glare, and turmoil of the town; but one resource, little thought of in general, is highly appreciated by a few unfashionable people: the Middle Bridge, leading from the base of the Petit Champs, across the Golden Horn, to the quarter of Stamboul known as Oun-Capan. It is called the Middle Bridge, as lying between the steamer bridge of Karakeui and another—the Jews' Bridge, long since destroyed—that spanned the water between Piri Pasha and the Jewish suburb of Balata.

The Middle Bridge was built by Sultan Mahmoud

and given by him to the people, free of toll, but the old structure has vanished, and for the passage of its modernised successor the usual charge is now exacted.

The view from this point embraces the most interesting monuments of the city, the greater number being what are called church-mosques—Christian churches of the Greek Empire converted into mosques after the conquest. It is very pleasant to stroll along the wooden pathway, and watch the deepening glory of the sky behind the clear silhouette of dome, and minaret, and cypress. The beautiful grey and green masses of the old Seraglio are too much veiled by the masts and spars of the crowded harbour to be distinguished; but the small yellow dome of St. Irene is seen on the crest of the second hill, in the broad shadow of the massive pile and heavy minarets of St. Sophia. Below, and near the water's edge, rise the fine proportions of the Yeni-Djami. After this, the ground sinks slightly, then swells into the third hill, crowned by the Solimanieh and by the lofty tower of the Seraskierate. This height, covered with konaks and gardens, the palace of the Sheïkh-ul-Islam, the mansion of a Grand Vizier, by hundreds of picturesque wooden buildings in every variety of form and colour, falls rapidly into the grey misty shadow of a deep valley, from out of which the half-ruined aqueduct of Valens starts into bold relief against the glowing amber of the sunset. It arches over the slope of the fourth hill; slightly below it you may see a cluster of small domes, marking the Zeïrek-Djami, formerly the Church of the Pantocrator, and, on the neighbouring summit, the noble mosque of Mohammed the Conqueror covers the site of the once celebrated Church of the Twelve Apostles, where the last Constantine passed in prayer and penitence the night preceding his heroic death. In a crowded mass of buildings near the shore, stands the small Vefa'a-Djami, once dedicated to St. Theodore. Looking quite up the Golden Horn, the mosque of Selim, with its two slender minarets, points a bold spur of the succeeding hill and seems to overhang the Gul-Djami, or Rose Mosque, the Church of St. Theodosia. Beyond all this, the Fatiyeh-Djami rises above a wilderness of wooden houses and gardens and ruined walls: it was the Church of the Virgin, and the burial-place — amongst others of their Imperial family—of the Emperor Alexis and of his celebrated daughter, Anna Comnena. More distant still, and faintly traced in the softening glow of the sunset, you divine the beautiful "mosaic" Kahireh-Djami (the Church of the Saviour) and the venerable towers and line of wall that mark the western boundary of the city.

Look now along the waters of the Golden Horn;

there are wonderful pictures to be discovered amongst the shipping. Strange, fantastic craft are thickly crowded near the bridge on the side towards Stamboul; boats from the Black Sea with high beak-like prow, and stern richly carved and gilt and coloured; the turbaned crews lounge about the low decks, forming unconscious "subjects," as the light brings out a spot of carmine from girdle or jacket, and glorifies the faded blues and greens of their weather-stained garments. The coarse sail-cloth drooping heavily from the long lateen yard is of a brown and dingy hue; pierced by the golden rays, it is flecked with dashes of orange and glowing red against a background of tender grey and melting purple shadows.

The bridge is very quiet, for little traffic sets in this direction. Now and then a laden horse or donkey drags along the heavy planks fastened to its sides; they thump and jolt along the uneven roadway; a talika may also break the stillness with its jangling progress. A few loungers saunter on; some stop to lean their arms upon the iron railing, gazing idly down on the rush and flow and hurry of life streaming through the arch on the side towards Azap-Capou.

Crowds of people are returning from the bazaars and different business places of the city in every variety of boat and caïque; on they come—all in the same direction—to their homes in the suburbs of Balata, Hasskeui, Eyoub, and other villages fringing the Horn: the Jews predominate. One, two caïques—then three or four in a cluster, hurrying to shoot the arch before it can be reached by that unwieldy mahone, which is being heaved along by two men, who mount on the thwarts at each pull of the monster oars, throwing the whole weight of the body into the downward effort. The slender caïques shoot past, light and rapid as the "lost souls" skimming the tranquil water; other boats are streaming upwards from as far as one can see, singly and in groups. Now a cargo of Turkish women; next two Persians in their pointed caps; then a boat full of mollahs with turbans white and green, and in soft tinted pelisses; the rose-coloured cotton jacket of the negro boatman, though full of stains and patches, is perfect in effect against the bluish grey of the water.

There is a moment's lull: a tiny skiff dances gaily out of the sunshine and glides into the shadow of the bridge; then a regular, majestic, ponderous thud of oars. It is a Pasha's five-pair caïque; the great man sits, heavy and solemn, in the bottom of the boat, which is steered by an attendant, crouching on the scarlet cloth thrown over the raised part of the stern. The silken gauze sleeves of the caïqdjies wave in unison with the ten firm even strokes, that sound as one. Some little flitting "one pairs" gracefully make way, and the great official disappears also into the gloom. More caïques darting, hurrying, shooting along; two sandals side by side freighted by a festive party—in one boat, the musicians, in the other the revellers, shouting and singing. The sounds are frightfully discordant, but the authors of them enjoy them mightily. Behind these boisterous travellers comes a man-of-war's boat, taking an officer to the great ironclad at anchor just above the bridge; then a cluster of bright colours draws near slowly, a bazaar caïque, carrying passengers at a lower rate than the steamers. This omnibus-boat holds from twenty to thirty persons of various classes and nationalities. We look down upon turban, fez, caftan, feràdjé, and yashmak, the felt hat of the dervish, the curly lambskin of the Circassian, a gold device set in the crimson and black cap of a Montenegrin, a faded parasol or two at the end reserved for the women: all these rainbow hues in a ponderous boat, painted green, with a band of bright red along the edge. The five rowers, with bare brown legs and arms, toil heavily as they rise and sink; an old man, wearing a shawl girdle and an enormous black turban, stands on the raised point, guiding the huge beam of the rudder.

The light caïques are still darting about; they crowd near the passage of the bridge; the great boat comes heavily onwards; the boatmen shout, the caïqdjies scream—there will be an accident! Ah! that little caïque on the left! it will be run down! The great prow touches it—no, it is safe; the caïqdjie watches his moment, and, with a vigorous push, sends his slender craft back from the dangerous neighbourhood, and the bazaar-caïque, with its load of life, passes also away into the shadow of the arch.

The bright rays have faded; the picture has become dull and grey; but it may be seen to-morrow or the next day, or indeed on any day throughout the year, with additions and improvements on the Fridays, especially during the spring season, for then the movement is heightened by crowds of gay pleasure-seekers returning from the favourite promenade of Kiat-hané, the Sweet Waters of Europe.

XX.

FACTS, FANCIES, AND FOLK-LORE.

Festival of the Firstborn.—Turkish Caudle.—Tchinganas.—A splendid Bed and Cradle.—Naming the Infant.—Precautions against the "Evil Eye."—The use of Incense.—Dog-bread.—A Faulty Pattern.—Polite Spitting.—The Value of Old Shoes and of Blue Beads.—Breadcrumbs and Scraps of Paper.—Infused Writing.—The Seven Holy Nights.—The Night of Terror.—The Night of Power.—Aschourah and Névrouzié.—Invention of Confectionery.—Garlic and Onions.—A Kurd's Appreciation.—Shem and his Bees.—Balkiss, Queen of Sheba, and her Difficulties.—Solomon, a Basket-Maker.—Concerning Mangals.—The Origin of the Deluge.—The Old Woman of Kufa.—Carrier Pigeons, and the Fate of Yezid and Djebada.—Dyvits invented by Enoch.

THE birth of the first child, in a Mussulman family, is always an occasion of especial rejoicing; in the case of the lady whom we were invited to visit it is a more than usually happy event, for Sabiha Hanum, the only wife of Ahmet Effendi, after fourteen years of marriage, is a mother for the first time. In many cases a poor wife so circumstanced, would long ago have been politely returned to her family, with her marriage dower as consolation; but Ahmet is a kind-hearted man, very fond of his gentle Circassian wife, and is now doing his best to welcome the arrival of the firstborn child, although, alas! only a little girl.

The konak in Stamboul is brilliantly lighted, and the handsome reception-rooms, on the first-floor, are crowded with women—a very mixed company, as some are handsomely, others simply and even poorly dressed; but class distinctions have not the same force here as with us, and all the guests seem at their ease, and quite disposed to make the most of the joyful occasion, after their fashion.

The customary coffee is followed by cups of *warm sherbet*—answering to our old-fashioned "caudle." It is offered only on occasions of birth festivities.

The people crowd more and more into the principal room; a row of female musicians—tchinganas, or gipsies—crouch on the ground, animating, by very discordant strains, the movements of four professional dancing women. The dress of these last consists of a close-fitting red velvet gold-embroidered bodice, detached from the rest of the costume, to permit of full freedom for the movements of the arms; a tunic fringed with gold, and wide trousers of the same material; but black-heeled boots, and a general look of fade and tarnish, detract considerably from the glories of their appearance. They move round the room, winding in and out amongst the crowd, sometimes gracefully, more frequently in distorted attitudes: now they whirl along separately; now take hands, winding and unwinding a graceful chain, and from time to time burst into song, or rather a screaming chant, that has no connection whatever with harmony or music.

We find Sabiha Hanum reclining on a French bedstead, richly gilt and heavily draped in costly blue silk, looped with gold cords and tassels; a coverlet of the same magnificently embroidered in gold. A pillow is placed at the back of the bed, on which is displayed a diamond brooch, worth £800, given that day by the father to his wife. In the centre of the costly silk and gold draperies hangs a little bunch of pink gauze, enclosing charms against the "evil eye,"—a blade of garlic, some blue beads, and various herbs. At the head of the bed, a copy of the Koran, carefully folded in silk, is fixed to the bedpost.

The infant's cradle stands beside the mother's bed; it is adorned in the same manner with rich blue silk and gold, and has its small gold-worked coverlet. The occupant is invisible beneath a veil of pink gauze, but a bunch of charms at the head of the little couch must surely counteract all evil influences.

To increase the display, the Hanum's new "keurk" (a cloak of crimson velvet lined with fur) is laid out to the best advantage; and streams of light from several lamps fall on French couches, armchairs, and velvet-piled carpeting.

Our compliments are quickly paid, and we retire, for poor Sabiha Hanum, in spite of her new-born happiness, looks flushed and wearied. The noise, the movement in the house, and the long continuance of the rejoicings, which have been going on for six days and nights, since the birth of the child, would seem almost enough to kill the delicate mother.

An infant is, most usually, named on the sixth or seventh day after the birth; this is done by the father or grandfather, or by the imām in his character of chief magistrate of the *mahallé* or quarter. Any present which he may receive on the occasion is quite a voluntary offering. At the time of the name-giving, the imām, or the male relation, takes the infant, and, after pronouncing the name agreed upon, whispers into one ear the call to prayer, and into the other an invocation; but the child would be admitted even without this ceremony, into the fold of Islam, by the fact of its having been born of Moslem parents, and acknowledged by them.

Children are carefully and specially protected from the evil eye: their little caps are frequently adorned with a large gold or gilt medal, embossed with writing from the Koran; hanging to this is a bunch of three bead drops enclosing, respectively, the clove of garlic, the blue bead, and the safety-giving herbs. In addition, a careful mother or nurse will not forget to adorn the infant, between the eyebrows, with a blue or black mark, endowed with the same precautionary virtues. Both mother and child are frequently "incensed" during some weeks after the birth.

The use of incense is frequent amongst the inmates of a harem. Guests arriving on the occasion of any great festivity—such as a betrothal or marriage—are incensed at the foot of the great staircase; their hands, especially, are thus perfumed, as a token of rejoicing. Incense is used, also, as an antidote to sorrow or misfortune; young ladies suffering from *ennui* apply to the chafing-dish as a supreme resource. A prayer-carpet is spread, and a small brasier with lighted charcoal placed on it; a piece of aloes-wood, on the burning embers, sends up a delicious vapour, across which the patient steps three times; the incense is also waved about her head and person. When this valuable remedy fails, another method for driving away "evil influences" is adopted: the use of the "dog-bread." A handkerchief, or towel, being held at the four corners, over the head of the sufferer, some small rolls of bread are broken into it. This, we must imagine, absorbs the noxious power which is producing headache, heartache, ill-humour, or misfortune, as the case may be. The broken bits are then given to the dogs, who, doubtless, find them poor food, but no worse than usual.

Amongst the familiar superstitions in daily use is the custom of leaving some small defect or unfinished part in every work, some slight irregularity in a design or pattern. This is meant to indicate that man should not assume the power of bringing anything to perfection, as perfection is an attribute of the Almighty.

Vanity is reproved by the habit of adding "Mashallah!" when praising the beauty of personal appearance, especially when speaking of the prettiness of an infant, for whom precautions against the "evil eye" are multiplied indefinitely. Some people will be so intensely serious in their desire to counteract all bad effects, that they favour you by spitting while uttering the well-intended compliment.

An old shoe has its virtues in the East, as with us, and a rare specimen may be frequently seen dangling from the corner of a newly-laid house roof, in company with garlic and other charms, to keep the djinns from the unfinished dwelling.

Horses and oxen, and even ugly buffaloes, are tenderly hung with blue beads and bright bits of colour, to attract the gaze of envy from their useful forms; and the white fleece of the pet lamb, or monstrous Caramanian sheep, is not neglected.

The feeling or custom which forbids a properly

disposed Turk to tread on fragments of bread is to be respected, as teaching due regard for one of the best gifts of the Creator. A person eating bread will carefully collect the crumbs; they may be thrown into the water, as profitable to the fishes, or given to a dog, but not cast upon the earth to be soiled and destroyed by the foot of man. It is quite customary to see men, even laden with burdens, checked in their progress by the sight of a stray crust, and stooping to remove the morsel from the thoroughfare to cast it to a neighbouring dog.

Stray bits of paper also are carefully picked up by the respectable Mussulmans, and thrust into a crevice in the first rough stone wall they may come to: the name of the Almighty may be written or printed on the scrap, and should not be exposed to be trodden under foot.

Stray bits of hair and nail-parings take us back again amongst the terrors of the evil eye; such fragments of humanity (say the superstitious) must not get into the possession of strangers, lest an evil charm should be cast by their means. Great care is taken to prevent these accidents.

Sick people will drink—with perfect faith in its potency—water in which a piece of paper, armed with words from the Koran, is soaking; and little bags even are suspended round the throat, containing equally efficacious scraps of written sentences.

You must enter a dwelling for the first time with the right foot, and to stumble on the threshold conveys a warning of the most dismal omen.

To enter fully on the vast list of superstitions concerning lucky and unlucky days, would be a hopeless task, wandering into the subject of religious belief; but it may be interesting to give some explanation of the seven holy nights, during which all pious Moslems are expected to abstain from worldly enjoyment.

The two first commemorate the birth of Mahomet; on the third—the Miradj Guidjessy—the assumption of the Prophet is celebrated. After the fourth namaz of that day an offering of milk is made to the Sultan and his fellow-worshippers in the mosque; this is done in remembrance of Mahomet's having been offered by the angels milk, honey, and wine, of which he accepted the milk only.

The fourth of the holy nights is the Bérat Guidjessy, or Night of Recording. It is a night of terror: the Recording Angels (Kiramen, Kiātibinn), stationed on each side of every mortal, to record the good or bad actions of the year, now deliver up their books and receive new registers to continue their work. Azraël (the Angel of Death) also at this time delivers up his record, receiving a new scroll on which to inscribe the names of those predestined to death.

The fifth is the Kadir Guidjessy, the Night of Power, endowed, in Mussulman belief, with a strange mystery, in which a deep sense of the adoration due to the Creator of the Universe is surrounded with the halo of a wildly poetic superstition. On this Night of Power all inanimate nature is supposed, during certain moments, to adore the Creator: the waters of the ocean become (for the time) fresh; all birds, beasts, and fishes—the mountains, the valleys, and the rocks; the forests, the plants, and flowers, are influenced by this night to acknowledge in some invisible and mysterious way the power and majesty of the Almighty. Prayers offered during this night become as meritorious as those that could be repeated during a thousand consecutive months. The exact time during which this supernatural influence prevails has never been revealed to any prophet or saint, but being supposed to occur during one of the "uneven" nights of Ramazan, it is always celebrated on the 27th of that month.

The sixth and seventh nights are those preceding the two festivals of Baïram.

On each of the seven holy nights the mosques are illuminated both within and without; the return of the Sultan from the mosque on the Kadir Guidjessy is greeted with general illuminations and fireworks.

The tenth day of Mouharrem—the first month of

the religious year—is, with the two days following, regarded as a period of mourning in commemoration of the tragical death of Hossein at Kerbela. It is also considered as an unfortunate time, at which no great undertaking should be inaugurated. A sweet soup, called aschourah (from the Arabic "ashar," ten), composed of ten ingredients, is distributed on this occasion to the poor; it is also sent round as a present to friends.

There is another sweetmeat endowed with mysterious powers—the névrouzié, which is distributed at the commencement of spring.

Whilst on the subject of legendary lore, we may gather a few more examples connected with objects in familiar and daily use; they are extracted from "White's Constantinople," and were, most of them, translated from old Arabic authors.

Speaking of confectionery and sweetmeats, of which there is a great consumption in the harems, we find that "Adam has the credit of having invented confectionery; but the patron of all trades connected with sweet condiments is Omer Halvadjy, a contemporary and kinsman of the prophet. He it was who had the honour of making *kadaïf halwa* and *rahat lokoum* for Kadija, Ayesha, Zenab, and the rest of the family. But the Prophet, although a great advocate for the use of *shékerlémé* (sweetstuff) by others, seems to have had more substantial tastes.

According to tradition, his favourite dish was a haggis of sheep's head stewed in garlic, or a plate of young camel's tripe and onions. The latter was declared by him to be the 'lord of all dainties.'"

While adverting to the Prophet's predilection for these two bulbs, it may be mentioned that we are originally indebted to Satan for their production. According to a vulgar belief, when the King of Darkness first touched earth, after his expulsion from Paradise, pungent garlic sprung up beneath his right foot, and honest onions under the left. From this cause, perhaps, garlic is held not less sacred by the Persian Yezidy, or devil-worshippers, than was the Nile lotus by the ancient Egyptians.

The Kurds also pay great respect to onions. They call them "your excellency," and look on them as "the pearl of vegetables." One day a Kurdish chief came to Stamboul, saw the Sultan, and exclaimed, "Great as may be the Padishah, I only envy him on one account. May he not every day dine on the core of onions? Can we Kurds do that?"

The wax-chandlers' guild venerate Shem, son of Noah, as their patron. He it was that invented wax tapers. When the ark was already floated, a swarm of bees settled upon the roof. Shem, seeing this, removed them carefully to a warm corner, where they hived and multiplied. When the ark rested upon Mount Ararat, near the spot where the convent of Etchmiazim now stands, Shem took the wax, melted it in an earthen pot, and dipped therein strips of wool. These, when cool, he rolled in his hands, and thus made the first twisted taper. From this cause Shem is also venerated as the patron of apiaries.

The guild of bakers, cornfactors, and millers admit that Adam was the first of their craft. He is supposed to have been taught by the Archangel Gabriel to bruise wheat between two stones, and having made dough therewith, to bake it in a hole in the ground.

The "tepsi," wooden trays covered with brightly-polished metal which are used as dining-tables in old-fashioned Turkish houses, owe their origin to the Queen of Sheba. Tradition has it that this celebrated beauty, when upon her road to meet Solomon, was accustomed to employ for this purpose a large inverted salver of gold, on which the dishes were placed in succession. This invention served also for another object: being brilliantly burnished, they produced the effect of mirrors, and the fair Queen was enabled to gratify simultaneously her vanity and her hunger. Although glass mirrors seem, from this, to have been unknown to Balkiss (said to have been the twenty-second queen of Yemen), plate glass was already in use at the court of Solomon. It is stated, upon the authority of the Arabian author, Jallal'uddin, that transparent glass was employed in profusion at the period in question.

Balkiss having accepted the invitation to Solomon's court, was received by the monarch seated upon a throne entirely composed of precious stones, elevated at the extremity of a vast hall built of gold and silver bricks. The floor of this gorgeous apartment was made of transparent glass, placed over a stream of running water, filled with living fish. The object of this singular flooring was to impress Balkiss with an idea that she was about to step into real water, and thus to induce her to exhibit her ankles; for Solomon had heard that her majesty's nether limbs were covered with hair "like unto those of a she-ass."

The stratagem succeeded. Balkiss, not aware of the existence of glass, no sooner approached the entrance than, supposing she must plunge into water, she slightly lifted up her robe. This natural precaution proved that the report was true, and Solomon, though mightily struck with the beauty of her face, was grievously disgusted at the disclosure of her shaggy heels, and could not be brought to marry her. However, some of the genii in his suite forthwith came to his assistance, and, literally, smoothed all difficulties; they composed a powerful depilatory paste, which, having been applied without loss of time, relieved the lovely queen from this unsightly appendage, "so that her feet became fair and downy as the cheeks of a new-born infant."

This beautiful Queen Balkiss was (say the legends) a sad slattern. Solomon, we are told, having discovered that his new wife was untidy, and accustomed to cast her raiment into corners, made for her several baskets, which he presented with a suitable admonition; for the great Solomon, whom the basket-makers venerate as their patron, amused his leisure hours in the useful and innocent manufacture of baskets. But the art of covering these baskets with leather is supposed to have been invented, at a much later period, by an Afghan, named Seid Dabbaghy, who first introduced an improved system of curing skins. This man is patron of the tanners' company.

Considerable difference of opinion exists as to the original invention of mangals. Some pious brasiers, who are supported by a few sectarian charcoal-burners, affirm that Nimrod is entitled to this honour, inasmuch as it was he who caused an enormous vessel of molten brass to be made, and then filled with burning charcoal, in order that he and his court might warm themselves during the building of Babel. Through the aid of a trifling anachronism, they likewise add that Nimrod, thwarted in his intentions, determined to revenge himself upon

Abraham, who was bound and about to be cast upon the burning pile, when the Lord caused the brass to melt. The flaring metal, streaming towards the spot where sat the mighty hunter, chased him and his attendants away, and Abraham, being thus rescued, departed into Egypt.

According to Eastern tradition, grounded on the Koran, the Deluge gushed from a mangal (fire-pot) near the spot where Kufa now stands, and streamed irresistibly forth until the world was submerged; and some mangal-makers declare that the first employer of brasiers was the old woman of Kufa from whose oven the flood is said to have issued. But not being disposed to allow merit to an old woman whose name is coupled with such terrible evidence of Almighty wrath, popular tradition prefers to ascribe the invention of this useful household article to Noah, who, when the rains had ceased and the waters were dried up from the earth, went forth and made a pilgrimage to Kufa, where he found the mangal whence the Deluge had proceeded, and preserving it carefully, handed it down as a model to posterity.

The art of training carrier pigeons is not unknown to Orientals. The first inventor of this means of communication is said to have been a native of Bagdad, who trained pigeons for the Abasside kaliph, Yezid III., in order that he might swiftly correspond, when absent, with a favourite slave named Djebăda, of whom he was tenderly enamoured. The devotion of this prince to his lovely captive was carried to most romantic and fatal extremes. The plague chancing to break out in Bagdad, this lady was among its victims. No sooner did the dread apparition of the black dog arise before the unfortunate girl and the fatal spots indicative of the malady appear upon her person, than the devoted Yezid clasped her to his heart. Then, waiting upon her as a faithful nurse, he remained at her side until the Angel of Death struck the last blow. After closing her eyes with his own hands, he cast himself beside the body, and continued three days in this state, refusing food and consolation. At length his vezir and courtiers, employing respectful force, tore him from the insensible remains, which were committed to earth with regal pomp.

Yezid died—as the poets of Arabia affirm—of a broken heart; but, in fact, he had taken the infection, and followed Djebăda to the tomb on the ninth day.

The dyvit is an article somewhat in the form of a short pistol, made of brass or silver. Ink is contained in the butt or projecting part, and the reeds (used as pens for Turkish writing), the knife and ivory for rubbing and splitting the reeds, in the barrel, which opens at the muzzle. They are worn by men with the elongated part thrust into the girdle or bosom pocket.

The use of these **dyvits** is traced up to the Prophet Enoch, who is supposed to have been the inventor of writing as well as of weaving. He it was who—instructed by the Archangel Gabriel—made the first reed pen, much as they are used in the present day. He also constructed the first distaff. According to modern belief, Enoch was the son of Berd, and the most learned and studious of all the sons of men. Thence the epithet "Idriss" added to his name. Moslems believe in his translation at the period mentioned in Holy Writ.

END OF VOL. I.

www.ingramcontent.com/pod-product-compliance
Lightning Source LLC
Chambersburg PA
CBHW020240240426
43672CB00006B/593